ENACTING CATHOLIC SOCIAL TRADITION

ENACTING CATHOLIC SOCIAL TRADITION

The Deep Practice
of Human Dignity

Clemens Sedmak

ORBIS BOOKS
Maryknoll, New York 10545

ORBIS BOOKS
Maryknoll, New York 10545

Founded in 1970, Orbis Books endeavors to publish works that enlighten the mind, nourish the spirit, and challenge the conscience. The publishing arm of the Maryknoll Fathers and Brothers, Orbis seeks to explore the global dimensions of the Christian faith and mission, to invite dialogue with diverse cultures and religious traditions, and to serve the cause of reconciliation and peace. The books published reflect the views of their authors and do not represent the official position of the Maryknoll Society. To learn more about Orbis Books, please visit our website at www.orbisbooks.com.

Copyright © 2022 by Clemens Sedmak.

Published by Orbis Books, Box 302, Maryknoll, NY 10545-0302.

All rights reserved.

No part of this publication may be reproduced or transmitted in any form or by any means, electronic or mechanical, including photocopying, recording, or any information storage or retrieval system, without prior permission in writing from the publisher.

Queries regarding rights and permissions should be addressed to: Orbis Books, P.O. Box 302, Maryknoll, NY 10545-0302.

Manufactured in the United States of America

Library of Congress Cataloging-in-Publication Data

Names: Sedmak, Clemens, 1971- author.
Title: Enacting Catholic social tradition : the deep practice of human dignity / Clemens Sedmak.
Description: Maryknoll, NY : Orbis Books, [2022] | Includes bibliographical references and index. | Summary: "Emphasizes that Catholic Social Tradition stems not from arbitrary laws laid down by Church leaders, but from moral guidance inspired by Scripture"—Provided by publisher.
Identifiers: LCCN 2021043074 (print) | LCCN 2021043075 (ebook) | ISBN 9781626984691 (trade paperback) | ISBN 9781608339310 (epub)
Subjects: LCSH: Christian sociology—Catholic Church. | Catholic Church—Doctrines. | Christian ethics—Catholic authors.
Classification: LCC BX1753 .S43 2022 (print) | LCC BX1753 (ebook) | DDC 261.8—dc23
LC record available at https://lccn.loc.gov/2021043074
LC ebook record available at https://lccn.loc.gov/2021043075

*I dedicate this book to my friend and mentor Bill Purcell,
who enacts Catholic Social Tradition
in a prophetic and compassionate way.*

Contents

Acknowledgments ix

Abbreviations xi

Introduction: Enacting and Applying Catholic Social Tradition xiii

1. **Enacting Human Dignity** 1
   Fragility 2
   Catholic Social Tradition and "Doing Dignity" 7
   Applying Catholic Social Tradition: The Meaning of Context 15
   The Deep Practice of Human Dignity 21
   The Power of the Deep Practice of Human Dignity 27

2. **The Portrayal of Principles** 32
   Portraits beyond Principalism 34
   On "Painting Principles" 41
   Example 1: A Portrait of the Concept of Solidarity 47
   Example 2: A Portrait of the Concept of the Common Good 58

3. **Raw Thinking** 73
   Raw Thinking and Catholic Social Tradition 77
   Disciplined Raw Thinking 84
   Example 1: The Ethics of Taxation 90
   Example 2: A Just Wage 97
   Raw Thinking as Thinking as Pilgrims 113

4. **Experiments with Truth** 116
   On the Concept and Dynamics of Habits 121
   Experimenting with Habits 127
   Experimenting with Lifestyle 130
   A Case Study: *Laudato Si'* 136
   Experiments and Growth 155

5. **Catholic Social Teaching as *Regula* and Therapy**   159
   Archbishop Óscar Romero   161
   Seven Criteria and Two Perspectives   167
   Catholic Social Teaching as "Therapy"   180
   A Therapeutic Reading of Catholic Social Teaching
      Documents   182
   The Church as Field Hospital   188
   The Reality of a Field Hospital   193

Index   199

Acknowledgments

I would like to thank all those who have supported me in the process of writing this book, especially the colleagues and friends at the Center for Social Concerns here at the University of Notre Dame. I would like to thank colleagues who have provided inspiration on the path to a deeper understanding of Catholic Social Tradition, notably Sister Helen Alford, Anna Blackman, Mathias Nebel, Margie Pfeil, Kelli Reagan, Martin Schlag, and Günter Virt. Special thanks to Elizabeth Rankin for her work on the manuscript. I am grateful to Orbis Books for accepting this book and working with me, especially to Jill O'Brien for her careful editing.

Abbreviations

AL   *Amoris Laetitia (The Joy of Love)*, Francis I (2016)

CA   *Centesimus Annus (On the Hundredth Anniversary [of Rerum Novarum])*, John Paul II (1991)

CCC   *Catechism of the Catholic Church*

CSDC   *Compendium of the Social Doctrine of the Church*, Pontifical Council for Justice and Peace (2004)

CV   *Caritas in Veritate (Charity in Truth)*, Benedict XVI (2009)

DV   *Dei Verbum (Dogmatic Constitution on Divine Revelation)*, Paul VI (1965)

EE   *Ecclesia in Europa (The Church in Europe)*, John Paul II (2003)

EG   *Evangelii Gaudium (The Joy of the Gospel)*, Francis I (2013)

EN   *Evangelii Nuntiandi (In Proclaiming the Gospel)*, Paul VI (1975)

EV   *Evangelium Vitae (The Gospel of Life)*, John Paul II (1995)

FR   *Fides et Ratio (Faith and Reason)* John Paul II (1998)

FT   *Fratelli Tutti (On Fraternity and Social Friendship)* Francis I (2020)

GS   *Gaudium et Spes (Pastoral Constitution on the Church in the Modern World)*, John XXIII (1965)

LE   *Laborem Exercens (On Human Work)*, John Paul II (1981)

LG   *Lumen Gentium (The Dogmatic Constitution on the Church)*, Paul VI (1964)

LS   *Laudato Si' (On Care for Our Common Home)*, Francis I (2015)

MM   *Mater et Magistra (On Christianity and Social Progress)*, John XXIII (1961)

OA   *Octogesima Adveniens (Eightieth Anniversary [of Rerum Novarum])*, Paul VI (1971)

PP   *Populorum Progressio (On the Development of Peoples)*, Paul VI (1967)

PT   *Pacem in Terris (Peace on Earth)*, John XXIII (1963)

QA   *Quadragesimo Anno (On Reconstruction of the Social Order)*, Pius XI (1931)

RN   *Rerum Novarum (Rights and Duties of Capital and Labor)*, Leo XIII (1891)

SRS   *Sollicitudo Rei Socialis (On Social Concerns)*, John Paul II (1987)

Note: All official church documents are available in English on the Vatican website, www.vatican.va.

Introduction

*Enacting and Applying
Catholic Social Tradition*

This book is a reflection on how to apply and enact Catholic Social Tradition. The question itself can be considered dangerous. Let me explain.

There is a story about a failed development project in Haiti. A well-meaning person procured an expensive water filter and donated it to an orphanage. The orphanage staff was properly instructed on the use of the filter, and the benefactor was willing to send them new cartridges once the filter went through the first twenty thousand gallons. However, because the filter was so expensive, it was locked in a closet, and rarely, if at all, taken out and used. In addition to the lack of benefit to the orphans' health, this situation was also a missed opportunity to work together with the local community, which could have benefited from the filter in a way that would have strengthened relationships between the orphanage and the community. This story may be reminiscent of the parable of the Talents, in which the person who had received just one talent told the Master, "Master, I knew that you were a harsh man . . . so I was afraid, and I went and hid your talent in the ground" (Mt 25:24–25). However, the true story above (as well as the biblical lesson of the buried talent) may also apply to the way we deal with Catholic Social Tradition: it is officially held in high regard, but also carefully stored away and thus deprived of its fruitfulness.

Catholic Social Tradition (and, less broadly, Catholic Social Teaching)[1] are not harmless ideas, but rather serve as a thorn in the flesh. The teachings are part of the effort to make the kingdom of God more present; they are part of the message: "The time is fulfilled, and the kingdom of God has come near; repent, and believe in the good news" (Mk 1:15). For an example of the challenging nature of Catholic Social Thought, we may look to the teaching on the nonabsolute nature of the right to private property, for example, in *Populorum Progressio*:

---

[1] The distinctions between these (as well as Catholic Social Thought) will be discussed below.

"He who has the goods of this world and sees his brother in need and closes his heart to him, how does the love of God abide in him?" [1 Jn 3:17]. The Fathers of the Church laid down the duty of the rich toward the poor in no uncertain terms. As St. Ambrose put it: "You are not making a gift of what is yours to the poor man, but you are giving him back what is his. You have been appropriating things that are meant to be for the common use of everyone. The earth belongs to everyone, not to the rich" [*De Nabute*, c. 12, n. 53: PL 14.74722]. These words indicate that the right to private property is not absolute and unconditional. No one may appropriate surplus goods solely for his own private use when others lack the bare necessities of life.[2]

Let me repeat the last sentence: "No one may appropriate surplus goods solely for his own private use when others lack the bare necessities of life." This statement has explosive potential if applied and taken seriously. However, the precise meaning of "surplus" is a key question. There is a beautiful Swedish word, *lagom*, which means "exactly the right amount." What is exactly the right amount of ties and toys, shoes and shirts, cars and condos?

The assertion also asks a lot from its intended audience. This is a sentence from a normative document that does not intend to just make inspiring suggestions. The claim is deeper and higher—it is a normative message that calls for a conversion and a particular form of life, similar to the Gospel passage "It is easier for a camel to go through the eye of a needle than for someone who is rich to enter the kingdom of God" (Mt 19:24). I stumble over this sentence, knowing that in comparison to the vast majority of people on this planet, I am "rich." If the world were a village of one hundred inhabitants, about twenty-nine would not have access to fresh drinking water, and about fifty-five would not have access to a safely managed sanitation service. I am rich. Why is it hard for me to enter the kingdom of heaven? This is a tough question.

My suspicion is that the rich person is tempted to take certain standards for granted and to consider himself or herself in full control of matters. There is so much money can buy. Wealth gives power over things and circumstances; it prevents problems from arising. If you have stable access to material resources you would likely not even be aware that certain situations, like a legal dispute with the authorities or a minor health issue, could become dramatic challenges. Money buys choices. It buys

---

[2] Paul VI, *Populorum Progressio*, "On the Development of Peoples" (1967), no. 23, hereinafter *PP*.

Introduction

independence—or the illusion of independence, the illusion of the "self-made." This illusion is like a wall between the person and God. We are creatures; God is the creator. The question "What do you have that you did not receive?" (1 Cor 4:7) holds a universal truth. *Deep knowledge* that our life depends on God may require experiencing that material security is not a given. A personal remark: I may be rich by some standards, but not by others. My very real worries about how to pay certain bills (e.g., medical or tuition bills) induce much-needed humility in my life, and gratitude if the bills can be paid after all. This is an experience that puts me in the childlike position of having to trust the heavenly Father. The questions then become: Does being rich in a humble way mean being rich in humility? And also: Is that hard to do?

These are (tough) questions to be asked. And we have not even reached the reality of "application" and "enactment." The Christian invitation to repent and believe is not a harmless endorsement of the culture of the convenient and the comfortable. Lessons about the demanding nature of the Christian message and our relationship with God were learned the hard way and communicated in moving letters by the Jesuit priest Alfred Delp. He experienced the "realness" of the Christian message in prison; he had been involved in the Kreisau Circle, which discussed Germany's social order and democratic future and was linked to the failed July 1944 attempt to kill Hitler. Delp was arrested and tortured and then transferred to Berlin, where he spent Advent 1944. In his cell, he wrote letters and meditations, reflecting on the core of the Christian message.[3] He discovered "Advent" in a new way, maybe even as the very point of Christian life.[4] To him, "Advent" stands for "wilderness" and "repentance" and "utter dependence on God."[5] There in prison, Delp rediscovered Catho-

---

[3] Thomas Merton observed in his preface to Delp's *Prison Meditations*, "Written by a man literally in chains, condemned to be executed as a traitor to his country in time of war, these pages are completely free from the myopic platitudes and the insensitive complacencies of routine piety" (Alfred Delp, *The Prison Meditations of Father Alfred Delp* [New York: Herder and Herder, 1963], vii–xxx, at vii).

[4] "Alfred Delp was in Tegel Prison in Berlin from the end of July 1944 until the end of January 1945, during which time the Church passed through the liturgical seasons of Advent and Christmas. Advent had always been the liturgical season to which he had been most drawn. In prison, as he paced three steps in one direction, three steps in the other, his hands nearly always in handcuffs, the 'Advent discovery' that Delp made was that God was present in the midst of his desolation" (M. Coady, "Truth Hidden in Untruth: Thomas Merton and Alfred Delp," in Angus Stuart, ed., *Across the Rim of Chaos: Thomas Merton's Prophetic Vision* [Stratton-on-the-Fosse, Radstock: Thomas Merton Society of Great Britain and Ireland, 2005], 81–88, at 85).

[5] "You need to have sat in a small room with your hands in irons and have seen the shredded flag of freedom standing in the corner, in a thousand images of melancholy. The heart flees from these images again and again, and the mind strives to lift itself free, only to awaken even more sharply to reality at the next guard's footsteps sounding in the hall

lic Social Teaching, especially the encyclical *Quadragesimo Anno*.[6] The testimony of his life and death—he was sentenced to death in January 1945 and executed on February 2, 1945—serves as a reminder that the Catholic Social Tradition is ultimately about our relationship with God, and is an expression of our deep belief that as creatures and sinners we depend on God.

Catholic Social Tradition, Thought, and Teaching

This book sets out to explore issues related to the enactment of Catholic Social Tradition, Catholic Social Thought, and Catholic Social Teaching. The relationship between these terms can be described as follows: The rich and broad tradition of Christianity has led to the generation of a way of thinking about social issues called Catholic Social Thought, and the tradition has been condensed into a more clearly defined body of texts, called Catholic Social Teaching. However, even in this normatively binding form, the documents of Catholic Social Teaching are contextual in nature; they reflect responses "to concrete circumstances rather than the handing down of already traditional doctrine."[7] In this book, I am particularly interested in the enactment of human dignity as the central principle and commitment of the human person. I explore the appropriation of principles as well as concrete experiences and experiments within the Catholic Social Tradition, and offer a therapeutic reading of Catholic Social Teaching.

The book has five chapters. The first chapter introduces the key term of human dignity as the guidepost for the enactment of Catholic Social Tradition; it explores the connection between the experience of human vulnerability and the discourse on dignity, and discusses the enactment of human dignity. Chapter 2 offers a new way to think about the principles

---

and the next clanking of keys. Then you know that you are powerless. You have no key, and your door has no inner keyhole, and your window is barred and set so high that you cannot even look out. If no one comes and releases you, you will remain bound and poor in misery. All the mental struggles do not help at all. This is a fact, a condition that exists and must be acknowledged" (Alfred Delp, *Advent of the Heart: Seasonal Sermons and Prison Writings, 1941–1944* [San Francisco: Ignatius Press, 2006], 112–13.)

[6] Pius XI, *Quadragesimo Anno*, "On Reconstruction of the Social Order" (1931), hereinafter *QA*.

[7] H. McCabe, *God Still Matters* (London: Continuum, 2002), 86. This point has to be kept in mind when working through the hermeneutics of Catholic Social Teaching documents, since magisterial documents have a tendency to be self-referential; i.e., it is part of the linguistic scheme of magisterial documents that they refer to previously published magisterial documents, thus creating a set of growing discursive commitments.

developed in Catholic Social Tradition; it paints "portraits" of principles, making use of multiple sources to provide a rich and thick understanding of these principles and their relevance for moral judgment and moral clarity. The third chapter introduces the concept of "raw thinking," which produces nonpolished reflections on open questions. Raw thinking, as opposed to the presentation of final and elaborated products, encourages the honest and tentative engagement with questions about the practical implications and the practical relevance of Catholic Social Tradition. Chapter 4, titled "Experiments with Truth," describes the role of personal and social experiments in trying to enact Catholic Social Tradition, in order to translate into practice the principles and ideas of the social tradition. The final chapter presents Catholic Social Teaching as a rule of life (*regula*) and a therapeutic means, working closely with Archbishop Óscar Romero's example of bringing Catholic Social Teaching to life in his prophetic ministry. The main point of the book is to show that Catholic Social Tradition responds to the wounds of the time, which is why the book ends with the image of a field hospital.

Catholic Social Tradition is not an optional add-on to the Christian message; it is the expression of the social dimension of the Christian faith. The 1971 Synod "Justice in the World" summarized this call: "Action on behalf of justice and participation in the transformation of the world fully appear to us as a constitutive dimension of the preaching of the Gospel, or, in other words, of the Church's mission for the redemption of the human race and its liberation from every oppressive situation."[8] In other words, you cannot credibly live the gospel without social and political commitments and engagements. This has traditionally been expressed as the unity between love of God and love of neighbor.[9] In his Apostolic Exhortation *Evangelii Gaudium*, Pope Francis makes this point forcefully when he writes, "A personal and committed relationship with God . . . at the same time commits us to serving others."[10] Catholic Social Tradition, one could say, is a spirituality rather than a doctrine, a *regula* to be lived rather than a rule to be followed, as this book suggests.

Catholic Social Tradition has a theological and not a philosophical foundation; that is, it is ultimately based on the encounter with Jesus, the Christ, and a personal relationship with God. But this relationship cannot be lived without "a turn to the other." As the first letter of John puts it succinctly, "Whoever does not love their brother and sister, whom they

---

[8] World Synod of Catholic Bishops, "Justice in the World" (1971), no. 6.
[9] See Karl Rahner, *Theological Investigations*, "Reflections on the Unity of Love of Neighbor and Love of God," vol. 6, trans. Karl-H. Kruger and Boniface Kruger (London: Darton, Longman and Todd, 1969), essay 16, 231–49.
[10] Francis, *Evangelii Gaudium*, "The Joy of the Gospel" (2013), no. 91, hereinafter *EG*.

have seen, cannot love God, whom they have not seen" (4:20).

Only in the late nineteenth century, with the publication of *Rerum Novarum* in 1891,[11] do we observe the beginnings of a magisterial tradition that explicitly offers "Catholic Social Teaching," especially through social encyclicals. But the social dimension of the faith has been an integral part of the Christian tradition from the very beginning. Underlining the importance of "love of neighbor" as a part of, expression of, and consequence of love of God, the most often-quoted Gospel passage in the first six centuries is Matthew 25:31–46, reading, "Whatever you did for one of these least brothers [and sisters] of mine, you did for me." This phrase again shows the specific Christian framing of the turn to the other (although it does carry with it the temptation of instrumentalizing the most disadvantaged for one's own spiritual edification).

The first centuries of the Christian era saw the rise of a social theology, but these developments were clearly not purely theoretical. We find many examples of concrete action, beginning with the Book of Acts in the New Testament, where we read that "there was no needy person among them" (4:34) and that there was a daily distribution for the widows (6:1). The year 368 was of special importance in this regard. People in Cappadocia suffered from a cruel famine, due to a severe drought, and the moral paradigm at the time was "indifference." Bishop Basil of Caesarea (today a saint) preached a sermon titled "In Time of Famine and Drought," and organized famine relief activities. He established a *ptochotropheion* (poorhouse or hospital), and bought available local grain from wealthy landowners that he distributed to the starving. His whole family engaged in these relief efforts, motivated by a new way of seeing society as a community and the human person as a being with dignity.[12] Peter Brown described this new way of seeing the person and community as "a revolution of social imagination": Christian Social Tradition stretched the imagination of Basil's contemporaries and continues to do so today. The values of dignity and solidarity were translated into practices and institutions, along with a new language to talk about community and justice.[13] Stretching the imagination so that it can inform proper action is a key point in the enactment of Catholic Social Tradition.

Delving into social issues does not come without risks. When Pope Leo

---

[11] Leo XIII, *Rerum Novarum*, "Rights and Duties of Capital and Labor" (1891).
[12] S. Holman, *The Hungry Are Dying: Beggars and Bishops in Roman Cappadocia* (Oxford: Oxford University Press, 2001), 64–98.
[13] P. Brown, *Poverty and Leadership in the Later Roman Empire* (Hanover, NH: University Press of New England, 2002), 1; see also P. Brown, *Through the Eye of the Needle: Wealth, the Fall of Rome, and the Making of Christianity in the West, 350–550 AD* (Princeton, NJ: Princeton University Press, 2012).

XIII issued *Rerum Novarum,* addressing the situation of workers—and talking about just wages, labor unions, and the right to private property and its social function—he chose the path of using magisterial authority not to talk about matters of revelation, but rather about social realities. This was risky because social realities change, are always "particular" (rather than "general"), and are never exhausted by analysis. Their changeability stands in contrast with eternal truths. This does not mean, however, that the literary genre of a social encyclical is primarily based on social science. The biblical roots and thus the roots in revelation are as obvious as the anchoring in tradition and magisterium. The rootedness of Catholic Social Teaching in the Gospels deserves special attention since the Gospel foundations make it clear that enacting Catholic Social Teaching is discipleship, a way of following Christ. Catholic Social Teaching is not a social theory, based on certain key arguments and principles, but a social imperative, based on an encounter: the encounter with Christ. The gospel foundation has been present from the very beginning of systematic papal Social Teaching: in writing the social encyclical in 1891, Leo XIII incorporated biblical sources. Let us take a closer look at the way the encyclical works with biblical sources to explore the "gospel closeness" of the papal text.[14]

One example of this is found in section 22 of *Rerum Novarum.* It refers to the spiritual challenges of wealth (in the "camel through the eye of the needle" quote from Mt 19:23–24 as well as in the quotation from Lk 6:24–25: "But woe unto you who are rich; because you have no more consolation to expect. Woe to you who are now full; because you will starve. Woe to you who are laughing now; for you will complain and cry"). The same section also quotes Luke 11:41, which expresses the obligation of almsgiving, and cites the passage on the final judgment in Matthew 25, in connection with the description of the duty of solidarity (Mt 25:40).

References to the Sermon on the Mount are made in two sections of *Rerum Novarum,* namely 24 and 57: on the Beatitude of the poor (Mt 5:3; section 24) and in section 57 on the primacy of the kingdom of God (Mt 6:32–33). The primacy of the kingdom of God and eternal life is also underlined with the quotation from Matthew 16:26: "What good is it to a man if he gains the whole world, but at the same time pays with his life? At what price can a man buy back his life?" (section 57).

Section 24 of the encyclical indicates an "option for the poor"—here

---

[14]It can be argued, however, that Catholic Social Teaching would benefit from an even more serious engagement with the Bible, and with the practical wisdom of the experiences and practices of Church engagement with social issues: see D. McLoughlin, "Catholic Social Teaching and the Gospel," *New Blackfriars* 93 (2012): 163–74.

the reference to the first beatitude is mentioned, along with a reference to the invitation to the burdened: "Come to me all you who are struggling and carrying heavy burdens, I will give you rest" (Mt 11:28). In this way, the Gospel references convey sociocritical thoughts, that is, comments on the prevailing social relationships—"the rich" versus "the poor" and orientation toward the primacy of the kingdom of God, along with a view to a final judgment—and the admonition to solidarity based on the Gospel. At the same time, the text appeals to common sense.

Rerum Novarum is an important normative document that gives us a sense of the risks of applying the gospel to social realities. Exploring this connection between the gospel (discipleship) and the social world is the project of this book. Enacting Catholic Social Tradition (and Thought and Teaching) is the commitment of following Christ in the social world.

"Applying" and "Enacting" Catholic Social Tradition

The story of Alfred Delp shows that the question of "applying Catholic Social Thought" is ultimately very simple: it is an invitation to a conversion, a permanent and recurring invitation. But as always, the question of "right application" is delicate and difficult.

The English word "apply" is etymologically linked to the French word "*plier*" (to bend), indicating that applicability and flexibility are interrelated. "*Plier*" can also mean "to fold"; there is a suggestion of the malleability of the material that can be adjusted to particular circumstances. This image expresses a specific epistemological aspect of the challenge of applying Catholic Social Tradition: how much flexibility or pliability can there be, and how much stability is necessary? This book discusses this question of the applicability of key values of the Catholic Social Tradition with a primary intention to understand the depth of the question.

The "application discussion" is also familiar from applied ethics, in which a common conception is the idea that one starts from a set of principles—such as autonomy, benevolence, welfare, nonmaleficence, and justice—and then transfers them to a specific area. Media, sports, or medical ethics are then understood not as special ethics that follow their own principles, but as reasonably well-defined contexts in which principles are brought into dialogue with particular situations. The much-cited "reflective equilibrium" is generated when common principles and the dynamics of a specific situation have been brought into balance.

Now this image—here the basket of principles, there the basket of special situations—does not seem implausible, but it has its pitfalls, which can be articulated in the form of questions:

- Does a principle change when it is confronted with a certain context? Are we talking about the same principle when we speak of the "autonomy principle" in the context of high-performance sports or in the context of a hospice? Does a principle remain stable when applied in different contexts?
- Is the context in question clearly distinguishable? How many ethically relevant preliminary decisions are already expressed in the profiling of a context?
- What does it mean to apply a principle? Can one imagine this application in terms of "entering into a dialogue" between a value and a social reality? Will this application also presuppose a personal "power of judgment," so that a subjective moment necessarily takes place, and statements in applied ethics necessarily reflect the personal attitude of the judging agent?

These many questions point to the depth of the larger question of what it means to apply and enact the Catholic Social Tradition.[15] The principle of subsidiarity is not something to pull off the shelf and easily implement. Subsidiarity in unstable social situations—such as transitional justice contexts—may mean something different from subsidiarity in a politically stable situation. Solidarity in a context of an overabundance of material goods may be different from solidarity in a context of massive inequality. Of course, one could argue that the main message is the same, but the kinds of examples used, the ways in which the concepts and principles can be introduced, the challenges on the ground in taking the principle seriously, may be quite different. Ingrid Betancourt had this experience when she was held as a hostage by FARC[16] rebels in Colombia for six-and-a-half years. The practical meaning of terms like "human dignity" and "solidarity"—that is, the ways to enact them—changed significantly during her captivity in the jungle. Respecting human dignity did not mean "politeness," but fighting dehumanization; living in solidarity did not mean "giving out of one's surplus," but "sharing the bare necessities."[17] Ingrid Betancourt repeated the key concept of "dignity" as a reminder, as an anchor, as a reference point, to protect her innermost integrity:

---

[15] See C. Sedmak, "Enacting Human Dignity," in P. Carozza and C. Sedmak, eds., *The Practice of Human Development and Dignity* (Notre Dame, IN: University of Notre Dame Press, 2020), 27–45.

[16] The Revolutionary Armed Forces of Colombia, founded in 1964.

[17] Cf., I. Betancourt, *Even Silence Has an End: My Six Years of Captivity in the Colombian Jungle* (New York: Random House, 2010).

> I had decided that they would not hurt me. Whatever happened, they would not touch the essence of who I was. I had to cling to this fundamental truth. [. . .] My father's voice spoke to me from very afar, and a single word came to mind, in capital letters. But I discovered with horror that the word had been completely stripped of its meaning. It referred to no concrete notion, only to the image of my father standing there, his lips set, his gaze uncompromising. I repeated it again and again, like a prayer, like a magical incantation that might, perhaps, break the evil spell. DIGNITY.[18]

The notion of dignity is a reminder that we are part of something bigger that transcends the observable dimension and concrete circumstances. There is something powerful in the term that suggests that we do not fully grasp what it means to have dignity or to live with dignity. There is a moment of elusiveness here that also serves as a source of a particular encouragement. Betancourt tried very hard to enact the principle of dignity—accepting the term as a reminder that we owe something to ourselves and to others on its basis. She was "holding on to dignity."[19] As she observes, a sense of dignity is incompatible with certain types of behavior:

> I refused to be treated like an object, to be denigrated not only in the eyes of others but also in my own. For me, words had a supernatural power, and I feared for our health, our mental balance, our spirits. When I heard the guerrillas refer to us as "cargo," as "packages," I shuddered. These weren't just expressions. The point was to dehumanize us. It was simpler for them to shoot at a shipment of goods, at an object, than at a human being. I saw it as the beginning of a process of degradation, which I wanted to oppose. If the word "dignity" had any meaning, then we must not allow them to treat us like numbers.[20]

Reducing people to numbers, to objects that can be replaced and disposed of, is a well-known strategy for dehumanizing persons. A person loses her face, her identity, and her uniqueness when reduced to a number. This human uniqueness calls for a particular attention to what each person brings to the world (which would not be part of the world otherwise) and for a particular attention to what we lose when we lose a person. It is not trivial to say, "A human being died that night" (the title of Pumla

---

[18] Ibid., 15.
[19] Ibid., 465.
[20] Ibid., 253–54.

Gobodo-Madikizela's account of her painful interviews with Eugene De Kock, a state-sanctioned mass murderer who served the apartheid regime in South Africa).[21] Human dignity means that each person's life matters.

Ingrid Betancourt describes some of her struggles with dignity and upholding respect for human dignity. A particularly moving scene in Betancourt's memoir is her insistence on honoring the death of a fellow human being. A colleague had been killed and everyone had learned about it. It was mealtime: "Everyone hurried to stand in line, lost in thought." But Betancourt stood up. "'Companions!' I shouted, in a voice that I wished were louder. 'Pinchao is dead. I would like to ask you to observe a minute of silence in his honor.' "[22] This seems like a small gesture, but may go a long way in its symbolic power, pointing to something invisible and intangible within tough circumstances. Enacting principles requires both faithfulness to their established meaning and sensitivity to the local situation and the given context. Betancourt's memoir is a testimony to the commitment to honoring dignity even under adverse circumstances. There was no textbook or script telling her how to do it; she had to use her personal understanding of the dignity of the person.

Enacting principles (or concepts or values) requires, first, a moment of appropriation (of making it one's own), a moment of translation, a moment of anchoring; the principle (e.g., the principle of human dignity) has to be made one's own before it can be "inhabited." This distinction between "inhabited" and "noninhabited" has been inspired by Aleida Assman's distinction between "inhabited memory" and "noninhabited memory."[23] The latter points to museums and archives and memories that do not stir emotions, that do not lead to conversations, that do not play a role in people's lives; the former, "inhabited memory," refers to cultures of remembering that show people's emotions and shape communication and interactions. An inhabited principle has been personalized and reflects the style and personality of the person working with it; it is not enough to quote what has been stated or repeat what has been taught.

Second, principles have to be translated into practices, into habits and decisions, into particular actions and ways of exercising agency. The concept of human dignity, for instance, has to be translated into personal and institutional practices in daily life, since living values are nurtured from and within the everyday. Principles have to be translated into conversations and choices, into rituals and routines. And then, third, the mosaic of

---

[21] P. Gobodo-Madikizela, *A Human Being Died That Night: A South African Story of Forgiveness* (Boston: Houghton Mifflin, 2003).

[22] Betancourt, *Even Silence Has an End*, 513.

[23] A. Assmann, *Cultural Memory and Western Civilization: Functions, Media, Archives* (New York: Cambridge University Press, 2011), 119–35.

choices and habits will fill in, shaping a form of life that creates a culture and a climate that influence perceptions and judgments. The principle is then anchored in a way of life, in a particular way of being-in-the-world. One of Swiss philosopher Peter Bieri's deep insights into the concept of human dignity is his claim that our understanding of human dignity constitutes a particular form of life and facilitates a particular way of experiencing the world.[24] The "work" that the concept of human dignity is able to do affects our judgments and our perceptions. "Doing dignity" lays the foundation of a form of living; as Wittgenstein writes, for a concept to work, "there must be agreement not only in definitions but also (queer as this may sound) in judgments."[25] And not only in judgments, but also in perceptions; developing a common ground of both judgments and perceptions means that principles (appropriated, translated, and anchored) can shape emotional landscapes and the dynamics of perception.

Let me give one example, which may not be obvious at first glance. Environmental scholar Farhan Sultana talks about the emotional aspect of ecological matters,[26] pointing out that principles of ecological justice are in reality not applied as rational arguments, but come with heavy emotional baggage. Sultana describes a case study of contaminated drinking water in Bangladesh: many wells are unsafe due to arsenic, which puts women who provide the drinking water for their families under pressure to perform emotional labor.

> [Women] will carefully monitor their behavior and emotions around those they are dependent on for safe water, so as to not upset tenuous relations that enable them to obtain water. Any social infractions such as disagreements, perceived lack of respect (on the part of the well owners), insufficient expressions of gratitude or providing free labor (in return for safe water) can jeopardize the right to access a safe well. As one young woman put it: "We suffer for water in many ways, and put up with a lot everyday just so that we can have some water to drink."[27]

Women suffer indeed for clean water, since they also suffer from unsafe water. This suffering says a lot about the emotional aspect of the principle of "care of creation." It reaches the level of human perception.

This "emotional turn" in political ecology has been observed

---

[24]P. Bieri, *Human Dignity: A Way of Living* (Oxford: Wiley, 2017).

[25]L. Wittgenstein, *Philosophical Investigations* (Oxford: Blackwell, 1967), 242.

[26]F. Sultana, "Suffering *for* Water, Suffering *from* Water: Emotional Geographies of Resource Access, Control and Conflict," *Geoforum* 42 (2011): 163–72.

[27]Ibid., 169.

elsewhere,[28] allowing for the discussion of issues such as the role of emotions in power relations, the emotional attachment to place and emotional geographies, and the role of collective emotions as triggers for collective action—but also revealing the connection between emotions and overexploitation exemplified in

> the paradox of fishermen with strong emotional attachments to the sea that end up overexploiting it. . . . While their attachments to the sea and cooperative daily practices on board their boats can result in self-regulating fishing efforts, in policy meetings, where decisions about quotas, fishing effort, etc., take place, they feel uncomfortable when labeled by powerful others (e.g., trawlermen) as unruly, which provides a strong disincentive for self-regulation.[29]

The CST principle of "care for creation" is indeed a deeply emotional one, and Pope Francis acknowledges this dynamic in *Laudato Si'*:[30] "If we feel intimately united with all that exists, then sobriety and care will well up spontaneously" (*LS* 11). This feeling of union and closeness is also a source of the kind of pain necessary to overcome indifference: "God has joined us so closely to the world around us that we can feel the desertification of the soil almost as a physical ailment."[31] The encyclical underlines the importance of feelings as forces that sustain the motivation to enact the principle of "care for creation." Commenting on small, microlevel actions, such as "avoiding the use of plastic and paper, reducing water consumption, separating refuse, cooking only what can reasonably be consumed, showing care for other living beings, using public transport or car-pooling, planting trees, turning off unnecessary lights," Pope Francis observes,

> We must not think that these efforts are not going to change the world. They benefit society, often unbeknown to us, for they call forth a goodness which, albeit unseen, inevitably tends to spread. Furthermore, such actions can restore our sense of self-esteem; they can enable us to live more fully and to feel that life on earth is worthwhile.[32]

---

[28] M. González-Hidalgo and C. Zografos, "Emotions, Power, and Environmental Conflict: Expanding the 'Emotional Turn' in Political Ecology," *Progress in Human Geography* (January 2019): 1–21.
[29] Ibid., 5.
[30] Francis, *Laudato Si'*, "On Care for Our Common Home" (2015), hereinafter *LS*.
[31] *LS* 89, quoting *EG* 215.
[32] *LS* 211 and 212, respectively.

Bringing emotional components to bear on discussions of a seemingly abstract principle show that we have left the level of mere intellectual concerns. Because of the emotions involved, however, it is not surprising that enacting principles can lead to serious conflict since they touch upon questions of human identity and human integrity.

Conflicts

Enacting values and principles is clearly not as simple a process as, say, thawing frozen goods. One of the well-known challenges vis-à-vis the concept of human dignity is that participants in a controversy can make use of the same principle and idea and yet arrive at diametrically opposing views. Both proponents and opponents of abortion rights invoke human dignity, and same-sex marriage is both defended and rejected on the basis of human dignity.[33] The principle of dignity is also used by those fighting against and by those arguing for physician-assisted suicide, with both sides using language like "dying with dignity." Agreement on the importance of the principle and—to some significant extent—its content does not guarantee agreement in applying or enacting that principle.

The same can be said about Catholic Social Teaching more widely, and its application. Persons referring to Catholic Social Teaching may arrive at different and even contradictory positions. For example, while invoking Catholic Social Teaching, Catholics can disagree on the issue of free markets and market regulations, and on border control and migration management. Catholic Social Teaching can be used to justify support for opposing political parties and their candidates. In fact, the teaching gives the impression of having a certain elasticity.

A famous example of this dynamic in the history of American Catholicism is the 1949 cemetery workers' strike against the Archdiocese of New York. The conflict was significant:

> On January 13, 1949 approximately two hundred forty members of the Calvary unit of Local 293, UCW struck the archdiocesan operated Calvary Cemetery, New York City's largest burial ground. The walkout was total, and included all classes of workers—gardeners, gravediggers, chauffeurs, machine operators, foundation workers, and maintenance men. Located in Middle Village, Queens, Calvary

---

[33]See R. B. Sigel, "Dignity and Sexuality: Claims on Dignity in Transnational Debates over Abortion and Same-Sex Marriage," *International Journal of Constitutional Law* 10, no. 2 (March 30, 2012): 355–79.

Cemetery averaged ten thousand interments a year; in 1949 it held nearly two million departed within its four hundred acre tract.[34]

From a Catholic Social Teaching perspective, workers' rights as well as aspects of the common good were at stake. The history of the negotiations between the employer (the Archdiocese of New York) and the employees reveals different linguistic tactics. The former was employing the feudal language of managerial paternalism, with the benevolent Father offering paid employment and showing voluntary generosity. The latter were using a democratic language of rights and entitlements and the employer's duties. There was clearly a lack of consensus on the meaning and weight of equality in employer-employee relationships.

The figure of Cardinal Spellman, carrying the political and financial power of his elevated position, aggravated the effects of this managerial paternalism. His eminence kept a low profile at first, but became visibly involved in the strike negotiations in the second half of February. In spite of *Rerum Novarum*'s defense of unions in section 49, the cardinal (concerned about leftist tendencies) offered the strikers a flat 8 percent wage increase, "but with the proviso that they return to work free of union membership by noon the following day."[35] When they refused the offer, Cardinal Spellman took action and became a strike breaker, organizing seminarians to dig ninety graves, as reported by the *New York Times*.[36] This created quite an uproar:

> The grave diggers were dumbstruck when they saw his Eminence enter Calvary Cemetery in Queens accompanied by three busloads of seminarians, but of course, this was precisely the effect that Spellman had hoped for, spouting to the press that he was proud of his strike breaking. . . . No less a personality than Dorothy Day served notice to the Cardinal that what he really buried was Catholic social teaching.[37]

---

[34] A. Sparr, "The Most Memorable Labor Dispute in the History of U.S. Church-Related Institutions: The 1949 Calvary Cemetery Workers' Strike against the Catholic Archdiocese of New York," *American Catholic Studies* 119, no. 2 (Summer 2008): 1–33, at 3–4.

[35] Ibid., 6.

[36] W. Lissner, "Cardinal Directs as His Seminarians Dig Niney Graves; Spellman Leads 100 Past the Strikers at Calvary—Offer to Use Pick Declined," *New York Times*, March 4, 1949.

[37] P. J. Hayes, "Estote Firmi: New York's Local Church under Cardinal Spellman's Watch," in Christopher D. Denny and Christopher McMahon, eds., *Finding Salvation in Christ: Essays in Christology and Soteriology in Honor of William P. Loewe* (Eugene, OR: Wipf and Stock, 2011), 23–48, at 35.

In her letter to Cardinal Spellman, dated March 4, 1949, Day made it very clear that the (Catholic) workers rejected support by communists and were instead supported by the Catholic Worker Movement. She supports the strike since it is about "not just the issue of wages and hours. ... It is a question of their dignity as men, their dignity as workers, and the right to have a union of their own, and a right to talk over their grievances."[38] She appealed to the cardinal to go out as "father" to the children, especially since it is easier for the powerful to give in than for the poor. What is at stake in this controversy is the understanding and application of Catholic Social Teaching, based on the social encyclicals *Rerum Novarum* and *Quadragesimo Anno*. In the words of David Gregory, "Dorothy Day and the *Catholic Worker* bore profound and direct witness to the Cardinal's egregious repudiation of Catholic social teaching on the rights of workers."[39]

One of the negotiators for the Archdiocese of New York, Godfrey P. Schmidt, a Fordham Law graduate, questioned the reading of Catholic Social Teaching by New York's labor priests and their allies, and published an article in 1947 calling for the establishment of a commission of Catholic theologians to translate abstract principles and apply them to the realities of life.[40] He felt the need for a Catholic casuistry to deal with the day's challenges, in a context that differed from 1891, when *Rerum Novarum* was published. He named the challenge of translating and applying and enacting the abstract ideas and general principles of Catholic Social Teaching. As he pointed out, the texts of social encyclicals leave space for conflicting interpretations in concrete situations. The 1949 cemetery-worker strike also draws attention to the possibly severe divide between Catholic Social Teaching and Catholic institutional practices.

If we try to interpret the undeniable historical fact that Day and the cardinal disagreed about the moral status of the strike, we can identify several different possibilities:

- Cardinal Spellman and Dorothy Day agreed on the content of Catholic Social Teaching about workers' rights, such as the right to unionize, but did not agree on the application of these papal teachings to the concrete situation on doctrinal grounds (given a

---

[38] Dorothy Day, *All the Way to Heaven: The Selected Letters of Dorothy Day*, ed. Robert Ellsberg (New York: Image Books, 2010), 219.

[39] D. Gregory, "Dorothy Day," in John Witte Jr. and Frank Alexander, eds., *The Teachings of Modern Roman Catholicism on Law, Politics and Human Nature* (New York: Columbia University Press, 2007), 336–67, at 357.

[40] G. P. Schmidt, "Moral Theology and Labor," *America*, April 26, 1947, 95–97.

particular interpretation of the teachings that rejects communism as much as it supports workers' rights, for instance).
- Cardinal Spellman and Day agreed on the content of Catholic Social Teaching in its statements about workers' rights, but did not agree on the application of these papal teachings to the concrete situation on pragmatic grounds. Perhaps Spellman did not want to suffer economic disadvantages and social inconvenience as a result of the teachings that he had accepted, or maybe he operated under the assumption that Catholic Social Teaching ad intra (i.e., applied to Catholic employers), is softer than Catholic Social Teaching ad extra (i.e., applied to non-Church institutions and agents).
- The cardinal and Day disagreed about the content of the teaching given the variety of interpretations available for relevant texts as well as the variety of relevant texts.

We have reasons to believe that both Spellman and Day had good knowledge of *Rerum Novarum* (1891) and *Quadragesimo Anno* (1931), with both accepting the normativity of these papal documents. It is also safe to believe that they both shared a sense of the dignity of the human person created in the image and likeness of God. They seem to have disagreed on the relationship of principle to a concrete situation, and it seems plausible to see their dispute as a question of proper application. They made different judgments about the role and meaning of human dignity, the dignity of workers and work, and the common good in this particular context.

The Necessity of Judgment

Issues of application arise because of the elasticity of the material at stake. The 1949 dispute over labor rights would not be possible without this flexibility, which permits the application of social doctrine to be a personal interpretation rather than a mechanical implementation. You can only apply what can be formed or molded to the relevant situation, which differs from other situations, and the molding is done by someone with the necessary expertise. Here, the personal commitment of the epistemic subject is required; the judgment cannot be delegated to chains of citations. In application, the selection as well as the bending of the material has to be performed by the judging and interpreting subject—thus it cannot be standardized. This is also the place where biographical elements may enter the process of judgment. The life worlds of Dorothy Day and Cardinal

Spellman were clearly different; this influenced their individual readings of the situation and the relevant papal texts.

The disagreement in 1949 illustrates the need for judgment in the selection, interpretation, and application of Catholic Social Teaching. A principle can only provide concrete orientation if it is properly applied, with the particular reality in mind. Let us take the issue of migration, for instance. As a document defending human rights, the encyclical *Pacem in Terris*, completed by Pope John XXIII shortly before his death, is an influential source of orientation for the matter of migration. We read in section 25, "When there are just reasons in favor of it, he [the person] must be permitted to emigrate to other countries and take up residence there."[41] The Latin text speaks of "*iustae causae*" or "just reasons." We are, however, not told what these just reasons might be, especially in the changing circumstances of our times. In the same encyclical we see a further statement defending the right to migration:

> Among man's personal rights we must include his right to enter a country in which he hopes to be able to provide more fittingly for himself and his dependents. It is therefore the duty of State officials to accept such immigrants and—so far as the good of their own community, rightly understood, permits—to further the aims of those who may wish to become members of a new society.[42]

The key passage here is the caveat "so far as the good of their own community, rightly understood, permits." Again, by which criteria can we decide what "the good of their own community permits" and what it means to understand this good "rightly"? Judgments connecting the general statement and its applicability within concrete realities are indispensable.

The document *Ecclesia in Europa* mentions "intelligent acceptance and hospitality"[43] in the context of migration as a challenge for Europe. What then is an intelligent elaboration of the concept of intelligent acceptance? The *Catechism of the Catholic Church* provides a general orientation with regard to migration when talking about general duties of wealthy nations: "The more prosperous nations are obliged, to the extent they are able [*in quantum fieri potest*], to welcome the foreigner in search of the security and the means of livelihood which he cannot find in his country

---

[41]John XXIII, *Pacem in Terris*, "Peace on Earth" (1963), 25, hereinafter *PT*.
[42]*PT* 106.
[43]John Paul II, *Ecclesia in Europa*, "The Church in Europe" (2003), no. 101, hereinafter *EE*.

of origin."[44] We need to make judgments about the application of this implicitly invoked "ability-to-pay principle," the principle that holds that those who *can* pay *should* pay. Judgments do not follow mechanically; we are left with the necessity to exercise the key skill of Immanuel Kant's third Critique: *The Critique of Judgment* (1790). We need this ability to make appropriate judgments in concrete situations.

Working with Catholic Social Teaching *in concreto* leaves us with the challenge of how to identify and select an appropriate textual basis given the vastness of the body of relevant texts. This unavoidable selection of the texts is a further call to judgment. "Official Catholic social doctrine" is not as simple as a strictly ordered set of sentences, as we find in Spinoza's *Ethics* or in Wittgenstein's *Tractatus Logico-Philosophicus*; these two texts are examples of buildings in which each sentence has its place in the structure. In the case of the *Tractatus*, they are also numbered, and the claim is not only that of freedom from inconsistency but also of the validity of well-considered architecture, in which one sentence is built upon the other, no sentence is superfluous, and no sentence is missing. We do not have that with regard to Catholic social doctrine. And even if there were agreement on the selected set and the weight of relevant texts, one would need to take into account the signs of the times when making judgments. Sister Carol Keehan, president of the Catholic Health Care Alliance, for example, sided with President Barack Obama in the political debate surrounding the Affordable Care Act in the United States; the US Conference of Catholic Bishops had rejected the draft. Keehan's argument was that one cannot wait for the perfect statute, but must have, in addition to principles, preferences and priorities.[45] These preferences and priorities inform judgments about courses of action, allowing for a pragmatic approach that recognizes that the moral landscape is nuanced. Such preferences and priorities are formed on the basis of deliberations of "relevance," a category that cannot be separated from pragmatic considerations, which in turn inform judgments.

Judgments are not achieved by reiterating well-known statements. It is not enough to repeat the official general doctrine in concrete situations with their specific demands. It is not just about the what, but also about the how. There is more to the application of principles than their normative expression. Purely mechanical repetition of doctrine can even be dangerous since it could lead to numbness and indifference: "The message

---

[44]*Catechism of the Catholic Church* (Vatican City: Libreria Editrice Vaticana, 1997), no. 2241, hereinafter CCC.

[45]C. Keehan, "Time to Collaborate," *Modern Healthcare*, March 30, 2009.

is one which we often take for granted, and can repeat almost mechanically, without necessarily ensuring that it has a real effect on our lives and in our communities. How dangerous and harmful this is, for it makes us lose our amazement, our excitement and our zeal for living the Gospel of fraternity and justice!"[46] A judgment in the spirit of a fresh outlook cannot be realized in a mechanical way; in fact, in a sense, it surprises the person doing the judging, as philosopher Ted Honderich was surprised by his own analysis of moral rights in relation to terrorism.[47] Any judgment inhabited by an epistemic subject has a "subjective" dimension, which means that there is no guarantee that two individuals posing the same question will come up with the same conclusion or solution—and in the event of their conclusions being similar in content and results, the basic tenor of their arguments can still be different.

The enactment of Catholic Social Teaching calls for fresh judgments. These judgments are not arbitrary; they are guided by Catholic Social Teaching itself. If we take the category of "Catholic social doctrine" as part of moral theology and the magisterium, we find hints to its own application in the doctrine itself. Part of the essence of the social doctrine of the Church is "to apply the Word of God to the lives of people and society, as well as to the related earthly realities."[48] Here, the biblical foundation is stressed as well as the challenge, known from the art of homiletics, to translate the Word of God into life realities. The apostolic letter *Octogesima Adveniens* contains important notes on the application of social doctrine: we read that social doctrine does not present a prefabricated pattern, works in a solution-oriented manner, and is constantly applied to the changing course of things.[49]

Repeating doctrine is not enough, as has been explicitly stated in the encyclical *Mater et Magistra*: "All social teachings, however, must not only be recited, they must also be realized. This is especially true of the social doctrine of the church."[50] A list of core principles of Catholic

---

[46]*EG* 179.

[47]T. Honderich, *After the Terror* (Edinburgh: Edinburgh University Press, 2003). Honderich embarked on a journey of analysis and reflection after 9/11 and arrived—to his own surprise—at the conclusion that there is such a thing as a moral right to terrorism. I am not emphasizing this claim here, but rather the moment of surprise in the process of deliberating and judging.

[48]John Paul II, *Sollicitudo Rei Socialis*, "The Social Concern" (1987), no. 8, hereinafter *SRS*.

[49]Paul VI, *Octogesima Adveniens*, "Eightieth Anniversary [of *Rerum Novarum*]" (1971), no. 42, hereinafter *OA*.

[50]John XXIII, *Mater et Magistra*, "On Christianity and Social Progress" (1961), no. 226, hereinafter *MM*. Section 229 reflects on the difficulties in application and implementation: "The transition from theory to practice is already difficult. It is even more difficult to put the social doctrine of the Church into practice. The reasons for this are the unbridled

Social Doctrine can be quickly created and effortlessly memorized, and basic definitions of "subsidiarity" and "common good" are simple to draw from easily accessible sources. More is obviously needed to apply Catholic social doctrine. A suggested scheme for the project of applying Catholic Social Teaching is the "see-judge-act" approach,[51] which calls for a proper consideration of social realities and the signs of the times, a well-justified judgment, and a consistent translation of this judgment into action. In this see-judge-act process we see a particular concern of good judgment, namely, moral clarity. One cannot act upon diffuse and unclear judgments, and moral clarity about crucial ethical questions cannot be separated from spiritual identity and belonging. This is not only a matter of intellectual judgment, but more so, an existential question and a matter of spirituality.

Moral Clarity

Especially amid the complexity and fragility of our lives, moral clarity is hard to find; it is relatively easy in situations with clear boundaries, but boundaries shift and become blurred. Moral clarity can be hard won and then can get lost again; the December 1984 UN Convention against Torture and Other Cruel, Inhuman or Degrading Treatment or Punishment was adopted in the wake of many atrocious experiences and moral disasters. The text of the convention arrives at moral clarity with its absolute understanding of the prohibition of torture, stating explicitly in article 2.2: "No exceptional circumstances whatsoever, whether a state of war or a threat of war, internal political instability or any other public emergency, may be invoked as a justification of torture." After 9/11, the commitment to the absolute prohibition of torture weakened, especially in the United States. Jeremy Waldron, defending its absolute prohibition ("My personal conviction is that torture is an abomination, to be excluded from consideration in all circumstances, even in the ticking-bomb scenarios"[52]), appeals

---

selfishness of man, the materialistic world-view that is spreading in society today, and the difficulty of determining what justice demands in the concrete situation." There are both social and epistemological hindrances in applying Catholic Social Teaching. Universal principles can touch local realities only in a certain way; they are limited in their capacity for making directive statements and providing judgments in particular circumstances. They can serve as a point of departure and reference point, but not as the final result of local deliberations. There is no alternative to personal judgment and "local moral knowledge."
[51] *MM* 236.
[52] J. Waldron, "What Can Christian Teaching Add to the Debate about Torture?," *Theology Today* 63 (2006): 330–43, at 335; cf. J. Porter, "Torture and the Christian Conscience: A Response to Jeremy Waldron," *Scottish Journal of Theology* 61, no. 3 (2008): 340–58.

to specifically Christian sources to defend moral clarity with regard to torture: Christians should have a sense of absolute prohibition of torture, given the sacredness of the human person, the sacredness of norms, and the spiritual dangers of breaking the soul through torture.[53] Waldron even quotes F. S. Cocks, a UK delegate to the 1949 negotiations preparing the European Convention on Human Rights, who noted affirmatively that "The Consultative Assembly . . . believes that it would be better for a society to perish than for it to permit this relic of barbarism to remain."[54]

The challenge of applying principles in concrete situations consists of achieving moral clarity without losing a handle on the complexity of the situation at stake. And given our human condition, there are many complexities to negotiate. Wheaton College graduate Darren Yau authored the award-winning essay in the 2017 Elie Wiesel Foundation for Humanity's Ethics Essay contest. Titled "Truthfulness and Tragedy: Notes from an Immigrant's Son," his piece talks about two situations where persons struggled with integrity and truth.[55] In the 1970s his great-grandfather, a citizen of the People's Republic of China, was falsely accused of being a Nationalist sympathizer; he refused to sign a false confession and brought danger and shame to his family. Imprisoned, he was released after seven months in jail. In the spring of 2012, the author's uncle was notified that he had stage IV pancreatic cancer and refused to let his father (then in his late nineties) know; he was buried without his own father knowing of his son's illness and passing. In the first situation, a person refuses to lie, and in the second situation, a person refuses to tell the truth. Yau makes the point that in both situations a particular person—his great-grandfather, then his uncle—had acted to preserve and honor his integrity, and that the situations revealed a sense of the tragic character of our lives. Quoting a line from Alasdair MacIntyre's *After Virtue*—"The true genre of life is neither hagiography nor saga, but tragedy"[56]—he characterizes tragedy as "a drama wherein the actors are motivated by fundamentally conflicting cares and loves that inevitably lead to some demise."

---

[53] Waldron, "What Can Christian Teaching Add to the Debate about Torture?" 337–40.

[54] Ibid., 336n14. Christian sources of moral clarity are also evident, for example, in any Catholic Social Teaching–inspired discourse on migration, since the priority of the sacredness of the human person and the universal destination of goods over national sovereignty is well established in its documents (see, e.g., *PT* 105; Benedict XVI, *Caritas in Veritate*, "Charity in Truth" [2009], 62, hereinafter *CV*).

[55] Darren Yau, "Truthfulness and Tragedy: Notes from an Immigrant's Son," Elie Wiesel Foundation, 2017, http://eliewieselfoundation.org/wp-content/uploads/2017/12/Truthfulness-and-Tragedy-3.0-Formatting.pdf, 3.

[56] A. MacIntyre, *After Virtue: A Study in Moral Theory*, 3rd ed. (Notre Dame, IN: University of Notre Dame Press, 2007), 247.

There is a lot of wisdom in these observations. Not all of those refusing to respect article 2.2 of the UN Convention quoted earlier did so lightheartedly. For instance, Alan Dershowitz's claim to accept certain cases of justifiable torture reflected a process of careful deliberation.[57] There are painful situations that convey the tragic character of life; we may find ourselves in circumstances where moral clarity comes with a price that seems too high to pay, but concerns a good too precious not to procure. Human dignity is the most precious good that we have as creatures created in the image and likeness of God and saved into the image of Christ.[58]

There are situations in which it seems easy to protect and respect the dignity of the human person, such as in the moving Easter celebrations in a parish community or the joy of celebrating the birth of a child. And then in some situations tragedy strikes, and the path toward respecting human dignity becomes more fraught. For instance, it is tragic to be diagnosed with an inoperable tumor on the spine when one is a man in his mid-fifties, as Jeffrey Spector was, faced with the challenge of "living human dignity" after the diagnosis.[59] It is tragic to have a son, born with cardiofaciocutaneous syndrome, who is in danger of seriously hurting himself, whose behavior is unpredictable, and whose sleeping patterns do not align with his parents' needs for rest. Journalist Ian Brown describes this journey with his son to both heaven and hell in his book *The Boy in the Moon*.[60] Again and again he finds himself in situations that challenge categories like "family life," "tenderness," or "love." It is in such circumstances that we are called to "a deep practice of human dignity," to a practice that holds onto the dignity of the person under adverse circumstances. Tragedy is a framework whereby a person makes the experience of being "an unwelcome guest in the world"; tragedy leads to the exposure to "forces which neither be fully understood nor overcome by rational prudence"; tragedy brings with it a moment of irreversibility

---

[57] A. Dershowitz, *Why Terrorism Works: Understanding the Threat, Responding to the Challenge* (New Haven, CT: Yale University Press, 2002).

[58] Cf. Col 1:15; 1 Cor 15:49; 2 Cor 3:18; 2 Cor 4:4.

[59] Jeffrey Spector decided to end his life in Switzerland and was celebrated as a "hero of life" in certain circles in the United Kingdom; see A. Grey, *Dignity at the End of Life: What's beneath the Assisted Dying Debate?* (London: Theos, 2017), 23–27. Spector's case reminded many of that of paralyzed UK citizen Diane Pretty, who went all the way to the European Court of Human Rights to claim the right to assisted suicide; see M. Freeman, "Denying Death Its Dominion: Thoughts on the Diane Pretty Case," *Medical Law Review* 10 (2002): 245–70; see also S. B. Chetwynd, "Right to Life, Right to Die, and Assisted Suicide," *Journal of Applied Philosophy* 21. no. 2 (2004): 173–82.

[60] I. Brown, *The Boy in the Moon: A Father's Journey to Understand His Extraordinary Son* (New York: St. Martin's Press, 2011).

and irreparability, a sense of excessive suffering.[61] But in the words of George Steiner, "Yet in the very excess of his suffering lies man's claim to dignity."[62] Our sense of human dignity is shaped and molded by the tragic. Enacting Catholic Social Tradition happens in the space between the obvious and the impossible.

Alfred Delp found moral clarity and a new understanding of the price of Catholic Social Teaching in prison. His experience of the clear moral vision of the right and the wrong in politics was like his experience of Advent—and not only because he spent the crucial months of Advent 1944 in prison, preparing for the trial that would lead to his sentencing and execution. Advent, as Delp experienced it, challenges comfort, indifference, and ambiguity. Advent turns out to be the time of decision,[63] the time in which we must see things as they are.[64] Advent is the time of decision because the prophetic call to conversion compels a decision; it opens up a horizon of decisions on which people have to take a position. The possibility of indifference is no longer an option given the radical difference between what is, and what is preached as future reality. Advent is a time of a new realism, entailing a new discipline to see things as they are—including an understanding of what really counts when measuring and weighing what is. Advent lets us experience the temporary nature of the ephemeral structures of our lives, which increases the need for moral clarity and support beyond the variable and changeable. And this moral clarity can be drawn from an understanding of the absolute.

Delp experienced Advent as both an encounter with the absolute and a time of truth. Such an experience of truth in the wrong, as Delp had in prison (Coady called it "Truth Hidden in Untruth"[65]), stands in the way of the famous Adorno statement: "There is no right life in the wrong one."[66] Delp experienced truth "in the wrong life," in an injustice. This does not justify the wrong life, but strengthens our hope and trust both in the power *of* good and the power *for* good. Seen in this way, Advent becomes an exercise in overcoming comfort and indifference. In prison, Delp was shaken to the core. And this shock continued, since it went hand in hand with a deeper sense of incompleteness and sinfulness, and a need

---

[61] G. Steiner, *The Death of Tragedy* (New York: Oxford University Press, 1980), xi and 8, respectively.
[62] Ibid., 9.
[63] Delp, *Prison Meditations*, 33.
[64] Ibid., 47.
[65] Coady, "Truth Hidden in Untruth."
[66] "Es gibt kein richtiges Leben im falschen" (T. W. Adorno, *Minima Moralia: Reflexionen aus dem beschädigten Leben*, Gesammelte Schriften 4 [Frankfurt/Main: Suhrkamp, 1997], 43).

for conversion. Advent does not give freedom to those who think they have already converted. Advent provides moral clarity, precisely because the essential is separated from the nonessential. Catholic Social Teaching is an invitation to build the kingdom of God, to renew the commitment to a new social order. It is, in this sense, an expression of "an Advent spirituality."

1

Enacting Human Dignity

The principle of human dignity and the commitment to honor the dignity of each human person are at the center of Catholic Social Tradition. However, honoring human dignity in practice is part of the challenge of "enactment" mentioned in the introduction. What does it mean to respect human dignity in stress-filled situations or in situations of conflict? What do we mean when we say that human dignity has been violated, even though we believe in the inviolability of dignity?

There are many questions around human dignity—questions about definition and meaning, about justification and sources, and about practices and policies. All these questions are important. But there seems to be a particularly troubling challenge related to the enactment, realization, or implementation of human dignity. It is revealing that judges disagree about whether the dignity of a person has been violated in concrete cases and particular situations. Consider the well-known Benetton print advertisement that displayed naked human buttocks stamped with the phrase "H.I.V. POSITIVE," with the clothing company's name in small letters underneath. Does this ad violate human dignity? There was notable disagreement about this question.[1] So perhaps even if we had a clear definition of human dignity, and even if we were clear about the justification for it, disputes might still take place about whether it had been enacted.

Mary Robinson, UN High Commissioner for Human Rights from 1997 to 2002, mentioned the need for human rights practices at the end of a 2002 Tübingen lecture, "Ethics, Human Rights, and Globalization," stating, "I am struck by the fact that we have no need for new pledges and commitments. They are all there in solemn language. We need something more prosaic: implementation, implementation, implementation!"[2]

---

[1] See C. Smith, "More Disagreement over Human Dignity: Federal Constitutional Court's Most Recent Benetton Advertising Decision," *German Law Journal* 4, no. 6 (2003): 533–39.

[2] M. Robinson, *Ethics, Human Rights and Globalization, Second Global Ethic Lecture, The Global Ethic Foundation* (Tübingen: Global Ethic Foundation, 2002), 8.

1

Implementation is not an academic or abstract or elitist mandate. Eleanor Roosevelt famously stated that human rights have to begin at home:

> In small places, close to home—so close and so small that they cannot be seen on any maps of the world. Yet they are the world of the individual person; the neighborhood he lives in; the school or college he attends; the factory, farm, or office where he works. Such are the places where every man, woman, and child seeks equal justice, equal opportunity, equal dignity without discrimination.[3]

The enactment of human dignity in concrete situations is the basis for a culture of dignity. Concepts and conceptual clarifications do a certain type of work, practices and habits another.

Enacting dignity can be—and too often has been—a literal matter of life and death. Our experience with a culture of respecting human dignity is complex, from saints and moral leaders to indifference and destruction.

Fragility

Our experience is also dark: human dignity is precious because it is fragile—that is, it can be violated, trampled upon, not properly honored. In fact, it is amazing what human beings are willing and able to do to each other. In his moving *Notes from the Warsaw Ghetto*, Emmanuel Ringelblum provides particularly painful examples of humiliation that illustrate the violation of human dignity:[4]

> Women in fur coats. They're ordered to wash the pavement with their panties, then put them on again wet. (17)
>
> Several Jews were pressed into pulling an auto that was stuck and then ordered to march in line, saying: "Good luck." They were forbidden to turn around. They walked and walked for a long time, unaware that no one was following them. (17)
>
> A lawyer covered his arm band with his briefcase. They put his fur coat on him backwards and commanded him to walk the streets that way. (18)

---

[3] Eleanor Roosevelt, quoted in M. Ignatieff, "Human Rights, Global Ethics, and the Ordinary Virtues," *Ethics and International Affairs* 31, no. 1 (2017): 1–16, at 1.

[4] E. Ringelblum, *Notes from the Warsaw Ghetto*, trans. J. Sloan (New York: Schocken Books, 1974). Page numbers in parentheses.

> The workers are ordered to beat one another with their galoshes. A Jew who was taken to the garages wearing phylacteries for prayer was forced to work all day in them. A rabbi was ordered to shit in his pants. (19)
>
> Heard that the president of the Jewish Council of Warsaw ... was kept standing in a German office for eight hours and not offered a chair. (53)
>
> A Jew was ordered to kneel, and they urinated on him. (91)
>
> For some offense (presumably smuggling), a few seven- or eight-year-old children and a Christian woman were forced to do calisthenics for more than an hour, touching their toes. Afterward ... one child couldn't move. (142)
>
> Heard from a Lodz refugee that the editor of the Lodz newspaper, a former anti-Semitic National Democrat called Kargel, ordered the Jewish artist Hanemann to paint him standing on the ruins of Warsaw in the pose of a conqueror. Naturally, the portrait was to be signed by an Aryan artist. (164)
>
> [A rabbi] was ordered to sweep the street. Then he was ordered to collect the refuse into his fur hat. (167)

The situations speak for themselves, but they all involve the experience of not being able to freely choose dignified agency, of not being a full member of the human family, because of the doings of others. What is at stake here is not to be grasped in categories of "doing" (i.e., A experienced *x* because A committed action *y*), but rather in categories of "being." The fundamental "fault" of the Jewish person in this context was simply "being Jewish." All these situations involve agency insecurity, based on "ontological insecurity"—the insecurity resulting from loss of one's identity and place in the world. A number of situations also involve intentional pointlessness; they are part of a system that made it impossible for a person to live without humiliation. As Ringelblum wrote, "The only way Jews can live these days is to break the law" (27); the point of the law was not to enable, but to disable life and cooperation. "They beat up people for saluting them ('I'm no friend of yours'). And they beat up people for not saluting them" (53); similarly: "A decree was published forbidding Jews to salute the Others by removing their hats. A placard to this effect was posted in the streets. But now some of those people who fail to salute the Others are being beaten" (124).

Here, humiliation results from the persistently and publicly failed attempt to make a bid or claim to a certain social status: "What is denied is not only the status claim itself, but also and more fundamentally the individual's very status to have made such a claim at all."[5] This way of humiliating a person has undermined any sense of basic respect owed a human being (if one defines "respecting X" as "recognizing X as a source of normative claims"). A person, then, is not fully accepted as a person.

Humiliation is an obvious and tangible way of disrespecting a person's dignity. We do not have to refer to extreme situations like the Warsaw ghetto; humiliations happen in all societies, every day. People are humiliated when they are "invisible," when they are not invited to occupy public spaces. The shaming and shame endured by homeless persons in their experience of not being welcome points to humiliation; persons are humiliated when they have reasons to feel out of place. Persons in low-paid jobs, like street sweepers and office-cleaning personnel, complain about being ignored. French journalist Florence Aubenas, who worked undercover as a cleaner for twelve months, was told, when she was trained, that she should not expect anyone to pass the time of day with her, recognize her presence, or see her as a person; this was something she would have to get used to.[6] It is a social imperative for custodians and cleaners to remain invisible, and taking cleanliness for granted is perceived as part of a well-functioning institution: "Most of us know when somewhere has not been cleaned but few of us, we suspect, stop to think much about the laboring processes which go into maintaining spaces as clean."[7] A similar experience is recounted by Anna Sam, who, as a student in social anthropology, worked as a cashier in a supermarket. Customers were quite often oblivious to the fact that a human individual was operating the till, often ignoring her completely, without so much as a look or a word.[8] Axel Honneth has identified the experience of "seeing through or past" a person as an indication of a social pathology.[9] There are different ways of not showing a person respect, such as acting as if she were not present, an object, or not a full person. All these are frustrations of recognition and respect.

People are humiliated when they are reduced to epistemic objects, that is, to representatives of a group rather than as an individual person. This can happen in the context of a medical encounter, where a (vulnerable) person is labeled as "patient" and reduced to being a member of the

---

[5] W. J. Torres and R. M. Bergner, "Humiliation: Its Nature and Consequences," *Journal of the American Academy of Psychiatry and the Law* 38, no. 2 (2010): 195–204, at 199.

[6] F. Aubenas, *Le quai de Ouistreham* (Paris: Éditions de l'Olivier, 2010), 45.

[7] A. Herod and L. Aguiar, "Cleaners and the Dirty Work of Neoliberalism," *Antipode* 38, no. 3 (2006): 425–34, at 427.

[8] A. Sam, *Checkout: A Life on the Tills* (London: Gallic Books, 2009).

[9] See A. Honneth, "Invisibility: On the Epistemology of 'Recognition,'" *Proceedings of the Aristotelian Society, Supplementary Volume* 75, no. 1 (2001): 111–26.

group "patients."[10] This is an instance of what Avishai Margalit has called "blindness to the human aspect."[11] This blindness implies restricted or diminished awareness of the presence of a human being, a dysfunctional vision comparable to color blindness. Such dysfunctional vision is a key element in colonial literature, in which people look through others or ignore them as though they were not there.[12] Those who run the greatest risk of falling victim to such treatment are the socially vulnerable. As an important and disturbing way to violate a person's sense of dignity, humiliation can be "any sort of behavior or condition that constitutes a sound reason for a person to consider his or her self-respect injured."[13] Self-respect is the kind of respect one owes oneself purely because one is human. Being rejected from the human family is the strongest kind of humiliation.

There are many ways to violate a person's dignity—humiliating, objectifying, degrading, and dehumanizing are methods for denying the status of "person" to a human being. Instances of violations to human dignity are windows into the concept and into the work the concept can do. There is a clear link between dignity and vulnerability; in fact, we would not have discourse on human dignity without the experience of vulnerability. The 1848 French decree abolishing slavery (it said that "slavery is an assault upon human dignity"[14]) presupposed the atrocious experience of slavery and slaves. After the atrocities of World War I, which left many people without the means to live their lives in dignity, the 1919 Weimar Constitution aimed to deliver dignity-affirming basic rights, with article 51 stating, "The economy has to be organized based on the principles of justice, with the goal of achieving life in dignity for everyone."[15] The 1948 Universal Declaration of Human Rights and the Federal Republic of Germany's 1949 Basic Law were designed and debated after looking into the abyss of the World War II and the Holocaust. The Basic Law prominently declared in article 1.1: "Human dignity shall be inviolable. To respect and protect it shall be the duty of all state authority." In short, the discourse on human dignity is based on the experience of human vulnerability and the exploitation of this vulnerability. The concept of human dignity "seems particularly apt as

---

[10] See A. Lazare, "Shame and Humiliation in the Medical Encounter," *Archives of Internal Medicine* 147, no. 9 (1987): 1653–58.

[11] A. Margalit, *The Decent Society* (Cambridge, MA: Harvard University Press, 1996), 96–103.

[12] Ibid., 102.

[13] Ibid., 9.

[14] Decree of the Abolution of Slavery in the French Republic, April 27, 1848.

[15] "Die Ordnung des Wirtschaftslebens muß den Grundsätzen der Gerechtigkeit mit dem Ziele der Gewährleistung eines menschenwürdigen Daseins für alle entsprechen."

part of a description of such morally repugnant acts and practices that form a part of our modern experience of the world. . . . Any satisfactory conception of dignity should . . . not be detached from concrete occurrences and interpretations in social life."[16] This approach is inductive and experiential.

At the same time, we need to have a sense of the symbolic in order to make sense of the concept of dignity and its violation. The term "human dignity" expresses, among other important aspects, the idea that the material and tangible and visible aspects of the world and the human condition do not have the final word. That is why Hannes Kuch constructs dignity as symbolic vulnerability connected to the dependency on recognition: "Honor as well as dignity can be seen as constituted by a symbolic sphere surrounding a person to which others have to pay attention in their behavior and which can easily be threatened by the actions of others, namely by their symbolic actions."[17] The human person is a "citizen of two worlds": the material and the immaterial. Human dignity refers to an immaterial dimension of human life that cannot fully be grasped by a language that describes the person as a "utility-maximizer." The immaterial, symbolic sphere of our human condition opens up additional cruel ways of violating a person's dignity. When Jewish citizens were forced by the Nazis to scrub the sidewalks, they were not only physically abused, they were also—and even more fundamentally—abused symbolically. The material and the immaterial are inextricably linked in matters of dignity; indeed, one elementary way of violating a person's dignity is making her lose control over her basic bodily functions. Human dignity is not constituted by bread alone, but also by a person's hunger for justice. However, as accounts of cruel famines remind us, maintaining a sense of human dignity without bread is next to impossible.

Human dignity, then, is upheld and defended by respecting both the need for bread and the transcendence of the human person who does not live by bread alone. Reporting from an eight-country research project that engaged with poor and extremely poor people, Michael Ignatieff observed, "For those living in such extreme poverty, is not life a battle for survival rather than a struggle for meaning? On the contrary, it was soon obvious that even in the most desperate shantytown or the most crime-ridden housing project, life remained a search for moral order of

---

[16] P. Kaufman et al., "Human Dignity Violated: A Negative Approach—Introduction," in P. Kaufmann et al., eds., *Humiliation, Degradation, Dehumanization: Human Dignity Violated* (Dordrecht: Springer, 2011), 1–5, at 1–2.

[17] H. Kuch, "The Rituality of Humiliation: Exploring Symbolic Vulnerability," in Kaufmann et al., *Humiliation, Degradation, Dehumanization*, 37–56, at 50.

some sort."[18] The human person does not live by bread alone. This is one building block in our understanding of human dignity.

Catholic Social Tradition and "Doing Dignity"

Commitment to the dignity of the human person is at the very core of Catholic Social Tradition, with its adherence to a normative tradition that holds that each person is created in the image and likeness of God. The basic message is clear: the *imago Dei* idea has an equalizing effect since it states that *all* persons are created in the image and likeness of God, thus assigning equal rank to each person as highest in the order of creation.[19] The *Compendium of the Social Doctrine of the Church* leaves no room for doubt about the central place of the commitment to human dignity: *The whole of the Church's social doctrine, in fact, develops from the principle that affirms the inviolable dignity of the human person.*[20] Acknowledging the dignity of the human person means acknowledging the person in her uniqueness, in her mystery, in her special place in creation that cannot be mistaken for a capability-based or a meritocratic or even a civic understanding of dignity.[21] "Value the human person for she is

---

[18]M. Ignatieff, "Human Rights, Global Ethics, and the Ordinary Virtues," *Ethics and International Affairs* 31, no. 1 (2017): 1–16, at 7.

[19]See J. Waldron, "The Image of God: Rights, Reason, and Order," in J. Witte Jr. and F. Alexander, eds., *Christianity and Human Rights: An Introduction* (Cambridge: Cambridge University Press, 2010), 216–35. Waldron makes the point that the *imago Dei* approach to dignity has something unique to offer since it talks about the (equal) rank that we hold in creation and the connection to three basic rights: the right to life, welfare rights, and the right not to be subjected to degrading treatment. The *imago Dei* idea supports an anthropocentrism that is undeniably part of the Christian theological tradition; this anthropocentrism is defended in *Laudato Si'* in at least two passages: "At times we see an obsession with denying any pre-eminence to the human person; more zeal is shown in protecting other species than in defending the dignity which all human beings share in equal measure. Certainly, we should be concerned lest other living beings be treated irresponsibly. But we should be particularly indignant at the enormous inequalities in our midst, whereby we continue to tolerate some considering themselves more worthy than others" (90); "Christian thought sees human beings as possessing a particular dignity above other creatures; it thus inculcates esteem for each person and respect for others" (119) (Francis, *Laudato Si'*, "On Care for Our Common Home" [2015], hereinafter *LS*).

[20]Pontifical Council for Justice and Peace, *Compendium of the Social Doctrine of the Church* (2004), no. 107, hereinafter *CSDC*.

[21]Q. I. T. Genuis, "Dignity Reevaluated: A Theological Examination of Human Dignity and the Role of the Church in Bioethics and End-of-Life-Care," *Linacre Quarterly* 83, no. 1 (2016): 6–14, esp. 8–10; for two other versions of dignity, see J. Ober, "Meritocratic and Civic Dignity in Greco-Roman Antiquity," in *The Cambridge Handbook of Human Dignity*, ed. M. Düwell et al. (Cambridge: Cambridge University Press, 2014), 53–63.

human" is a short formula for this understanding of dignity.[22] This commitment informs the way we look at the person, at interactions with one another, at rules and regulations. It has been argued that human dignity opens the door to a particular form of life with specific actions, attitudes, and perceptions, as I mentioned in the introduction. One example of the way a sense of human dignity makes us "see" can be found in J. M. Coetzee's disturbing novel *Waiting for the Barbarians*. The protagonist defends four prisoners who are about to be killed with a sledgehammer. "Not with that!" I shout, . . . You would not use a hammer on a beast. . . . Look at these men. . . . Men!"—and also: "Look! We are the great miracle of creation!"[23] A sense of human dignity changes our judgments and our perceptions.

The outcry at this particularly disturbing scene is a reminder to see human beings *as* human beings, to see people *as* persons with dignity. The protagonist wants to say, "*Don't you see that these are human beings?* If you were to *see* that, you would not even think of torturing them!" The heart of the matter is not an analysis, not a series of arguments—it is a question of perception. Dignity is not only a concept, it is a way of perceiving. How can we learn to see clearly—to recognize and address structural injustice, racism, prejudice, and systemic and systematic discrimination and lift up the dignity of those who have been denied it?

The outcry "These are human beings!" has been heard the world over during the COVID-19 pandemic. It was heard in Spain, when soldiers helping to fight the pandemic found "elderly patients in retirement homes abandoned and, in some cases, dead in their beds."[24] The same outcry could be heard in the United Kingdom where care homes felt "completely abandoned" as the pandemic swept across the country.[25] The same outcry again in Italy, where commentators observed a "silent massacre" in nursing homes.[26] In the United States, in reaction to the all-too-familiar fate of George Floyd, the outcry against brutal individual and systemic racism—*This is a human being!*—resonated around the world, where a chorus of voices cried, "I can't breathe." We have been confronted with a terrifying reminder that misperception—blindness to systemic injustice—is more than just the indifference of the innocuous bystander. By failing to see, we deny dignity.

---

[22] See C. McCrudden, "In Pursuit of Human Dignity: An Introduction to Current Debates," in C. McCrudden, ed., *Understanding Human Dignity* (Oxford: Oxford University Press, 2013), 1–58, esp. 15–23.

[23] J. M. Coetzee, *Waiting for the Barbarians* (New York: Penguin, 1981), 106.

[24] "Coronavirus: Spanish Army Finds Care Home Residents 'Dead and Abandoned,' " BBC News, March 24, 2020.

[25] "Coronavirus: Care Homes Felt 'Completely Abandoned,' " BBC News, May 14, 2020.

[26] Greta Privitera, "The 'Silent Massacre' in Italy's Nursing Homes," Politico, April 30, 2020.

Dignity as a concept, as an attitude, as a way of seeing, and as a set of practices makes a difference—it *needs* to make a difference.

Dignity is a lofty concept, so it needs to be grounded. One important difference between a particular philosophical approach and Catholic Social Tradition is that the latter can refer to practices on the ground. Whatever happens in parishes and Catholic schools, Catholic hospitals, and mission bases is part of a rich and dynamic tradition. This may make it easier to deal with the suspected "elitism" of the discourse on human dignity. Partly shaped by a preferential option for the poor,[27] Catholic Social Tradition can move beyond an elitist discourse that seeks the universal category and the generalizable rule. Ignatieff has observed that there seem to be two different approaches to human rights:

> In the moral universe of the human rights activist and the global ethicist, the object of ultimate concern is the universal human being. Human differences—of race, class, or situation—are secondary. In this conception of moral life, one's primary duty is to be impartial, to regard the distinction, for example, between a citizen and a stranger as morally irrelevant. In our conversations surrounding the moral universe of the ordinary virtues, on the other hand, the universal human being was rarely, if ever, the object of ultimate concern. The most striking feature of the ordinary virtue perspective is how rarely any of our participants evoked ideas of general obligation to human beings as such; and how frequently they reasoned in terms of the local, the contingent, the here and now—what they owed those near to them and what they owed themselves.[28]

---

[27] The idea of a preferential option for the poor has been summarized in *Sollicitudo Rei Socialis* 42: "This is an option, or a *special form* of primacy in the exercise of Christian charity, to which the whole tradition of the Church bears witness. It affects the life of each Christian inasmuch as he or she seeks to imitate the life of Christ, but it applies equally to our *social responsibilities* and hence to our manner of living, and to the logical decisions to be made concerning the ownership and use of goods. Today, furthermore, given the worldwide dimension which the social question has assumed, this love of preference for the poor, and the decisions which it inspires in us, cannot but embrace the immense multitudes of the hungry, the needy, the homeless, those without health care and, above all, those without hope of a better future" (John Paul II, *Sollicitudo Rei Socialis*, "The Social Concern" (1987), hereinafter *SRS*).

[28] Ignatieff, "Human Rights, Global Ethics and Ordinary Virtues," 10. The "nonelites" have deep moral concerns, but not the abstract language that allows for generalization: "As we listened to favela dwellers, inhabitants of informal settlements, farmers in their fields, monks in their places of worship, we began to see that most ordinary people do not generalize or systematize their thinking. A global ethic, applicable to all mankind, is unimaginable and irrelevant to them. This is not because ordinary people do not reflect deeply about the injustice of the world and imagine a better one. It is because the validity of a moral proposition for them does not turn on whether it can be universalized or generalized. Its validity turns instead on whether it is true for them and their immediate

This creates a creative tension between intellectual elites living in the world of ideas and poor people dealing with life struggles. With the principle of human dignity, Catholic Social Tradition can offer contributions from both ends of this wide spectrum of engagement.

The enactment of human dignity can follow a script with thick examples in the tradition, a script that tells stories about saints who were committed to a form of life that breathed respect for the dignity of the human person. Concrete examples of lives dedicated to upholding the dignity of each person can be found in Catholic Social Tradition; these examples offer concrete descriptions of what an enactment of human dignity can look like. The witness of Dorothy Mae Stang may come to mind: an American-Brazilian religious sister who was killed in the Amazon Basin of Brazil after having advocated for the rights of the poor and the needs of the environment—killed because of her fight for dignity. Here again we see that enacting Catholic Social Tradition is not harmless but comes with costs and sacrifice.[29] It requires "deep practices," as we shall see, practices that are faithful to moral and spiritual demands, even in the face of adversity.

In studying the enactment of Catholic Social Tradition we can refer to a rich tradition of examples and practices. This is obviously not a ready-made script that an actor playing a role can follow, but there is a richness that deepens the loftiness of the concept, paradoxically through the dust and blood of real lives.

Again: dignity is a lofty concept. It helps us celebrate the beauty of the human person; it helps us be reminded of a story too beautiful and powerful to be excluded from the public discourse and from civic life—that is, the story of the human person being created in the image and likeness of God. This story can serve as an expression of truth but also as a postulate in a Kantian sense.[30]

Catholic Social Tradition has found many ways to tell this story, beginning in the patristic era.[31] The most explicit and focused expressions of the understanding of human dignity in this rich tradition can be found in Catholic Social Teaching documents. The documents—which, as I try to emphasize, in no way exhaust Catholic Social Thought—give us more

---

community, and whether it makes sense even provisionally of their specific context and situation" (ibid., 8).

[29]See R. Murphy, *Martyr of the Amazon: The Life of Sister Dorothy Stang* (Maryknoll, NY: Orbis Books, 2007).

[30]A postulate is an assumption beyond rational proof that is accepted as true as the basis for important and desirable action or argumentation.

[31]See T. G. Weinandy, "St. Irenaeus and the *Imago Dei*: The Importance of Being Human," *Logos* 6, no. 4 (2003): 15–34.

than simply a deep theological concept; they also offer some tangible points for the enactment of human dignity.

Key documents of Catholic Social Teaching provide us with an understanding of the scope of violations of human dignity:

- *Whatever is opposed to life itself*, such as any type of murder, genocide, abortion, euthanasia, or willful self-destruction.[32]
- *Insults to a dignified life*, such as subhuman living conditions, arbitrary imprisonment, deportation, slavery, prostitution, the selling of women and children; or disgraceful working conditions, where people are treated as mere tools for profit, rather than as free and responsible persons;[33] no access to water;[34] and terrorism.[35]
- *Whatever violates the integrity of the human person*, such as mutilation, torments inflicted on the body or mind, attempts to coerce the will,[36] attempts to force internal compliance,[37] or use of drugs that undermine a person's inner freedom.[38]
- *Whatever exploits human vulnerability*, such as child labor.[39]

This list does not provide an exhaustive set of indicators, but inspirations for tangible points of respecting or violating the dignity of the human person. Lists are not the best instrument with which to approach a deep understanding of human dignity, just as documents are not the best tool for reflecting on the realities of doing dignity. Nonetheless, the documents point to something beyond the texts; they serve as the tip of the iceberg reflecting a rich tradition and providing in document-form a condensed version of a multilayered discourse. In the light of key Catholic Social Tradition documents we can list four central aspects of human dignity, as framed by Catholic Social Thought.

First, *human dignity is a concept that orders our relationship with God*; let us call this the *vertical* dimension of human dignity. One particular aspect of this vertical dimension is the inner and spiritual life of the person, a Sabbath dimension in his or her life: "To safeguard man's dignity

---

[32]John XXIII, *Gaudium et Spes*, "Pastoral Constitution on the Church in the Modern World" (1965), no. 27, hereinafter *GS*; Benedict XVI, *Caritas in Veritate*, "Charity in Truth" (2009), no. 75, hereinafter *CV*; and *CSDC* 553.

[33]Francis, *Evangelii Gaudium*, "The Joy of the Gospel" (2013), no. 27, hereinafter *EG*.

[34]*LS* 30.

[35]*CSDC* 514.

[36]*GS* 27.

[37]John XXIII, *Pacem in Terris*, "Peace On Earth" (1963), no. 48, hereinafter *PT*.

[38]John Paul II, *Centesimus Annus*, "On the Hundredth Anniversary [of *Rerum Novarum*]" (1991), no. 36, hereinafter *CA*.

[39]*CSDC* 296.

as a creature of God endowed with a soul in the image and likeness of God, the Church has always demanded a diligent observance of the third Commandment: 'Remember that thou keep holy the sabbath day.'"[40] This resonates with an understanding of the human person as striving for a "Magis": "Having created him in his image, he also establishes the transcendent dignity of men and women and feeds their innate yearning to 'be more.'"[41] In this sense, human dignity is concerned with orthodoxy, with our right relationship with God.[42]

Second, *within social and interpersonal relationships, human dignity is expressed and enacted*; an important aspect of this *horizontal* dimension of dignity is the recognition of the special status of certain relationships. Catholic Social Teaching is clear about the institution of marriage as a necessary condition for the recognition of human dignity: "When the inalienable right of marriage and of procreation is taken away, so is human dignity."[43] A further expression of this horizontal dimension of dignity is a commitment to solidarity as almost a direct translation of dignity: everyone must consider his or her neighbor without exception as another self, first of all taking into account their neighbor's life and "the means necessary to living it with dignity."[44] The language of dignity is explicitly used to curb extreme disparity.[45] With numerous implications, this reference to disparity is a strong statement, making a commitment to a deeper equality that underlies all types of differences. All persons "are equally noble in natural dignity, and consequently there are no differences at all between political communities from the point of view of natural dignity."[46] This dignity-based equality (and equality in dignity) also excludes the acceptance of any form of racism.[47] Another important element of this horizontal dimension of human dignity is the special attention to the weakest members of a community, since "Only the recognition of human dignity can make possible the common and personal growth of everyone (cf. Jas

---

[40] John XXIII, *Mater et Magistra*, "On Christianity and Social Progress" (1961), no. 249, hereinafter *MM*.

[41] CV 29.

[42] Leo XIII, *Rerum Novarum*, "Rights and Duties of Capital and Labor" (1891), no. 40, hereinafter *RN*.

[43] Paul VI, *Populorum Progressio*. "On the Development of Peoples" (1967), no. 37, hereinafter *PP*; cf. *CA* 39.

[44] GS 27.

[45] "For excessive economic and social differences between the members of the one human family or population groups cause scandal, and militate against social justice, equity, the dignity of the human person . . ." (*GS* 29); "The dignity of the individual and the demands of justice require, particularly today, that economic choices do not cause disparities in wealth to increase in an excessive and morally unacceptable manner" (*CV* 32).

[46] PT 89.

[47] PT 44.

2:1–9)."[48] Proper work for people with disabilities is demanded by their human dignity;[49] similarly the integration of immigrants is necessitated by the recognition of their human dignity.[50]

Third, *human agency, responsibility, and freedom constitute a dimension of human dignity* according to Catholic Social Tradition. Let us call this the *expressive* dimension. Dignity is given space and expression in a person's life through exercising personal initiative[51] and making up her own mind when she acts.[52] Moreover, the respect for personal dignity recognizes "in the person a subject who is always capable of giving something to others."[53] This understanding of the person as an agent, as both contributor and subject of contributive justice, could mean some rethinking of possible and valuable contributions beyond a standard model—for example, as to the important contribution of people with severe disabilities. This reminder of agency, of course, is not meant to reduce a person to her "productivity," but is rather a commitment to seeing the being of a person as a foundational, irreducible, and undeniable source of valuable contributions.

Fourth, *human dignity needs to be translated into rights and conditions*—what I refer to as the *legal* dimension. In fact, "The movement towards the identification and proclamation of human rights is one of the most significant attempts to respond effectively to the inescapable demands of human dignity."[54] The human dignity of workers is respected by appropriate working conditions[55] and a "just wage" that allows for a standard of living "consistent with human dignity."[56]

The vertical, horizontal, expressive, and legal dimensions of human dignity are interlinked in that the vertical dimension—connection to God—serves as foundation, reference point, and aim. The four dimensions and the points on this list just presented of dignity violations both give us a sense of what it means to translate dignity into practice, to enact human dignity. This is particularly important when we are faced with challenging circumstances such as huge inequalities or a "globalization of indifference."[57]

---

[48] *CSDC* 145.
[49] John Paul II, *Laborem Exercens*, "On Human Work" (1981), no. 22, hereinafter *LE*.
[50] *CSDC* 298.
[51] *MM* 83.
[52] *PT* 34; cf. *GS* 17.
[53] *CV* 57.
[54] *CSDC* 152.
[55] *MM* 21.
[56] *PT* 20. On the dignity of workers also see *RN* 20.
[57] See Michael Sean Winters, "Francis Continues to Critique Capitalism, Globalism of Indifference," *National Catholic Reporter*, November 29, 2017, www.ncronline.org.

Again, lists are not the best and most convincing way to do justice to the depth of the meaning of a concept; in fact, they may be obstacles to moral clarity. It is dangerous to organize the discourse on human dignity around lists of specifically human properties—such as the medieval discourse that developed rationality, freedom, social nature, moral capacity, and incommunicability as five "propria" of the human person.[58] Similarly risky is the contemporary discourse on "basic human capabilities," which contains a list of fundamental aspects of human agency.[59] A Christian understanding of human dignity moves beyond a capability-based understanding, which situates dignity within the context of certain capabilities that are quite often linked to cognitive faculties and reasoning skills.[60] The idea that the dignity of the human person is connected to what makes human beings distinct from other beings and animals is plausible, but it can easily lead us into the trap of isolating and listing essential features interpreted as necessary conditions of "being human" and "having dignity." Eva Feder Kittay, a philosopher and the mother of a daughter who does not fit into many philosophical textbooks' anthropological definitions, warned against a search for excluding and exhaustive characteristics, or for intrinsic properties of what it means to be human. In her presidential address at the 113th Eastern Division meeting of the American Philosophical Association, Kittay speaks with love and respect of her daughter:

> She has no measurable IQ and can do nothing for herself by herself. She defies philosophical characterizations of what is human, namely, the possession of certain essential attributes assumed to be definitive of the human. She is often written out of our moral treatises, though human she surely is. . . . The Kantian autonomy of the will may forever be beyond her grasp. Yet human she is. You know her humanity in every movement, every look, every response. You know it when you see her thrill to music, giggle at something she finds funny, or reach out her arms to embrace you; when she puts down her head

---

[58] See R. Imbach, "Human Dignity in the Middle Ages (Twelfth to Fourteenth Century)," in *Cambridge Handbook of Human Dignity*, ed. Marcus Düwell, Jens Braarvig, Roger Brownsword, and Dietmar Mieth (Cambridge: Cambridge University Press, 2014).

[59] See M. Nussbaum, *Women and Human Development* (New York: Cambridge University Press, 2000), 78–80; Nussbaum, "Capabilities as Fundamental Entitlements: Sen and Social Justice," *Feminist Economics* 9 (2003): 33–59. For a critical account, see S. Charusheela, "Social Analysis and the Capabilities Approach: A Limit to Martha Nussbaum's Universalist Ethics," *Cambridge Journal of Economics* 33 (2009): 1135–52, esp. 1138–39.

[60] Genuis, "Dignity Reevaluated," 8–10. Genuis, as indicated earlier, contrasts an understanding of dignity as "immutably given" with approaches that consider the concept of dignity as redundant or that view dignity through the lens of capabilities (especially connected to IQ).

shyly or beams when complimented. She has the feel and touch and smell of a human being. And above all, she is my daughter.[61]

We need to move into a second-person perspective, a perspective of encountering the person and "be *with* her" rather than (third-person) "talk *about* her." We need to move into the muddiness of experience if we want to "enact" the principle, value, and concept of human dignity.

Applying Catholic Social Tradition: The Meaning of Context

Human dignity is a principle that is presented with a claim to universality; it applies irrespective of cultural or historical context. The term "dignity" is used in a solemn way in serious documents such as constitutions, mission statements, papal letters, and Council documents, but there is a danger in using the concept as an aspirational term under ideal conditions, detached from real practices. As Ludwig Wittgenstein put it, "We have got onto slippery ice where there is no friction and so in a certain sense the conditions are ideal, but also, just because of that, we are unable to walk. We want to walk so we need friction. Back to the rough ground!"[62] We need the "friction" stemming from contact with the real ground, with real practices, best practices, everyday practices, and disturbing practices. Unless dignity is being practiced, it runs the risk of remaining a lofty concept without operational cash value or the moral importance of being a thorn in the flesh of institutional arrangements. We need to engage in "doing dignity," especially under challenging and adverse circumstances. Paradoxically, the universality of the principle of human dignity can only be justified if the principle is perceived to do justice to the local and particular context. The principle of human dignity does not operate in the abstract, but within concrete contexts of particular applications. Concrete application in particular situations, however, demands judgment, as we have seen. Such judgments have to take the local context into account in order to do justice to the particular situation.

Even a general principle like respecting the dignity of the human person arises against the background of an encounter with a concrete situation. A particular challenge in the application of principles is the question of how to honor changing circumstances and the signs of the times. The special history of World War II looms behind the general formulations of

---

[61] E. F. Kittay, "The Moral Significance of Being Human," *Proceedings and Addresses of the American Philosophical Association* 91 (2017): 22–42, at 24, and 28–29, respectively.

[62] Ludwig Wittgenstein, *Philosophical Investigations* (Oxford: Blackwell, 1967), 107.

the Universal Declaration of Human Rights, which in turn are invoked in specific contexts and have particular implications. General statements reflect a particular history; this history has to be understood in order to grasp not only the letter of the law but also its spirit. This requires a special relationship: in the famous passage on the letter that kills, Paul places emphasis, for good reason, on a special, trusting relationship with Christ: "Through Christ we have such great trust in God" (2 Cor 3:4). This trust is the foundation of our ability: "He has enabled us to be servants of the New Covenant, not of the letter, but of the Spirit. For the letter kills, but the spirit gives life" (2 Cor 3:6). Only the personal appropriation of the general (principle or law), which takes place in the particular (situations and circumstances), ensures this freedom of proper treatment. Doing justice to the letter and the spirit of the law (the principle) is not only a matter of proper judgment and reflective equilibrium, but also a question of spiritual identity. One wonders, perhaps, which suprarational motifs play a role in the verdicts of judges.

Let us deepen these points by looking at two decisions by the Grand Chamber of the European Court of Human Rights (ECHR). In a judgment from September 28, 2015, on the well-known case *Bouyid v. Belgium*, the ECHR Grand Chamber had to decide whether article 3 of the European Convention on Human Rights ("No one shall be subjected to torture or to inhuman or degrading treatment or punishment") had been violated by a police officer who had slapped seventeen-year-old Said Bouyid in the face when he protested his arrest at the police station. The Grand Chamber's assessment began with an expression of a commitment to a deep practice of human dignity: "Even in the most difficult circumstances, such as the fight against terrorism and organised crime, the Convention prohibits in absolute terms torture and inhuman or degrading treatment or punishment, irrespective of the conduct of the person concerned" (para. 81). Respecting article 3 and respecting human dignity are explicitly linked: "The Court has emphasized that respect for human dignity forms part of the very essence of the Convention" (para. 89); this is reiterated in paragraph 101 with, "Any interference with human dignity strikes at the very essence of the Convention." In the decision we find an explicit reference to a contextual "threshold aspect": "Ill-treatment must attain a minimum level of severity if it is to fall within the scope of Article 3" (para. 86), and there is a further elucidatory note on this question of "level of severity":

> Ill-treatment that attains such a minimum level of severity usually involves actual bodily injury or intense physical or mental suffering. However, even in the absence of these aspects, where treatment humiliates or debases an individual, showing a lack of respect for

or diminishing his or her human dignity, or arouses feelings of fear, anguish or inferiority capable of breaking an individual's moral and physical resistance, it may be characterised as degrading. (para. 87)

The general context of the case at stake (i.e., the type of situation in which Said Bouyid found himself) is taken into account with a reference to increased levels of vulnerability of the detained person: "Where an individual is deprived of his or her liberty or, more generally, is confronted with law-enforcement officers, any recourse to physical force which has not been made strictly necessary by the person's conduct diminishes human dignity and is in principle an infringement of the right set forth in Article 3 of the Convention" (para. 100).

The court's ruling is clear and expressed in clear language: "The Court emphasises that a slap inflicted by a law enforcement officer on an individual who is entirely under his control constitutes a serious attack on the individual's dignity" (para. 103). The expressed commitment to a "deep practice of respecting human dignity" is underscored in paragraph 108:

The fact that the slap may have been administered thoughtlessly by an officer who was exasperated by the victim's disrespectful or provocative conduct is irrelevant here. The Grand Chamber therefore departs from the Chamber's approach on this point. As the Court has previously pointed out, even under the most difficult circumstances, the Convention prohibits in absolute terms torture and inhuman or degrading treatment or punishment, irrespective of the conduct of the person concerned.

However, what is not clear is the role of context in the ruling. In paragraph 90, the judgment holds up the ruling irrespective of consequences and quotes another case (*Tyrer v. United Kingdom*, para. 33), which ruled, "Although the applicant did not suffer any severe or long-lasting physical effects, his punishment—whereby he was treated as an object in the power of the authorities—constituted an assault on precisely that which it is one of the main purposes of Article 3 (art. 3) to protect, namely a person's dignity and physical integrity." This paragraph 90 of *Bouyid v. Belgium* together with paragraph 103 seems to suggest that slapping a detainee is "intrinsically wrong," no matter the context or consequences.

This context-free reading is challenged on two grounds—first, by the text of the judgment itself. The court holds "that even one unpremeditated slap devoid of any serious or long-term effect on the person receiving it may be perceived as humiliating by that person" (para. 105). Hence, the aspect of subjective perception enters the argumentation. Second, and more seriously, a context-free reading of slapping is challenged by a joint, partly dissenting opinion by Judges De Gaetano, Lemmens, and Mahoney, who worry about the loss and lack of credibility of the application of the principles implied. After having stated forcefully that a slap by a police officer is unacceptable (para. 2–4), they call for a proper consideration of context. After asking, "Should it be accepted that any interference with human dignity constitutes degrading treatment and hence a violation of Article 3?" they raise the question of necessary "minimum levels of severity" that have to be attained in order for an act to violate article 3 (para. 5). The assessment whether this minimum has been met "depends on all the circumstances of the case." They criticize the judgment for not showing proper concern for the specific circumstances and for adopting "an eminently dogmatic position" (para. 6): "For our part, we consider that the specific circumstances are of fundamental importance. It is not for the Court to impose general rules of conduct on law-enforcement officers; instead, its task is limited to examining the applicants' individual situation." The context of the treatment, the kind of treatment, and the effects of the treatment need to be taken into account. Since this did not happen—thus, as one might say, constituting a sense of "absolute wrongs"—the three dissenting judges express the fear that

> the judgment may impose an unrealistic standard by rendering meaningless the requirement of a minimum level of severity for acts of violence by law-enforcement officers. Police officers may well be required to exercise self-control in all circumstances, regardless of the behaviour of the person they are dealing with [...] but this will not prevent incidents in which people behave provocatively towards them—as in the present case—and cause them to lose their temper. It will then be for the appropriate domestic courts, where necessary, to determine whether the officers' behaviour may have been excusable. (para. 7)

They explicitly point out that they respect the absolute prohibition of torture and inhuman or degrading treatment or punishment, but precisely because of the absolute nature of this prohibition there has to be a contextualized assessment of the level of severity. Their conclusion: "We should avoid trivialising findings of a violation of Article 3. The situation complained of in the present case is far less serious than the treatment inflicted by law-enforcement officers in many other cases that the Court has unfortunately had to deal with" (para. 7).

The discussion is of interest on many different levels: What is the relationship between "human dignity" and "degrading treatment," if one position opposes accepting that any interference with human dignity constitutes degrading treatment and hence a violation of article 3 of the ECHR? What is the role of the personal experiences and life histories of the judges involved?

The decisions allow deep insights into the concept and the operationalization of human dignity. As one scholar notes,

> The concept of human dignity is central, as the Court recognises, to delimiting at least some of these wrongs, not least degrading treatment or punishment. Substantively, human dignity has two interwoven aspects which are relevant to these wrongs: one is chiefly tied to the principle of treating persons with a special kind of respect which distinguishes them from objects or non-human animals; the other relates to providing or not denying the bare essentials required for human flourishing and personality development.[63]

These are helpful pointers to the anchoring of dignity in practice.

As a side note, the judgment discussing the police slapping the teenager's face makes an interesting observation about the connection between "human dignity" and "face": "A slap to the face affects the part of the person's body which expresses his individuality, manifests his social identity and constitutes the centre of his senses—sight, speech and hearing—which are used for communication with others. Indeed, the Court has already had occasion to note the role played by the face in social interaction" (para. 104).

A second interesting example of a discussion of "context" from the Grand Chamber of the ECHR is Judge Villiger's dissenting opinion in *Vinter and Others v. The United Kingdom* (July 9, 2013). The case dealt with criminals sentenced to lifelong imprisonment without the possibility of early release. The judgment declared, "For a life sentence to remain compatible with Article 3, there must be both a prospect of release and a possibility of review" (para. 110). The court justified this decision by noting the impossibility for the criminal to atone for an offense (para. 112) and by the failure of the penal system to aim for rehabilitation (para. 115), as well as by the statement, "It would be incompatible with the provision on human dignity in the Basic Law for the State forcefully to deprive a person of his freedom without at least providing him with

---

[63]N. Mavronicola, "*Bouyid v Belgium*: The 'Minimum Level of Severity' and Human Dignity's Role in Article 3 ECHR," *Cyprus Human Rights Law Review* 1 (2016): 1–16, at 13–14.

the chance to someday regain that freedom" (para. 113).[64] Judge Villiger partially disagreed with this judgment on epistemological and methodological grounds. He said he lacked the proper consideration of context pointing to consensus: "that whether or not an issue arises under Article 3 will depend on all circumstances of the individual case; that this provision contains different thresholds (namely 'inhuman,' 'degrading' and 'torture'); that a minimum of severity has to be reached to attain the first threshold; and that the assessment of this minimum will be relative." The judge notes that the judgment refers to the "standards" and "requirements" of article 3 without properly explaining what these standards and requirements are, a clear illustration of the challenge of "applying" and "enacting." Second, according to Villiger, there is undue generalization: "The judgment assesses the situation for all prisoners serving whole life orders, thus in fact providing for a generalised interpretation of Article 3. However, Article 3 would normally require an individualised assessment of each applicant's situation." In other words, there is a violation of the principle of subsidiarity in the handling of the case and in the way the Court overlooked different thresholds that must be taken into account. Again, Villiger articulates a plea for contextuality:

> The considerations in the judgment as to the problematic issues of irreducible sentences are relevant and valuable, but they have to be examined individually. Furthermore, in the context of such an individual examination, it is not the circumstances which existed at the outset of the sentence which are relevant, but rather the concrete circumstances which exist at the point in time when the Court comes to examine the case.

These considerations of legal reasoning concern an "ethic of thinking," an ethic of "crafting thoughts" and carving out judgments. Indeed, the text of the decision brings to light an interesting aspect of human dignity, expressed in the concurring opinion of Judge Power-Forde, who stated,

> I understand and share many of the views expressed by Judge Villiger in his partly dissenting opinion. However, what tipped the balance for me in voting with the majority was the Court's confirmation, in this judgment, that Article 3 encompasses what might be described

---

[64]In a 2017 decision in the case *Hutchinson v. the United Kingdom* (application no. 57592/08 [2016] ECHR 021) (January 2017) the Grand Chamber of the ECHR revisited the United Kingdom's life-sentencing regime, adding nuances to its earlier position and holding that the regime does not contravene the European Convention on Human Rights.

as "the right to hope." It goes no further than that. The judgment recognises, implicitly, that hope is an important and constitutive aspect of the human person. Those who commit the most abhorrent and egregious of acts and who inflict untold suffering upon others nevertheless retain their fundamental humanity and carry within themselves the capacity to change. Long and deserved though their prison sentences may be, they retain the right to hope that, someday, they may have atoned for the wrongs which they have committed. They ought not to be deprived entirely of such hope. To deny them the experience of hope would be to deny a fundamental aspect of their humanity and, to do that, would be degrading.

This explicit connection between "human dignity" and "hope" is insightful. It points to the implicit anthropology to be seen in judgments like these, and to hidden assumptions about human nature.

Both decisions invite a distinct effort to respect human dignity; I want to call a commitment to honoring human dignity even if it is costly, demanding, difficult, and challenging "a deep practice of human dignity." Such a practice upholds and defends respect for the dignity of the human person, even under adverse circumstances in which this respect may not be convenient or even prudent by worldly standards.

The Deep Practice of Human Dignity

A deep practice of human dignity is especially important in situations of increased vulnerability—both the vulnerability of a person to be harmed and the vulnerability of a person who acts against moral standards. In a report about his work experience, Jochen Temsch, a nurse working with an aggressive dementia patient, unabashedly described his revenge behavior: "I could strangle him with my bare hands! Yet, I decide for a more subtle revenge. Normally we use two washcloths: a bright one for the face and upper part of the body and a dark one for the legs and genitals. He, however, gets the dark washcloth for this bum as well as for his face."[65] Ralf Stoecker comments,

> Due to his dementia, the client presumably never realized what had been done to him. Moreover, there is no evidence in the report that the treatment harmed the old man's health. Hence, from the consequentialist perspective there is little reason to complain. And

---

[65] J. Temisch, "Das wird schon wieder werden," *Die Zeit* 48, November 25, 1994, 7.

although the client certainly would never have consented to having been washed with just one washcloth, it sounds somewhat forced to maintain that what is morally at stake in the example is merely a violation of autonomy. The young man's deed was so bad not just because he treated his client in a way that he would not have agreed to but because the treatment was deeply humiliating; it violated the old man's dignity.[66]

It is admittedly hard to honor the dignity of the person in one's behavior if confronted with a violent person; it is admittedly hard to hold on to a person's dignity if one has to shoulder responsibilities far beyond one's comfort zone or if pushed to the limits. But in these situations we find the litmus test of doing dignity. Practicing dignity under adverse circumstances can be called the "deep practice of human dignity." It should *not* be exceptional. Indeed, if we need to find cleverly construed arguments for honoring a human's dignity in these circumstances and contexts, quite a lot has already been lost. This is where the *imago Dei* story is more than a concept; it is a living tradition, an enacted narrative about the human person.

The story that can be told on the basis of the *imago Dei* understanding of the human person is essentially a story about the "*Magis*" (the "more") of the person. A person is so much more than her current role or status could express. Lisa Genova beautifully expressed this idea in her novel *Still Alice*. She describes a fifty-year-old Harvard psychology professor, Alice, who is diagnosed with early-onset Alzheimer's disease. Towards the end of the book Alice gives a talk at an Alzheimer's conference, not as a researcher, but as a patient—and she describes how she defined herself at first as an Alzheimer's patient. "But I am so much more than that!" She is wife and mother, soon-to-be-grandmother, as well as daughter, sister, and friend. She is "so much more" than any one role or particular aspect of her life. Respecting the dignity of a person means to accept the "more" of the person, the moment of mystery.

The instance Temsch describes in his article about his experience as a nurse is disturbing. Three weeks after his piece appeared, Gertrud Rueckert, the seventy-eight-year-old founder of a chain of nursing homes and senior citizen residences that invite young people in to spend a gap year, reacted to the article in a thoughtful essay. She challenged the young man—who was praised by some readers for his honesty and the sharing of very understandable emotions—by honestly expressing her fear of getting to

---

[66]R. Stoecker, "Three Crucial Turns on the Road to an Adequate Understanding of Human Dignity," in Kaufmann et al., *Humiliation, Degradation, Dehumanization*, 10–11.

the point of needing care. "I had come to realize how people may think in situations like these. I do not want to be judged in this undignified way."[67]

She observes how the young man has overstepped boundaries of decency in an almost autistic manner by not "seeing" another side; she notes how he has violated the dignity of the old man in his care. And she is worried about what will happen to her. Rueckert expresses her feeling that it can be hard, very hard, for an old woman to be undressed and washed by a young man who cannot hide his disgust. Rueckert expresses the hope that she will still belong to the human family as an old person, that her children will hold her the way she has held them when they needed their mother. We may not even need an understanding of human dignity based on the *imago Dei* to consider this the only appropriate way—but it does help. We can learn from Rueckert, who mentions a number of persons (people with disabilities, accident victims, the homeless) who may be at risk of being defined as useless members of society.

We need to practice and inhabit the deep practice of human dignity. Dan Coyle coined the term "deep practice" in his observations on high achievers.[68] He wondered about the remarkable soccer talent in Brazil and posited that training under adverse circumstances would constitute a "deep" way of developing a practice; if you have mastered the art of playing soccer on a rough *favela* lot with a makeshift ball made out of an old rug, how much easier would it be for you to excel at the game on a real soccer field, using a real soccer ball? Adverse conditions and deep commitments are characteristic of deep practices. You are faced with nonfavorable conditions that turn the practice into an uphill battle—and because of that you need to have access to strong beliefs, to robust concerns that will nurture the structures of your agency.

The deep practice of human dignity is a challenge in our everyday lives, but also on the theoretical level of diagnosis. The practice presupposes a strong sense of dignity and its violations, but it also has to work as "practice." That is to say, it has to be realistic given the pressures of and in everyday life. As an example, Maud Deckmar, in describing her experience raising her son Fred, diagnosed with autism, recounts two particular scenes:

---

[67]"Ich habe ja zur Kenntnis nehmen müssen, wie man in deren Situation denken kann. Und ich möchte nicht, daß man auch über mich so würdelos urteilt und möglicherweise die Erinnerung an mich nur lautet: "Vor zwei Tagen ist die Alte gestorben. Wir sind alle sehr zufrieden darüber" (G. Rueckert, "Eine Erwiderung: Gedanken einer alten Frau zur allerletzten Seite der Zeit," *Die Zeit*, December 16, 1994). Rueckert died at age ninety-four, by the way, in December 2011.

[68]D. Coyle, *The Talent Code* (New York: Bantam Books, 2009), part I.

Once, my mother had looked after Fred for a night, and I came to the farm to pick him up. She had tied one end of a long rope around his tummy and the other end round the trunk of a big tree. She had a lot to do, hanging laundry and couldn't stop doing all the chores around the place. The first thing I saw was my little four-year-old. My baby. A captive. Tied down with a rope. He was pulling at the rope that restrained him. I saw red.... I was used to not showing my anger and quietly went over to the tree and turned him loose.[69]

Her mother inquired whether she was upset: "'Yes, I damn well am,' I said indignantly. 'Do you have any idea how awful it seems, his being tied up like that?'" And the mother's reaction: "'Yes,' she answered quietly. 'But it was the only way for me to do anything but watch over him, and I don't honestly think it harmed him one little bit.'"[70]

I asked students to comment on this scene, specifically asking whether they thought Fred's dignity had been violated in this situation. The more than forty answers arrived unanimously in the affirmative. Their comments included,

- "While I think that the grandmother's actions were well-intended, I do read this situation as a violation of Fred's dignity—he was tied up 'like a captive,' infantilized."
- "This is degrading treatment."
- "The grandmother violated an important aspect of dignity, namely equality, and allowed Fred's being different to mitigate his dignity. She also failed to uphold subsidiarity—she didn't recognize Fred's ability to offer a positive contribution to her daily chores."
- "Fred was subjected to a situation where he could not exercise control over himself."
- "Fred was humiliated because this is something you might do to a dog, but not to a human being."
- "If I were tied to a tree I would feel useless, unwanted, unrespected."
- "Fred's dignity was violated because he was seen as an inconvenience, 'in the way' of the work; he was reduced to a 'burden.'"
- "By treating him this way the grandmother was not engaging with her grandson as a 'mysterious, relational being.'"
- "It is perhaps symbolic, in a way, that the boy was humiliated by being tied to a tree. Christ was also humiliated (in the sense that his human dignity was not recognized) when he was raised to the wooden cross."

---

[69] M. Deckmar, *My Son Fred: Living with Autism* (London: Jessica Kingsley, 2005), 33.
[70] Ibid.

- "Fred's dignity was violated; part of what makes this so clear is the fact that the reason for his captivity was not for his own safety, comfort or protection, but for the convenience of the caretaker."
- "Even if Fred was not physically harmed by his restraints, the symbolic sphere of vulnerability that surrounds him was not recognized by his grandmother."
- "'Doing dignity' is about operationalizing dignity in times when it is especially difficult. It is easy to recognize the dignity of others when our interactions are civil and polite. We must aspire to 'do dignity' when we are busy and have chores—when we feel as though we don't have the time."

The comments worked with the ideas that non-infantilization is an important aspect of respecting a person's dignity, that humiliation can be seen as a major indication of the violation of human dignity, and that one aspect of humiliation is induced loss of basic control.[71] The verdict was clear on the basis of a number of aspects; the story, however, becomes more complicated as one reads on:

> The next summer Maud and her husband went out for a picnic on Midsummer's Eve. The parents took turns to save the food, the garbage, the stereo, the china from their son Fred who would destroy everything he would get hold of. . . . Maud recounts: "I had packed everything with love and care, including napkins, a small Swedish flag and table cloth. All of no use. Why did I even try to make things nice and keep up a semblance of a festive mood? A dark rage came over me again. Fuck! He got hold of an egg and smashed it in his hand, threw himself over the rest of the food to find something else to smash. I helped him, threw an egg at a tree. It smashed. I didn't give a damn. His father said calmly:
> —"'I've got a 30-foot rope in the car. . . .'"
> —"'Get it!,' I said."[72]

Again, we are confronted with the question of how to comment on this situation from a human dignity perspective. Clearly, what is at stake is "respecting human dignity under adverse conditions," that is, a deep practice of human dignity. Raising a child with autism is highly challenging; there are adverse conditions, including the challenge of learning *how* to love an autistic child, an experience described by Sheila Barton,

---

[71]For this important aspect of honoring dignity by noninfantilizing the person, see J. Ober, "Democracy's Dignity," *American Political Science Review* 106, no. 4 (2012): 827–46.
[72]Deckmar, *My Son Fred*, 33–34.

who had to learn not to hug her son when he was banging his head against the wall.[73] Raising a child with autism makes families vulnerable, and raising a child with autism means raising a particularly vulnerable person. These challenges require deep commitments in order to endure and grow. In other words, raising a child with autism is a deep practice of living with a person.

Indeed, Deckmar is describing a situation that could qualify for the use of the term "humiliation": a child is tied up and loses some basic control; he could have reasons to feel his self-respect violated; he is exposed to a treatment routinely applied to dogs. However, Deckmar is not describing an institutionalized setting with a routine of restraining people to make life more efficient; different values are driving her decision. The situations she describes, in their full context, show aspects of a deep practice. There is a history, the acceptance of costly commitment, genuine interest in Fred as a person—and not as a "problem." The grandmother has to run a farm with daily chores that cannot be delegated, and at the same time she has to take care of a grandson who is at risk of disrupting his environment, thus not only damaging objects and hurting people, but also hurting himself. A deep practice of human dignity is an invitation to walk the extra mile in making an effort to explicitly honor a person's dignity, especially when we talk about the dignity of the most vulnerable members of society and the fundamental acts of the person, linked to her biological setup. This is where we find the highest demand for a deep practice of human dignity.

Upon reflection, the situation Deckmar described may not seem as clear a violation of human dignity as at first glance. The same situation taken out of context could understandably make us judge and assume that this was a classic case of the violation of human dignity. I would be cautious in arriving at this judgment since we do not want to enter into "dignity hysteria" and suspect violations of human dignity wherever we go. This is a trap, similar to the trap of scrupulosity in spiritual affairs—you can set the bar so high as to lose your agency. Indeed, in spiritual terms, over-ambitiousness can lead to moral exhaustion, to "acedia."

In the case of Deckmar's situational challenge you would also want to take into account structurally similar situations such as restraining a person in a nursing home or putting a child in a car seat. It is understood that, in the case of restraining a person: (1) the burden of proof lies with the person committing the act, (2) there has to be an element of "best interest of the person(s) involved" in the reflection process, and (3) the measure is "exceptional" and not the default position of institutional routine, with its tendency toward administrative convenience and the standardization

---

[73]S. Barton, *Living with Jonathan* (London: Watkins, 2012).

of procedures. However, we do know, as pointed out above, that dignity has a lot to do with a symbolic sphere, with "symbolic vulnerability" and "symbolic actions," so we should not underestimate the impact of certain situations and their acceptance on our judgments and perceptions.

The situation Deckmar described deserves much reflection—perhaps in the spirit of Polish pediatrician Janusz Korczak, who looked after orphans in the Warsaw ghetto and who advises us to think deeply about a child's behavior and situations involving children; we should be cautious and not rush to a final judgment. Also in the spirit of Korczak, when we implement a pedagogical measure we need to ask ourselves whether we are really interested in the well-being of the children or primarily in our own comfort.[74] We should even be prepared to live with open-ended questions—and with more questions than answers. With its commitment to reflection, this procedural element is one aspect of the deep practice of human dignity as I understand it.

I see four consequences of the deep practice of human dignity:

- There is no standard account of dignity.
- Any understanding of human dignity is constantly being challenged and faced with disruption.
- Due to its contextual nature there is a primacy of "how" over "what," of "how things are done" over "what is being done."
- Deep practice can change other practices. Enacting human dignity in deep practice will change our social perspective, our outlook on the world.

As a nurse interested in the ethics of her profession writes, "If we focus on caring relationships and the relationships between power and caring practices, such as bringing up children and caring for the sick, a radically different set of social arrangements will ensue."[75] There will be new arrangements and new ways of seeing the world.

The Power of the Deep Practice of Human Dignity

This practice is hard and may require aspects of moral heroism, but it can also look almost effortless. Kimberly White describes Jason, a custo-

---

[74] J. Korczak, *Wie man ein Kind lieben soll* (Goettingen: Vandenhoeck and Ruprecht, 2009), 182.
[75] S. D. Edwards, "Three Versions of the Ethics of Care," *Nursing Philosophy* 10 (2009): 231–40, at 233.

dian in a nursing home: "His primary job was running the floor machine. It was run every day in all the hallways and large rooms, and that's what he was paid for; that was his entire shift, all day, every day."[76] There is something remarkable about this man:

> He does more than he's strictly paid for. He knows every single last resident of the facility. Every day Jason can be seen to push wheelchairs to and from dining and activities or carrying blankets to an old lady who caught a chill or filling a water jug for an old man who can't fill it himself. None of these tasks are technically his job, but they are part of the job to him.[77]

Jason explains his particular way of inhabiting the job by pointing to the residents of the nursing home as his family. This frames his relationship with residents as special obligations toward especially important persons. This is a shift in perspective that ceases to see persons as objects. The sentence "This could be my mother" is a powerful statement. With reference points like these, Jason can engage in the deep practice of human dignity with a sense of the mystery of the person, a sense of a person's inexhaustible depth.

Eva Feder Kittay, in her earlier mentioned presidential address, works with vignettes that remind us of the humanness of the person. She mentions the experience of Albert Kurihara, a Japanese American who was interned after the attack on Pearl Harbor, who said, "I remember thinking, 'Am I a human being? Why are we being treated like this?'" Kittay also describes the cry of Abdel, a twenty-year-old from Afghanistan living in the "Jungle" of Calais, a makeshift camp in France, who says to his interviewer, "They treat us like animals.... We are human. They should treat us like humans.... These people are someone's son. They're someone's brother."[78] She develops the term "moral access," the state of having a window on moral significance. Jason, the custodian, has moral access to the people he works with; they are more than patients, they are somebody's son or daughter or mother or father or brother or sister. The deep practice of human dignity requires this sense of more (*Magis*), with a sense of the uniqueness and mystery of the person.

Let me mention another story of a hospital custodian: this story features Luke, who works in a major teaching hospital.[79] Luke had to

---

[76] K. White, *The Shift: How Seeing People as People Changes Everything* (Oakland, CA: Berrett-Koehler, 2018), 3–4.
[77] Ibid., 4.
[78] Kittay, *Moral Significance of Being Human*, 22.
[79] B. Schwartz, "Practical Wisdom and Organizations," *Research in Organizational Behavior* 31 (2011): 3–23, 6.

clean the room of a young patient who had fallen into a coma after a fight; the comatose patient's father had been keeping vigil for months at his son's bedside. One day the father left his place next to his son's bed and went out to smoke a cigarette while Luke cleaned the room. Later, Luke encountered the patient's father in the hall, and the father, furious, yelled at him that the room had not been cleaned. Luke apologized and cleaned the room a second time, while the father watched. Again, this is remarkable. Notwithstanding the possibility of a critical reading through a perspective of power relations, one could see this situation as a commitment to a deep practice of human dignity engaged in a deep reading of the person. Luke reflects,

> At first, I got on the defensive, and I was going to argue with him. . . . Something caught me. . . . I cleaned it [the room] so that he could see me clean it . . . I can understand how he could be. It was like six months that his son was here. He'd be a little frustrated, and so I cleaned it again. But I wasn't angry with him. I guess I could understand.[80]

We could argue that there is something like "deep perception" at work; it is remarkable that Luke saw the man who yelled at him as a deeply concerned and frustrated man. He saw the father as a human person who cared about his son, as a social agent with commitments, as a vulnerable being challenged by a frustrating experience with no end in sight.

The ability (and willingness) to engage in deep perception that reaches beyond the surface level and perceives various and complicated roles and functions is an aspect of "dignity literacy." Dignity therapy works with this very idea, that a person should not be reduced to one's present state or role. Looking for the richness and depth of a person is an intentional effort to respect that person's dignity.[81] In this sense a human person is a mystery that "never finishes saying what it has to say," to use Italo Calvino's famous characterization of "a classic." As in Jason's case earlier, we encounter a sense of the mystery of the person. A person is so much more than the role he or she inhabits—be it the role of a patient, a patient's family member, or a custodian. And sometimes we have to make an effort to see that more clearly—and this effort can express a commitment to a deep practice of human dignity.

Such deep practices, as I have mentioned, can be identified by looking

---

[80]Ibid.

[81]M. H. Chochinov et al., "Dignity Therapy: A Novel Psychotherapeutic Intervention for Patients near the End of Life," *Journal of Clinical Oncology* 23, no. 24 (August 20, 2005): 5520–25.

at especially vulnerable persons and by looking at fundamental human acts (actions connected to food, the human metabolism, hygiene, etc.). I would like to move away from extreme cases in human dignity discourse (such as torture, locked-in syndrome, and assisted-suicide issues) and rather focus on difficult moments in a person's everyday life. I suggest we start looking at issues of "body" and "power," which I believe point us in the right direction.[82] Showing respect for a person under adverse circumstances is an expression of a deep practice of human dignity. Not reducing a person to a means for an end, especially if it is difficult, also constitutes a deep practice of human dignity.

Reductionisms of all kind—reducing people to numbers, to expenses, to achievements, to problems, to illnesses, and so on—undermine the possibility for deep practices of human dignity, but real encounters with real persons make it more difficult to engage in reductionist approaches. We see this with Ian Brown, in his account of his life with his severely disabled son, when he tells of the demanding practice of being present, with his son needing constant attention. He describes in beautiful words his own transformation because of his son, the results of a "second-person encounter."[83] He is an ambassador of the deep practice of human dignity.

We need such ambassadors—these are "testimonial practices" in the sense that they give witness to the possibility of living a culture of dignity even under adverse circumstances. As we have seen, human dignity can best be enacted by undertaking practices that show firm commitments to the dignity of the human person in his or her uniqueness and vulnerability, even in difficult circumstances. The persons involved in these practices can serve as ambassadors to help us understand the concept of dignity. Enacting dignity and learning from its deep practice will and should lead to a transformation of the person, as Kimberley Brownlee has argued.[84] Vulnerable people and those living with them can also be ambassadors of deep practices of human dignity. This is why accounts like those of Martha Beck and Rachel Adams in their stories about their sons with Down syndrome are especially powerful.[85] Here we have access to "testimonial

---

[82] "Power is a particularly important value in shaping dignity outcomes. More than wealth, dispositions of power have perhaps the greatest impacts of any value dimension on dignity-relevant dynamics" (D. J. Mattson and S. G. Clark, "Human Dignity in Concept and Practice," *Policy Sciences* 44, no. 4 [2011]: 303–19, at 315).

[83] I. Brown, *The Boy in the Moon: A Father's Journey to Understand His Extraordinary Son* (New York: St. Martin's Press, 2011).

[84] K. Brownlee, "Normative Principles and Practical Ethics: A Response to O'Neill," *Journal of Applied Philosophy* 26, no. 3 (2009): 231–37.

[85] M. Beck, *Expecting Adam: A True Story of Birth, Rebirth and Everyday Magic* (New York: Three Rivers, 2011); R. Adams, *Raising Henry: A Memoir of Motherhood, Disability, and Discovery* (New Haven, CT: Yale University Press, 2014).

knowledge" of the deep practice of human dignity. And we experience "the poor" as teachers, in the spirit of *Evangelii Gaudium*.[86]

Catholic Social Tradition, I would like to suggest, is an invitation to engage in the deep practice of human dignity. Such an engagement requires robust concerns and strong commitments, which can be nourished by the belief that God has created the human person in God's likeness and image. This foundation of human dignity does not have to worry about the challenges of a capability-dependent understanding of dignity. It takes all persons, all of whom are created in the image and likeness of God, to get as close as we can to an understanding of the image of God. It takes deep practice for a deep understanding—a deep understanding of deep enactment.

---

[86] See *EG* 48, 123, 236.

2

The Portrayal of Principles

Consider the following statement from the encyclical *Laudato Si'*: We have "a sort of 'superdevelopment' of a wasteful and consumerist kind which forms an unacceptable contrast with the ongoing situations of dehumanizing deprivation."[1] Now consider the following experience of a volunteer working in a soup kitchen in a southern state in the United States:

> On Sundays, our organization receives fruit from a local grocery store. Anything deemed unsuitable for public consumption makes its way over to our house—enough produce to barely fit in the bed of a truck. This was the first shipment I'd ever seen, and I was immediately disappointed. The fruits and vegetables weren't just ugly, but rotten. The bananas were black, flies buzzed around an open melon, and some of the food reeked. In my eyes, none of this was good enough to eat. I prepared to throw a black banana into the trash, and a resident of the house stopped me: "No, está bien." I proceeded to watch the women cut rotten spots off of tomatoes, squeeze bananas to see if they were still firm, and sort through the fruit, rarely throwing anything into the trash. I couldn't judge them because I saw that under the black peels, the bananas still tasted sweet, and the peaches weren't rotten just because of one rotten spot. Today reminded me of how much food I waste, and made me appreciate how wise the women at the house are.

The experience sheds light on the statement from the encyclical. It offers "depth" and "richness" and "thickness," and can add to a more concrete understanding of the statement. Experiences like these offer insights into concepts as well as assertions; the term "superdevelopment," introduced by Pope John Paul II in 1987 and defined as "an excessive availability of

---

[1] Francis, *Laudato Si'*, "On Care for Our Common Home" (2015), no. 109, hereinafter *LS*.

every kind of material goods for the benefit of certain social group,"[2] can be understood as a real-life term with cash value in the light of experiences like the one recounted.

Consider another example: *Caritas in Veritate* states, "One of the deepest forms of poverty a person can experience is isolation."[3] A student working at a nongovernmental organization (NGO) wrote in his journal,

> I was approached by a homeless man. This man told me that he has made some mistakes in his life but is coming to terms with them and with God and is on his journey to making positive changes in his life. When he was done telling me his story he asked me if I would buy him a coffee or something to eat. I told him that I was very happy for him that he is going to make changes in his life but that I was sorry but I didn't have my wallet with me. I then said that I was going to serve lunch at the house.... He thanked me for the offer and said that he would be on his way. I told him that I was almost ready and he replied that he wasn't comfortable being around too many people because he was dirty and he smelled bad and he was ashamed.

Again, the experience is like a few strokes of a brush on a canvas, offering color to an otherwise rather abstract statement. Let us explore this metaphor a little further: A painter painting a portrait always makes statements in the picture about her relationship to the person portrayed. In the course of multiple sittings, she establishes a relationship with the other person; she struggles with details; she emphasizes certain aspects; she goes beyond the obvious to aspects that are not revealed at first glance and not even at second glance, but rather over the course of a story. A portrait displays the style of the painter, who, of course, takes inspiration from the phenomenology of the situation, but always inserts something of her own into the art, so that a series of portraits by the same artist bears family resemblances. Portraits are not reproductions of an object, but the end results of encounters and conversations between the artist and her "portrait partner."

If we emphasize the personal approach to the principles of Catholic Social Teaching and the irreducibly subjective element in making judgments about social realities, we may find reasons to see the technique of portrayals as relevant for enacting the Catholic Social Tradition, and for personally inhabiting the principles of Catholic Social Teaching.

---

[2] John Paul II, *Sollicitudo Rei Socialis*, "On Social Concerns" (1987), no. 28, hereinafter *SRS*.

[3] Benedict XVI, *Caritas in Veritate*, "Charity and Truth" (2009), no. 53, hereinafter *CV*.

Portraits beyond Principalism

Principles, as valuable as they are, are empty without a person inhabiting them. And again, there is no doubt that principles play an important role in the reception and application of Catholic Social Teaching—so much so that numerous introductions to Catholic social doctrine reduce it to its familiar and well-known principles such as human dignity, solidarity, subsidiarity, orientation to the common good, option for the poor, political participation, and preservation of the creation. This approach gives the impression that the application of Catholic social doctrine is above all a question of the application of general principles. In addition, these principles are presented with such a high degree of abstraction that they appear harmless and unlikely to make any difference in concrete situations. However, Pope Francis has drawn attention to the fact, "We cannot help but be concrete—without presuming to enter into details—lest the great social principles remain mere generalities which challenge no one. There is a need to draw practical conclusions."[4] Principles easily become trivialized if a certain level of abstraction is reached. They become harmless, unchallenging, and vague.

A personal appropriation of a principle can be likened to the painting of a portrait that reveals the style and approach of the artist. So let us ask the following questions: What can we learn about the appropriation of principles from the art of portraiture? How could we paint a "portrait" of a principle?

The portrait of a person always comes as a surprise to the painter:

> The finished portrait is explained by the features of the model, by the nature of the artist, by the colours spread out of the palette; but even with the knowledge of what explains it, no one, not even the artist, could have foreseen exactly what the portrait would be. For to predict it would be to produce it before it was produced.[5]

A portrait is the result of a dialogue—and the same time, the occasion of a portrait invites and facilitates a dialogue that can lead to fruitful results. Heinrich Schenker and Victor Hammer, for example, engaged in a deep and enriching dialogue on the relations between art theory and

---

[4] Francis, *Evangelii Gaudium*, "The Joy of the Gospel" (2013), no. 182, hereinafter *EG*.
[5] T. E. Hulme, "Bergson's Theory of Art," in T. E. Hulme, *Speculations: Essays on Humanism and the Philosophy of Art*, ed. H. Read (1924; London: Routledge, 2000), 141–69, at 144.

music theory when Schenker attended a number of sittings for his famous mezzotint portrait by Hammer in 1924–1925.[6] Entering into a dialogue with the person sitting for a portrait is an invitation to be transformed by this encounter.

Portraits call for deep engagement, for an intense encounter. One of the major projects of artist-priest Martin Nam Nguyen, CSC, is a series of hundreds of small facial portraits painted from photographs. After photographing a person, he spends three hours with the image, translating it into a painted face. It is a way to communicate with the person, a way to be close to them, and a way to study them. He has had hundreds of encounters with people in this way, all part of a growing work of art titled *Painting of the Social Network*, which he began in 2007. Some photos that he uses to create the paintings manifest significant moments in a person's life, such as last photos—like the image of Fr. Martin's father taken very shortly before his death. It is a demanding and intensive process to create the paintings, as testimonies of an encounter with a person in her uniqueness and in her mystery. It is a very particular way to give witness to the dignity of the human person.

In another artwork (*Lucie*), Fr. Martin created 365 drawings, from 365 photographs taken at the end of each day in a year in the life of a child named Lucie. This project oscillates between distance and closeness, as Brandon Gallaher observed: "On the one hand, the artist is many times removed from Lucie. He depicts an image from an image. . . . To create the moment of Lucie he must be alien to her. Yet, on the other hand, in contradistinction, the drawings are an attempt by the artist to cross space and time to enter into union with Lucie."[7] He achieves this by looking with a particularly intense gaze: "His is a gazing of what is always absolutely Other. Yet his gazing is a gazing into in an attempt to manifest the invisible gazing of Lucie of Father Martin himself."[8]

In both cases, an ill-informed spectator could say that she did not see the point in the process, since there are photographs available to capture each person and the moments of their lives. The act and effort of painting, however, allows Fr. Martin to inhabit the portraits in a special and different way. He has made the person he works with his own through a considered effort and investing in a relationship with the person he tries to capture.

---

[6] K. M. Bottge, "Lessons in 'Pure Visibility' (reine Sichtbarkeit): Victor Hammer's Correspondence with Heinrich Schenke," *Music Theory Spectrum* 37, no. 1 (2015): 25–50.
[7] See https://www.academia.edu/35383598/Painting_Time_A_Meditation_on_Fr_Martin_Lam_Nguyen_C.S.C._s_Moments_in_Martin_Lam_Nguyen_C.S.C._s_Moments_Dallas_Beatrice_M._Haggerty_Gallery_University_of_Dallas_2017_10-13—Gallahe.
[8] Ibid.

There is a certain authority of likeness to be observed in the case of portraits; this authority is ratified by recognition, by the experience of recognizing the depicted subject. The challenging question exists of what makes successful portraits successful. One could suggest that it is the likeness between portrait and the person portrayed. Which likeness, though? And who is the judge? Some people say close friends and the immediate family of the person represented are in the best position to judge a portrait's likeness. They have a deep sense of the inner world of the person who has been portrayed, and they may also be in a position to judge the relationship between the artist and the portrait's subject, since the artist's personality and the relationship with the sitter always enter the portrait.

Hence, the category "likeness" can also be applied to the artist; a portrait "can also present the subject's social position or 'inner life,' such as their character or virtues."[9] A portrait is not a copy, not a literal "quotation"; it carries the handwriting and style of the painter, and it reveals (sometimes invisible) features said to be characteristic of the model. Sometimes these invisible features can be aspirational, as in the case of Sebastiano del Piombo's portrait of Claudio Tolomei in the sixteenth century. Tolomei had asked the artist to create a "divine mirror" (*specchio divino*), a portrait of him that could serve as a model to nurture his longing for goodness. There is then also the authority of the artist: the artist seeks to go beyond the surface, to make subtle claims about the person beyond the obvious. These are also claims to likeness. A likeness exercises power and commands authority. Paradoxically, this likeness weakens the same authority since it is not "the original," but only a representation. Representation can bring the absent into the viewer's presence; it can even keep alive someone who is dead, in a certain manner. Jean-Luc Nancy observed in his studies of the portrait, "The role of the portrait is to look out for [*guarder*] the image in the absence of the person, regardless of whether this absence results from distance or from death."[10] In the Victorian period, portraits were supposed to allow a person looking at a painted image to imagine herself in the artist's place in the presence of the subject of the painting.

Portraits express memory labor, a commitment to remembering. In

---

[9] S. West, *Portraiture* (Oxford: University Press, 2004), 22. A social dimension has been recognized in an interpretation of African portraiture: "African portraits emphasize social identity rather than personal identity and evidence an aesthetic preference for the general and ideal rather than the idiosyncratic and representational, which is consistent with African cultural conceptions about personhood and ideas about individualism" (J. M. Borgatti, "Portraiture in Africa," *African Arts* 23, no. 3 [1990]: 34–39, at 37).

[10] J.-L. Nancy, *Portrait*, trans. S. Clift and S. Sparks (New York: Fordham University Press, 2018), 29.

as much as memory oscillates between preserving the past and finding orientation for present and future, a portrait oscillates between distance and closeness, between likeness as copy (reading) and likeness as interpretation (writing), between imitation and creation, between object and subject. A portrait says a lot about the painter—"In van Gogh's portraiture, for instance, the images referred primarily to the identity of the artist, as opposed to that of the sitter."[11] The same can be said about the portraits done by Paul Cézanne: his painting *Uncle Dominique as a Lawyer* could be interpreted as bearing witness "to his own intransigent status as an artist. Some years before, to the dismay of his affluent father, Cézanne had abandoned the study of law to become a painter; the crude bluster behind the portrait may reflect his own defiant choice of a vocation."[12]

Clearly, a portrait can be self-reflective. Austrian painter Johannes Gump created a self-portrait in 1646 that showed him looking into a mirror while painting himself. The painting makes statements about the artist, the subject, and the art of portraiture, all at the same time. The portrait as a piece of art is the third element in the encounter between artist and model. The artist cannot predict the final portrait. It comes as a surprise, and it is a statement of its own; it invites the artist as much as other viewers of the portrait to an encounter with its subject. For example,

> The American Antiquarian Society owns two miniatures of Edward Everett, one attributed to Sarah Goodridge c. 1825 (cat. 45), the other to Anson Dickinson c. 1828 (cat. 46). At first glance, these tiny pictures have much in common: both show the sitter bust-length against a neutral background wearing a plain, dark jacket and white cravat. Characterization of the young congressman from Massachusetts differs considerably, however. Goodridge paints him frontally, at closer range, with a penetrating gaze that rivets our attention. Dickinson depicts a more introspective individual, turned away from the viewer physically and psychologically. Taken together, these roughly contemporary works exemplify alternative artistic perceptions of a man embarking on a career in public life.[13]

---

[11] J. Woodall, "Introduction: Facing the Subject," in J. Woodall, ed., *Portraiture: Facing the Subject* (Manchester: Manchester University Press, 1997), 1–25, at 7.

[12] M. Tompkins, "Lewis, Faces, Figures and the Physicality of Paint: Cézanne's Portraits," in *Paul Cézanne: Painting People* (Princeton, NJ: Princeton University Press, 2017), 7–23, at 9.

[13] L. Docherty, "Portraits as Documents: Historical and Humanistic Reflection," *Proceedings of the American Antiquarian Society* 114, no. 1 (2004): 45–57, at 51–52.

Again, a portrait can make statements about itself as well as about the artist. Canadian artist Germaine Koh has engaged in the process of painting and overpainting her self-portrait, thus bearing witness to the process of change and aging. Each layer of the current self-portrait (including those made invisible by the respective new layer) reflects a particular stage in her life. The portrait has been taken into the sphere of the changing body; self-portraiture has become a medium for aging itself rather than merely documenting age. Portraits are not static descriptions, but they capture a story and invite a particular dynamic, a dialogue between the subject, the artist, and the observer.

An interesting question in this dynamic of describing the art of portraits is the subject: what can become the subject of a portrait? The artist can paint persons, animals, landscapes, interior spaces, clouds, artifacts. What about principles and the approach to principles?

The claim is that it can be fruitful and promising to make theological principles the subject of an effort to create portraits. Entering into a dialogue with a principle of Catholic Social Thought can be a truly transformative experience. Let us think, for example, of the principle of the common good and the simple question: what goods can we have only if we possess them together, by having them in community? This simple question can change our way of looking at goods, at community, and at our priorities. Communal experiences, friendships, and educational adventures with travel companions come to mind. Answering such a question is also a way of appropriating a principle, of making a principle one's own. This requires the "pliability" of principles that can move beyond a rigid word structure. The portrayal of principles would not be possible without this flexibility; it permits the application of social doctrine to be a personal acquisition rather than a mechanical implementation.

Then the question about "likeness": where principles are concerned, what is the likeness we seek and who can judge this likeness?

One answer to these questions would be to see the category "likeness" as a statement about the relationship between a principle and social realities. The gap between a principle (e.g., the common good) and the realities of social exclusion that we encounter points to the need for social transformation. And who is in the best position to judge? We could suggest that it is those who are at the margins. Pope Francis has talked about poor people as teachers: "They have much to teach us."[14] They can teach us a great deal about social realities and the cash value of principles, as they suffer from the nonimplementation of principles like solidarity, participation, and the common good. Poor people are in a privileged position

---

[14] *EG* 198.

to judge the quality of the portrait of a principle since they expect real change from a principle's proper appropriation.

These insights can be used methodologically in the social sciences. Based on a dialogue between art and science, Sara Lawrence-Lightfoot developed a social science method she called "portraiture." This method, at the interface of science and art, decisively brings the author's position into the telling of a story. It has its origins in Lawrence-Lightfoot's qualitative social research in six high schools, which she got to know intensively over the course of three years, as she created portraits of the organizational culture of these institutions. Explicitly, she introduced her own voice into her descriptions, as she does in relating a discussion about *Uncle Tom's Cabin*:

> Perhaps in response to the faraway looks in her students' eyes, Ms. Wood brings the discussion closer to home. She is trying to reveal the contemporary examples of enslavement all around them. "Having a slave in Highland Park is not the thing to do. . . . It's also slightly illegal. But can't you picture how some of the folks here would deal with slaves. . . . They are just as despicable as Beecher Stowe's characters!" Maybe they cannot hear the urgency in her voice, but the students' faces show no change. I cannot see the face of the one Black boy in the class who sits in front of the window, but I project pain onto him. How must he feel as this conversation swirls about him? And how does he experience the disinterest and distance of his peers?[15]

She clearly inserts herself into this description, with the authority and concern of an African American, a sociologist, and a citizen engaged by the education system. She is interested in drawing a portrait of the school, including its dynamics, using all the material she can access. She systematically developed this portraiture methodology in a book with coauthor Jessica Hoffman Davis.[16]

In addition to current experience, autobiography and stories play a major role in the approach, which entails "listening for a story" in order to be able to present as a product a story or a collage of stories. In the development of portraiture, Lawrence-Lightfoot drew on her own experiences, most specifically in sitting for a portrait herself. A woman painted

---

[15] S. Lawrence-Lightfoot, *The Good High School: Portraits in Character and Culture* (New York: Basic Books, 1983), 145.

[16] S. Lawrence-Lightfoot and J. Hoffmann Davis, *The Art and Science of Portraiture* (San Francisco: Jossey-Bass, 1997).

her as an eight-year-old, and at the age of twenty-five she was again asked if she would permit herself to be portrayed. As part of the process, Lawrence-Lightfoot had oriented herself to a key question: "Think of how you would like to have children remember you"[17]—a question she calls a "burning question" in another context, as the question that expresses what really interests her.[18] She found that she was disappointed with the result achieved by "a sensitive eye, a meticulous brush, and enduring patience."[19] She realized that the portraits "did not capture me as I saw myself, that they were not like looking in the mirror at my reflection. Instead, they seemed to capture my 'essence'; qualities of character and history, some of which I was unaware of, some of which I resisted mightily, some of which felt deeply familiar."[20] These insights were expressed in her idea of creating a portrait of social contexts. For her, it was not and is not about a full representation, but about "the selection of some aspect of, or an angle on, reality that would transform our vision of the whole."[21] Such reality is gathered from other contexts, such as from the use of literature in philosophy and sociology or from "clinical story telling." This approach gives social science research a personal touch and brings together the intimate qualities of personal appropriation with what is public in the field.[22] Emmanuel Katongole has made use of this method in his theological explorations of African political theology.[23]

Significantly, a discussion of the method debates whether the sentence "only Sara could do it" is correct.[24] In fact, it is crucial for the social science methodology of portraiture that the author contributes and does not retract, that the product bears the author's handwriting, and that different researchers in the same field do not get the same results. "Portraiture differs from traditional forms of qualitative research because the investigator's voice is purposely in the written document, called a portrait, which is created as a result of the researcher's interactions with the actors in the research setting."[25] The portraiture method brings biographical elements

---

[17] S. Lawrence-Lightfoot, "Reflections on Portraiture: A Dialogue between Art and Science," *Qualitative Inquiry* 11, no. 1 (2005): 3–15, at 4.

[18] S. Lawrence-Lightfoot, "Portraiture Methodology: Blending Art and Science," *Learning Landscapes* 9, no. 2 (2016): 19–27, at 22.

[19] Ibid.

[20] Lawrence-Lightfoot, "Reflections on Portraiture," 5.

[21] Ibid., 6.

[22] See J. Featherstone, "To Make the Wounded Whole," *Harvard Educational Review* 59 (1989): 367–78.

[23] E. Katongole, *Born from Lament: The Theology and Politics of Hope in Africa* (Grand Rapids: Eerdmans, 2017), 33–39.

[24] See the book review by E. Vallance of Sarah Lightfoot and Jessica Hoffman, *The Art and Science of Portraiture*, in *American Journal of Education* 107, no. 1 (1998): 66–71.

[25] D. G. Hackmann, "Using Portraiture in Educational Leadership Research," *Interna-*

into play and creates research that depends on a particular person; thus, she cannot simply be replaced by another researcher without significantly changing the results.

The art of biography, which paints a person's life, is yet another way to engage with a person. Richard Holmes, the well-known author of biographies of Percy Bysshe Shelley and Samuel Taylor Coleridge, mentions two important principles in his approach to biographies: the "footsteps principle"—physically pursuing the subject by going to all the places where the subject had ever lived or worked—and the principle of following a strategy of "double accounting," with a two-pronged approach comprising objective facts and subjective interpretations. "Only in this way, it seemed to me, could I use, but also hope to master, the biographer's most valuable but perilous weapon: empathy."[26] Again we see the importance of experience and effort, the negotiation of the space between facts and interpretations. Biographies are like portraits, depictions of moments in time, never definitive statements, but stories that can be retold, reconfigured, and reinterpreted. The person of the biographer inevitably enters the story since "All good biographers struggle with a particular tension between the scholarly drive to assemble facts as dispassionately as possible and the novelistic urge to find shape and meaning within the apparently random circumstances of a life."[27] The person of the painter or the biographer with her particular perspective and interest is an irreducible factor in projects of portrait or biography. A biography paints the life of a person. Can this exercise of struggling to achieve a personal sense of a subject (be it through a portrait or a biography) also be done for principles?

On "Painting Principles"

Can we "paint principles"? Can there be portraits of principles? Can the art of portraiture be applied to principles?

The main idea that arises in trying to respond to these questions is personal appropriation. A portraiture of principles calls for a special and personal approach to each principle, after a patient struggle against a background of what one might call "personal knowledge" or even "personal weighting." A portrait of a principle should convey a sense of

---

tional Journal of Leadership in Education 5, no. 1 (2002): 51–60, at 52.
[26]R. Holmes, *This Long Pursuit: Reflections of a Romantic Biographer* (New York: Pantheon, 2016), 6.
[27]Ibid., 59–60; cf. L. Edel, *Writing Lives: Principia Biographica* (New York: W. W. Norton, 1984).

the principle, inviting an audience to encounter the principle based on the author's own encounter with it. Personal examples, nuanced experiences, and even other inspirations, such as fiction or art, enter into the portrait of a principle.

One aspect in the art of portraying principles is the confrontation between Catholic Social Teaching statements and concrete experiences. For example, the principle of freedom, expressed in *Pacem in Terris*—"Man's personal dignity requires . . . that he enjoy freedom and be able to make up his own mind when he acts"[28]—can be deepened by this experience in a homeless shelter:

> I was on the soup line today and before serving them [the homeless clients] we ask, "Would you like potatoes, green beans, or whatever it may be?" After a couple people said no to her bread, the women standing next to me leaned over and said, "These homeless people are picky!" Although a seemingly insignificant comment and moment, it bothered me. I thought to myself that simply because a person is experiencing homelessness, it doesn't mean that that person no longer has preferences, things they like or dislike, etc. This is a small way that we ignore the dignity of some of our guests.

Similarly, the following passage from *Evangelii Gaudium*—"The poor and the poorer peoples are accused of violence, yet without equal opportunities the different forms of aggression and conflict will find a fertile terrain for growth and eventually explode"[29]—finds an illustration in a remark by a young man working with disadvantaged youth: "The boy I was helping told me the only reason he would not join a gang was because he was afraid of getting arrested. He said, however, if they offered him enough money, he would drive the car."

Or consider how this statement from *Evangelii Gaudium*—"Our commitment does not consist exclusively in activities or programmes of promotion and assistance; what the Holy Spirit mobilizes is not an unruly activism, but above all an attentiveness which considers the other 'in a certain sense as one with ourselves' "[30]—is colored and enriched by a student's encounter with a social worker:

> I interviewed a case support specialist working with unaccompanied refugee minors, who said that the best part of her job was being able

---

[28] John XXIII, *Pacem in Terris*, "Peace on Earth" (1963), no. 34, hereinafter *PT*.
[29] *EG* 59.
[30] *EG* 199.

to provide help for the family she served and being able to be the person with which they could *desahogar*—in English this means to vent, but in Spanish, the term carries a deeper definition. She meant to say that she could be the person they rely on in times of trouble and be the person of consistent support in lives of nearly consistent hardship. She mentioned that her job wasn't easy, especially with the weight of the problems that get vented to her daily. But, by wanting to be the open ear, the good radiates from her abilities.

The idea is simple—concrete experiences increase the tangibility and accessibility of general and abstract statements and principles, adding nuances, depth, and color. Portraits of principles allow for a thick description of the principle in question. Experiences that can be connected to Catholic Social Teaching content liberate such documents from the confines of the text and allow them to enter the way we experience reality as well as the way we think about the principles themselves. The official documents do not offer many examples; examples have to be brought to the texts. And examples serve more than just the purpose of illustration since they can communicate insights in a unique way. Just as a metaphor can express things in a way that a nonmetaphorical manner of speech cannot convey, an example can express aspects of a discourse that cannot be communicated without examples. They do not simply "illustrate" or "decorate" a discourse; they "deepen" and "widen" it. Examples shed light on a matter, and this can lead to a new way of perceiving and judging an issue.

A particularly relevant set of examples that can contribute to the portrait of a principle are "dignity experiences." The main concern of Catholic Social Tradition, I would suggest, is the commitment to a deep practice of human dignity. Catholic Social Tradition is a constant reminder to not fall into the trap of cheap dignity practices that make it too easy for us to claim that we do justice to the dignity of each and every human person. The portrayal of the principle of human dignity can benefit from concrete experiences; these points of friction with the rough ground can lead to a sharper attentiveness and a more nuanced sensitivity. A student working with an immigration agency wrote in her journal:

> Today, I let an immigrant father borrow my cell phone to message family on Facebook, in the hopes of getting a functional number for a relative in the United States. While sitting next to him, watching him like a hawk, I noticed that he smelled horrible. Detention centers don't often let you shower. You wear the same clothes every day. You sleep on the floor. The nickname for the rooms where you sleep is *hielera*. Freezer. Detention centers are an assault on human dignity.

The vulnerability that you have to adopt as an immigrant: trust these officers, who don't speak your language, who may not respect you, who make you sleep on the concrete floor with only an aluminum blanket for warmth, trust them with your whole life. Sitting next to this stinky father, I realized the truth of the horror stories I've heard about detention centers, and the immense position of vulnerability that comes with not having access to meeting your basic needs.

Such an experience is a moment of cognitive breakthrough, of being able to make connections between stories heard and personal emotional investment. Experiences are thick enough to make memories. There are dignity teaching moments in each person's life, such as the one related by a student in a service learning program who worked at a camp hosting persons with disabilities:

My camper Michael needs thickener in his drinks because he has weak throat muscles, and the liquid needs to be honey consistency in order for it to go down the right pipe. I am so new at this, but thank goodness that John, an older counselor, is there to advise me and help me out. One of the things he said to me really stuck, because it fit perfectly with the readings. The very first time I mixed in the powder to Michael's drink, I had the giant tub of thickener on one of the dining room tables and was mixing it in front of all the campers. John suggested that I make it in the privacy of the kitchen so that Michael could feel the same as everyone else, and not different because of his disability. This reminded me of the importance of human dignity, and how by making his drinks appear different from everyone else's, I was in a way taking a little bit of his dignity.

The deep practice of human dignity not only challenges us in the extreme conditions of extraordinary situations, but also in instances of everyday thoughtlessness or the little inconveniences of ordinary life—or through and in our bodies, in the experience of the everyday. An important aspect of human dignity is vulnerability, and an important aspect of vulnerability is body-related. This idea, that the respect for human dignity can be seen especially in situations involving a person's biology and bodily vulnerability, can be made much more concrete when looking at a very basic aspect of human life, namely human waste and sanitation. *Gaudium et Spes* states that subhuman living conditions insult human dignity.[31] A

---

[31] John XXIII, *Gaudium et Spes*, "Pastoral Constitution on the Church in the Modern World" (1965), no. 27, hereinafter *GS*.

basic human need is for food, and an accompanying secondary basic need is the proper processing of the food, that is, the question of disposal. "Going to the toilet when you want to" is an expression of human dignity that can serve as a basic indicator for dignity-consonant practices.[32] Women are especially vulnerable to sanitation-related dignity abuses.

A researcher who worked in Haiti collected experiences related to sanitation.[33] A thirty-eight-year-old woman reported, "I love my modern flushing toilet, but there is a problem getting water for flushing. Imagine that you really need to go but there is no water. I have to walk down the street to the tap, wait in line, fill my bucket, and then walk all the way back. If I really have to go, this is a very long time." Furthermore, "As a woman, all the responsibility falls to me. My husband and boys are very busy during the day and expect me to keep the toilet clean and retrieve all flushing water." And, "I am getting older and sometimes do not feel strong enough to carry the buckets. When I feel too weak, I use my friend's latrine even though one of the women who uses it has three children, and they do not keep it clean." A teenager recounted her anxieties around the latrine:

> I do not feel safe using my latrine. There is a child buried by the latrine, and we sometimes feel its spirit. I am a cowardly person, so at night, I am so scared to run to the latrine. The latrine is far from the house, and we have to share it with the whole yard. I am afraid of the spiders and frogs.

The researcher identified not only private homes as sources of sanitation-related shame and anxiety, but also and especially public places:

> One women told a particularly humiliating tale that exemplifies the vulnerability of inadequate sanitation. "I remember I have been to Harbicot (market in neighboring town) and I asked someone to use a toilet. The man took a machete and started to dig a hole in the ground. He told me to go in the hole and that he would walk away and come back when I finished. With no cover, no privacy, they just dig a hole and expect you to go! After you finish, they cover it with soil. He said they do that for everyone. I had no other choice."

---

[32] See Human Rights Watch Report, April 19, 2017, https://www.hrw.org/report/2017/04/19/going-toilet-when-you-want/sanitation-human-right.

[33] S. Pieslak, "Sustainable Sanitation as a Contribution to Restoring Human Dignity," research paper (Notre Dame, IN: Center for Social Concerns, 2018).

Human dignity is a principle that comes with official language and examples, but also with personal attitudes, social practices, and cultural perceptions. Similar to the "underside" of institutions explored by Erving Goffman, who was particularly interested in their "off-stage" aspects of society (as opposed to the official dimensions of social life), there is an underside to principles, an important role principles play in the sphere of human life that we try to keep hidden, private, shielded from view. The principle of human dignity plays a major role in questions of sanitation and defecation. In fact, the conditions of defecation in many cultures are an important window into the practice of human dignity.[34]

Portraits of principles provide these "windows" through relevant experiences and relevant concepts. In addition, "enacting principles" can be seen as the art of translating a concept into stable practices, of creating "testimonial practices," that is, practices that give testimony to the depth and richness of a concept's many semantic layers. Enacting principles and concepts suggests that the agent is the bridge between principles/concepts and practice, between semantics and pragmatics, between linguistic and extralinguistic practices. The agent is like the painter who is not "outside of the portrait." The role of the agent ensures that we cannot justify there being a clear line between a concept/principle on the one hand and human practices on the other; principles and concepts are embedded in and expressions of practices as much as practices are shaped by conceptual lenses that influence perceptions and appraisals.

A portrait of a principle could include a conceptual approximation through "bond concepts" or "bridge concepts," that is, through concepts that can contribute to the understanding of the principle at stake, either as semantically related ("bond") or as semantically unrelated ("bridge") concepts. For human dignity, examples of bond concepts would be respect or honor; examples of bridge concepts would be uniqueness or mystery. A portrait of a principle could also include relevant experiences (positive and negative) that can plausibly connect to a principle. It may also be a good strategy to inquire about "model situations" that could be used to introduce a principle—for example, the idea of a birthday cake to illustrate the common good. The cake itself is a competitive good that is reduced by sharing, but the joy and celebratory effect are increased by sharing, a good that can only be reached in company with others. A portrait of

---

[34]See S. van der Gees, "The Toilet: Dignity, Privacy and Care of Elderly People in Kwahu, Ghana," in S. Makoni and K. Stroeken, eds., *Ageing in Africa: Sociolinguistic and Anthropological Approaches* (London: Routledge, 2017), 227–43; S. van der Gees, "The Social Life of Faeces: System in the Dirt," in R. van Ginkel and A. Strating, eds., *Wildness and Sensation: An Anthropology of Sinister and Sensuous Realms* (Amsterdam: Het Spinhuis, 2007), 381–97.

principles could also include particular habits or an "operational translation"—that is, an attempt to translate a principle into concrete actions or indicators (e.g., instances of humiliation as an indicator that human dignity has been violated). In short, the portrayal of principles can work toward a personal appropriation of the principle, making use of all kinds of material approaching the issue from various angles, not so much with a Cartesian analysis, but with a "politeness of thinking" that we find in Pascale's *Pensées* or Montaigne's *Essais*.

I offer here two examples of a portrait of a principle, wrestling separately with the concepts of solidarity and the common good.

Example 1:
A Portrait of the Concept of Solidarity

Solidarity is both a moral virtue and a social principle of the Catholic Social Tradition; *Sollicitudo Rei Socialis* 38 defines it as "a *firm and persevering determination* to commit oneself to the *common good*."[35] Given this understanding, solidarity is a "second-order commitment," that is, a "commitment to commit oneself," a decision to enter commitments. The main features of this second-order commitment are firmness and perseverance, meaning that this commitment is accepted as a strong self-obligation that circumstances or obstacles cannot change. In this sense, solidarity requires the courage to hold onto labor for the common good even in the face of difficulties. The subjects of this commitment can be individuals as well as collectives. In fact, Catholic Social Tradition teaches that solidarity is to be translated into structures and institutional arrangements; relationships between persons and peoples "must be purified and transformed into structures of solidarity through the creation or appropriate modification of laws, market regulations, and juridical systems."[36] Solidarity has both an individual and an institutional face. The object of the second-order commitment of solidarity is the common good, which is explored later.

Solidarity can be seen as a response to the temptation of indifference. On October 16, 2017, on the occasion of the celebration of World Food Day, Pope Francis paid a visit to the Food and Agriculture Organization (FAO) headquarters in Rome. "Death by starvation or the abandonment of one's own land is everyday news, which risks being met with indiffer-

---

[35] *SRS* 38. Cf. Pontifical Council for Justice and Peace, *Compendium of the Social Doctrine of the Church* (2004), no. 193, hereinafter *CSDC*.
[36] *CSDC* 192.

ence," he said to the major UN organization dedicated to ending hunger and providing food security globally. "We cannot resign ourselves to saying: 'someone else will take care of it,'" the pope continued. "Therefore I ask myself—and I ask you—this question: is it too much to consider introducing into the language of international cooperation the category of love, understood as gratuitousness, equal treatment, solidarity, the culture of giving, fraternity, mercy?"

In other words, the pope asked about the integration of deep concerns as an antidote to indifference. The culture of indifference, though predicated on passivity, is a formidable opponent. Compatible with serenity and politeness, high levels of personal comfort, and the ultimate "value" of convenience, indifference authorizes a self-protecting withdrawal from others in their need.

In his encyclical *Fratelli Tutti* Pope Francis continued to denounce "a cool, comfortable and globalized indifference,"[37] which he also called "cruel."[38] In this regard, *Fratelli Tutti* can be read as an extension and elaboration of *Laudato Si'*'s condemnation of the "globalization of indifference,"[39] a widespread indifference to suffering,[40] and a "nonchalant resignation."[41] In the concluding prayer of *Laudato Si'* he even uses the term "the sin of indifference."[42]

One could read Pope Francis's messages to say in these texts that solidarity is not "optional," if one sees the human person as a social being in need of social friendship. Social friendship means that we care about each other. The question "Where is your brother, where is your sister?" is valid. A key message of *Fratelli Tutti* is indeed a reminder of the social nature of the human person: we only achieve who we are by our interactions with others; the good of the human person is a relational good. Pope Francis asks us to reimagine ourselves "as a single human family."[43] "We need to think of ourselves more and more as a single family dwelling in a common home."[44] This is more and more important since dreams of this unified vision of humanity have been shattered,[45] and we have fallen into the traps of "limitless consumption and expressions of empty

---

[37] Francis, *Fratelli Tutti*, "On Fraternity and Social Friendship" (2020), no. 30, hereinafter FT.
[38] FT 72.
[39] LS 52.
[40] LS 25.
[41] LS 14.
[42] LS 246.
[43] FT 8.
[44] FT 17.
[45] FT 10–12.

individualism."[46] We do not live as a human family, people and peoples are sacrificed,[47] human rights are not equal for all,[48] and "the sense of belonging to a single human family is fading."[49]

We are largely indifferent to the lives around us. Even the tragedy of the worldwide pandemic that is such a strong reminder of global interconnectedness[50] could not change that. We live in cultures of indifference that impede and erode a culture of solidarity. *Fratelli Tutti* urges a renewed and global commitment to love and solidarity as an antidote to indifference. Solidarity "finds concrete expression in service," whereby individuals learn to "set aside their own wishes and desires, their pursuit of power, before the concrete gaze of those who are most vulnerable."[51] Solidarity means much more than engaging in occasional acts of generosity. It means that "the lives of all are prior to the appropriation of goods by a few. It also means combatting the structural causes of poverty, inequality and the lack of work, land and housing, the denial of social and labour rights."[52] Solidarity means getting people to care about each other and the dignity of each person. This robust concern and sincere caring must be placed on the fundamental level of perception, of "seeing-as," as we have seen.

During the earlier-mentioned visit to the FAO in 2017, Pope Francis donated a marble sculpture; the statue depicts the tragic death of Alan Kurdi (also known as Aylan), a three-year-old Syrian boy whose body washed up on the shore of Turkey in September 2015 after a small boat holding a dozen refugees had capsized. Next to Aylan we find a childlike angel weeping over the boy's lifeless body. We see the lifeless boy and the suffering, helpless angel who could not prevent Aylan's tragic death. *Fratelli Tutti* reminds us that we share one world with our brothers and sisters. Aylan is our brother. We cannot be indifferent to the story of our brother or sister. We are called to social friendship and to solidarity.

Solidarity is a fundamental attitude that fosters habits that move a person beyond her immediate sphere of agency; solidarity makes a person acknowledge the bigger picture and the fact that we are part of a context that transcends us. Solidarity comes naturally to people who understand the first words God spoke to Cain after Cain murdered Abel: "Where is your brother Abel?" (Gen 4:9). And we learn that it does not do to say that we are not our brother's or our sister's keeper. We learn that it does not

---

[46] *FT* 13.
[47] *FT* 18.
[48] *FT* 22.
[49] *FT* 30.
[50] *FT* 32.
[51] *FT* 115.
[52] *FT* 116.

do to say that our sister's life or our brother's life is none of our business.

A portrait of the principle of solidarity could—and does in this case—entail bridge concepts, experiences, and a story.

Bridge Concepts

One way of coming to a deeper understanding of concepts such as solidarity is to identify bridge concepts that shed light on the chosen concept in more indirect, more surprising, and less established ways. Such concepts represent bridges between seemingly distinct discourses and semantic fields. As mentioned, the concept "mystery," for instance, can be a fertile bridge concept to illuminate our understanding of human dignity. British theologian James Hanvey has characterized mystery as "capacity for inexhaustible meaning," an important aspect of understanding the dignity of the human person, while German legal scholar Christoph Möllers has established a link between human dignity and the concept of mystery: "Human dignity guarantees a place of intimacy in which every human being must be left alone."[53] The concept of "chaos" has been used as a bridge concept to open up the term "mercy," as in "the willingness to enter into the chaos of another."[54] Bridge concepts provide what could be called "semantic bridge capital," which links different discourses in a fruitful way.

A helpful bridge concept for understanding solidarity is the concept of "loneliness." Solidarity can be approached as a response to or as protection from loneliness, which can be defined as a felt deficit of social relations. A subjective aspect in this definition could be an invitation to search for a subjective aspect of solidarity, there is an emotional aspect of loneliness (plausible also in the case of solidarity), and there is a social dimension. A few years ago Yale undergraduate Marina Keegan published "The Opposite of Loneliness," which after her tragic death was the lead text in a posthumously published collection. She ponders what she experienced at Yale, suggesting that she found the opposite of loneliness: "It's not quite love and it's not quite community; it's just this feeling that there are people, an abundance of people, who are in this together. Who are on your team. When the check is paid and you stay at the table. When

---

[53] J. Hanvey, "Dignity, Person and Imago Trinitatis," in C. McCrudden, ed., *Understanding Human Dignity* (Oxford: Oxford University Press, 2013), 209–28; C. Möllers, "The Triple Dilemma of Human Dignity: A Case Study," in McCrudden, *Understanding Human Dignity*, 173–87, at 178.

[54] James F. Keenan, *The Works of Mercy: The Heart of Catholicism*, 3rd ed. (Lanham, MD: Rowman and Littlefield, 2017), 5.

it's four a.m. and no one goes to bed. That night with the guitar."[55] The "opposite of loneliness" could also be used as a proxy for "solidarity." Loneliness—just like solidarity—can be understood on a micro level and on a macro level. On the micro level we have the painful experience of loneliness as a certain "lack of integration and inclusion," "ennui," and even "unwantedness."[56]

On the macro level we can observe that loneliness has been identified as a major social challenge. Olivia Laing's 2016 book on the urban experience of loneliness, *The Lonely City,* has been praised for its deep insight into one of the most important health challenges of our time, and loneliness has been viewed as a public health issue.[57] Loneliness has been linked to higher mortality risks, reduced stress processing, and a higher risk of mental health challenges. There is also a higher risk of loneliness for an aging population. All these insights can deepen our understanding of solidarity. A supporting concept on both the micro and the macro levels is the concept of "indifference." The experience of indifference can lead to the opposite of solidarity. Pope Francis lamented the globalization of indifference in his homily on the island of Lampedusa in July 2013, and indifference that nurtures attitudes of carelessness and moral exhaustion.

We could also use biblical lessons about loneliness to distinguish different types of loneliness: loneliness as shame (Adam), as not being understood (Job), as exhaustion (Elijah), as frustration (Jonah), as neglect (the nameless sick man at Bethzatha), as jealousy (Martha), and as remorse (Peter). And in this spirit, we can identify responses to these forms of loneliness, which would then give us reference points for solidarity. Helpful questions to be asked when trying to make sense of loneliness as a bridge concept to solidarity include: What does it mean to be connected? What is togetherness?

A further important bridge concept to shed new light on the principle of solidarity is the concept of kinship.[58] "Kinship" has been introduced by Jesuit Gregory Boyle (Fr. Greg) as an important term characterizing his work with former gang members in Los Angeles. In the recognition

---

[55] M. Keegan, *The Opposite of Loneliness: Essays and Stories*, introduction by Fadiman (New York: Scribner, 2014), 1.

[56] See Emily White's moving testimony about her personal experience of being lonely: E. White, *Lonely: A Memoir* (New York: HarperCollins, 2010).

[57] O. Laing, *The Lonely City: Adventures in the Art of Being Alone* (New York: Picador, 2016); see also Justin Worland, "Why Loneliness May Be the Next Big Public-Health Issue," *Time*, March 18, 2015.

[58] For an earlier version of these thoughts in the context of mission theology, see Clemens Sedmak, "Mission as Kinship on the Margins," *International Bulletin of Mission Research* 41, no, 4 (2017): 1–12.

that "We belong to each other," kinship grows when we refuse to forget that we belong to each other. Kinship is the experience of "being with" rather than "working for"; it is the driving force of building community, as well as the refusal to accept the claim that "there just might be lives out there that matter less than other lives."[59] The concept of kinship can shed light on solidarity in ways that make us perceive and shape solidarity practices differently than we otherwise might have.

"Kinship" expresses a particular connectedness between persons, and we can distinguish four types of kinship that I would like to name "blood," "milk," "water," and "wine." "Blood-based kinship" is kinship by birth, referring to a common descent, to common roots. The German word *kind* (child) expresses this kind of connection. Second, "milk-based kinship" is kinship by means of shared family life, offering protection and nurturing practices. It is a kinship expressed in rearing and caring, beautifully expressed in the Old English word *cynn*. "Water-based kinship" is kinship based on compassion, as in giving water to the thirsty; it occurs in seeing and listening to the other and can be linked to the word *cynde*, originally meaning to express the feeling of relatives for one another. Finally, "wine-based kinship" relates to celebration and companionship, characterized by presence and participation, as expressed in the German word *kennen* (to know). These four types of kinship—or solidarity—can change or transmute into one another. By accepting a baby into the family, we transform blood-based kinship into one that is milk-based (which is, one would say, a natural thing to do). Turning water into milk is the dynamism of accepting a stranger in need into the home as a member of the family; turning water into wine is the transformation of compassion into celebration, of support into community. The principle of solidarity can be elucidated by identifying kinship moments and kinship structures, that is to say, experiences of encounter and structural provisions that facilitate these moments by offering opportunities as well as protection.

Kinship moments and kinship structures are both exemplified in the work of Fr. Greg. He describes one kinship moment, when an ex-gang member feels compassion for the first time.[60] Boyle established kinship structures in giving marginalized young people opportunities to work, having understood that jobs are key to starting a new life;[61] he also started

---

[59] Gregory Boyle, *Tattoos on the Heart: The Power of Boundless Compassion* (New York: Free Press, 2010), 187, 192.

[60] Ibid., 82. Boyle characterizes compassion not as "a relationship between the healer and the wounded. It's a covenant between equals" (77). Further, inspired by Buddhist nun Pema Chödrön, he notes that the truest measure of compassion "lies not in our service of those on the margins, but in our willingness to see ourselves in kinship with them" (71).

[61] Ibid., 4. The workplace itself is a "kinship structure," a "place of second chances" (10),

a new school. These are structural responses based on a recognition and experience of kinship.

In this way, the two bridge concepts of loneliness and kinship can provide epistemic access to the principle of solidarity. Another element in the portrait of the principle of solidarity would be a description of solidarity experiences.

Solidarity Experiences

Undoubtedly, Fr. Greg lives and shapes the Catholic Social Tradition. The same can be said about Magnus MacFarlane-Barrow and his organization Mary's Meals. The story of this organization is an expression of lived solidarity, of a "firm and persevering determination to commit oneself to the common good."[62] Magnus founded Mary's Meals in 2003, an NGO with a particular commitment to Malawi.[63] In 2002 the media reported on a terrible famine in Southern Africa, especially in Malawi. Magnus traveled there and obtained firsthand knowledge of the situation; three months later he returned to the country, accompanied by two journalists. This time he explored the issue of structures of aid:

> I had realized by now that most effective emergency food-distribution projects were often being delivered by the churches, which had the advantage of a permanent structure which could be mobilized to create networks of community volunteers. On this visit I spent time with several groups of nuns and priests who were carrying out incredible work on a large scale. None seemed particularly shocked by this famine, and all had tried-and-tested systems they had been relying on and developing over many years.[64]

Within this context, Magnus had a decisive encounter:

> Father Gamba, a young friendly priest, then asked me if I would like to accompany him to the home of one of his parishioners, who was near death. Thus it was I came to meet that family whose picture remains on the wall above my desk: Emma surrounded by her six children, including fourteen-year-old Edward, who, when I asked him about his hopes in life, gave me an answer I will never forget.

---

and a combination of "worksite and therapeutic community" (9).

[62]*SRS* 38.

[63]M. MacFarlane-Barrow, *The Shed That Fed a Million Children: The Mary's Meals Story* (London: William Collins, 2015).

[64]Ibid., 133.

"I would like to have enough food to eat and I would like to be able to go to school one day" had been his stark, shocking reply to my question.[65]

This was the leap to establishing the mission of Mary's Meals.[66]

The simple idea of providing meals in schools led to practices of solidarity: Magnus and his organization cooperated with the local parent-teacher association. They also decided on the food to be served, namely Likuni Phala, a popular and nutritious porridge, the ingredients of which were sourced locally from smallholder farmers. This was the basis for the replicable model first used in January 2003. The basic idea, however, was just that: an idea, namely that we are our siblings' keepers and that all members of the human family are our siblings. Following from this was the idea that something can be done about hunger and lack of education. And since then, this idea has led to a huge impact involving thousands of persons. These experiences also illustrate solidarity as kinship.

Solidarity experiences make the principle of solidarity more tangible and also offer a fruitful way to ask questions such as: What is the role of institutions in living solidarity? What are material and monetary aspects of solidarity? Can there be "cold solidarity" (i.e., professional support of vulnerable population without inner emotional involvement)? What is the role of emotions in solidarity? Clearly, Magnus was moved by Edward's remarks about food and school. What is the cost of solidarity, including its opportunity costs? (The involvement in Africa, for instance, shifted the focus of Mary's Meals toward a particular region.) Does solidarity with X lead to new forms of exclusion of Y?

These questions can become even more urgent and more painful in situations of crisis like the coronavirus pandemic that began in 2020, where we saw many moving expressions of solidarity, but also disturbing forms of nationalism. The responses to the pandemic point to the macro level of solidarity; there is also a micro level, which I want to illustrate with a story.

A Testimonial

An important element of a portrait of a principle are testimonials, stories that serve as witnesses to solidarity. A testimonial story shows

---

[65] Ibid., 137.
[66] "Thus, the mission of Mary's Meals, to provide one good meal every day in a place of education, for hungry impoverished children, was launched by Edward's words" (ibid., 140). The mission was clear: "We all agreed that the vision of Mary's Meals should be for every child to receive a daily meal in their place of education" (142).

a paradigmatic, fundamental practice, the kind of practice that can be both the foundation and an expression of a form of life that embodies the principle at stake.

An inspiring story about solidarity is the life of Issa Grace, the fourth child of her parents, Sean and Felicia. The pregnancy was difficult, and Issa was born June 7, 2013, with Trisomy 18.[67] The doctors only gave the baby girl a few hours or at most a few days to live, but she beat the odds. Issa lived her life in the constant imminence of death, to which more than once she came extremely close. She drew dozens of people into a circle of living solidarity while learning about it, as verified in her obituary: "Issa guided and taught her family all the way through her final breaths." I was privileged to hold tiny baby Issa in February 2014, who was breathing with difficulty; it was an experience beyond words. I was overwhelmed with a feeling of peacefulness, a sense of protecting the vulnerable, and also an understanding of the fragility of humanity—and my own fragility.

Issa's mother wrote about the first moment of her baby's life:

> Her first cries are some of the happiest moments of my life.... She was too small and fragile to endure surgery. We were sent home under hospice care with no directions about how to care for her and an unknown timeline for how long she might live. It was terrifying. There was no roadmap; only a clear message that our days with our sweet daughter, Issa, were numbered. Issa was extremely fragile and needed to be held 24/7. Because of her reflux and heart complications she couldn't lie down for long. Her only comfort was being held chest to chest, heart to heart.[68]

On the day Issa Grace was born, June 7, 2013, Pope Francis addressed students, alumni, teachers, and parents of Jesuit schools in Italy and Albania in the Vatican's Audience Hall. It was the feast day of the Solemnity of the Sacred Heart of Jesus, understood as the devotion to a word that forges a unity that makes reality present to us, that comes to us as a gift[69]—just as Issa did on that very same day. Pope Francis talked

---

[67] Also called Edwards syndrome, Trisomy 18 is a chromosomal condition causing many different kinds of physical abnormalities.

[68] Felicia Johnson O'Brien, "The Gifts of Solidarity, Inspired by Issa Grace," in C. Sedmak, F. Johnson O'Brien, and L. Eid, *Issa, Teacher of Solidarity*, Center for Social Concerns Occasional Papers 17, no. 1 (Notre Dame, IN: CSC, 2017), 11.

[69] In his theological essay "Behold this heart: Preliminaries to a Theology of Devotion to the Sacred Heart," Karl Rahner wrote, "The words which by their charm forge a unity, make reality first present to us, make us subject to them, spring from our hearts, come to us as a gift and transport us—these I would like to call *primordial words (Urworte)*" (K. Rahner, *Theological Investigations* 3, trans. K.-H. and B. Kruger [London: Darton, Longman

about magnanimity, "the virtue of the great and the small." Issa's life is a testimony to magnanimity, her troubled heart embodying the greatness of human dignity and the smallness of human vulnerability. Solidarity is the attitude evoked by this "in-between" between greatness and smallness, this in-between full of undivided dignity and undeniable vulnerability.

The idea of solidarity is based on the acceptance of vulnerability, and the especially vulnerable are uniquely positioned to provide lessons on vulnerability. One could say that Issa demonstrated "the pedagogy of the weak"—she taught those around her important lessons about life in a way that only the most vulnerable, weakest, and most fragile can do. She had unique power—indeed, something like the power of the powerless, not unlike the newborn in the manger in Bethlehem. Issa inspired people to learn the languages of solidarity and love; you had to find a new language to express your love to Issa, her parents, her siblings, and her extended family and friends. Issa made it very clear that she was not someone to love with a sense of future (future achievements, future capabilities, college degrees, a career, etc.); she was not to be described in a vocabulary of progress. The solidarity she evoked was aimless in the sense that it was given in the moment, and taken one day at a time.

Issa inspired people to learn about solidarity by challenging boundaries—the boundaries between nuclear family, extended family, a circle of friends, and institutional support, for instance. The medical miracle of Issa's nine months on this planet was made possible by a kind of "permeability," an experience of openness of different contexts to other contexts (among the systems related to the family, neighborhood, official institutions, and health care). Issa also challenged the boundaries of giving and receiving, of teaching and learning, of living solidarity and experiencing solidarity. There was also an openness, a permeability to these categories. Issa bore witness to the "polyphony" of life, a term Dietrich Bonhoeffer used to describe the multifarious nature of life, the colorfulness of human existence in its many dimensions, even in a narrow prison cell.[70] Issa was a vulnerable baby in need of care, but she was so much more than that; she was a teacher and a guide, a mystery and a gift, a human being created in the image of God and a sign of God's presence. Her life was much

---

and Todd, 1967], 321n30, at 322). The Solemnity of the Sacred Heart of Jesus is a feast day celebrating solidarity, union, and reaching out, becoming part "in flesh" of a community.

[70] D. Bonhoeffer, *Widerstand und Ergebung. Briefe und Aufzeichnungen aus der Haft. Vollständige Ausgabe, versehen mit Einleitung, Anmerkungen und Kommentaren.* Edited by Chr. Gremmels, E. Bethge, and R. Bethge in cooperation with I. Tödt. Bonhoeffer Werke Band 8. (Gütersloh: Gütersloher Verlagshaus, 2011), 444. English edition: "Life, Even in prison, Is Kept Multidimensional and Polyphonous" (D. Bonhoeffer, *Letters and Papers from Prison* [London: SCM, 1971], 311).

more than a life of medically motivated attention—she was so much more than a "medical case." She was a teacher of solidarity without an explicit teaching mandate. And this teaching continues to travel deep and far.

Issa's life inspired dozens of people to show solidarity with the family, who needed support with cooking, cleaning, looking after Issa's three siblings, and holding the baby. When Issa was six weeks old, her mother wrote in her journal,

> People ask how we are doing, which is a hard question to answer. We're exhausted from sleepless nights and worry, and we're filled with awe and love for our sweet baby.... Our community here (and afar) continues to be an amazing support to us. We are filled with gratitude for your fellowship, prayers, letters, gifts, meals, hugs and visits. The outpouring of love that is showered on our family reminds us of the awe people must have felt at witnessing the first Christian community share and live so beautifully together.[71]

Solidarity is the experience of giving as much as it is the experience of receiving; solidarity illustrates aspects of agency and commitment, but is also an expression of "allowing to receive." In the seventh month of Issa's life, her mother wrote about "lessons on solidarity":

> It's humbling for me that I need so much help for our family to function; simple tasks that I used to do every day, I cannot get done. We need our community and are so incredibly grateful for the hundreds of people who literally come through our door to help out in one way or another. If I'm lucky, I leave the house one day a week to run a quick errand. I feel pretty isolated, but the world seems to come to us in different ways.... You, our community, have not given up on us or on Issa. We will always be grateful for the ways you accompany us each day.[72]

Coming out of this story is a connection between solidarity and humility[73]—a connection that is an interesting and rather unexplored aspect of solidarity. Solidarity is seen as a gift and as a burden, as a response and as a question, as a virtue and as concrete acts, as expressions of vul-

---

[71] Johnson O'Brien, "Gifts of Solidarity," 11.
[72] Ibid., 12.
[73] "Learning to ask for help in the early stages of pregnancy was a crucial time of building trust, honesty, and vulnerability with those willing to help us. On the flip side, I imagine that it took sacrifice, courage, reflection, planning, and working together to figure out how to help us" (ibid., 13).

nerability and of strength, as justice and as mercy. This testimonial can highlight these aspects. It has many things to teach us about solidarity, but a portrait of the principle cannot end there. There is so much more to learn, as Issa's mother reflected: "In some ways, modeling solidarity with Issa was easy. Who doesn't love a precious baby? Jesus pushes the envelope with solidarity and challenges us to extend it to those who are different than us, even to our enemies."[74]

Solidarity—as with any principle of Catholic Social Teaching—pushes the envelope and is a thorn in the flesh, a constant reminder of the need for conversion.

Example 2:
A Portrait of the Concept of the Common Good

The second example of the portrait of a principle focuses on the common good. How can we portray the principle of the common good? For the principle of solidarity, I have made use of bridge concepts, experiences, and a testimonial. For a portrait of the principle of the common good, I focus on three elements: fiction, indicators, and a "negative" approach.

Fiction

Novels can be seen to be "seismographs" of social phenomena and political developments, in that fiction deals with possible worlds that can serve as alternative or counterworlds to the experience of reality. Fiction also has the power to express deep insights into human nature, as George Steiner pointed out with characteristic confidence.[75]

Many books can be used to exemplify the principle of the common good (or its dismantling), but a particularly well-suited one is Upton Sinclair's *The Jungle*. Even though it has to be made very clear that the book is fiction,[76] working with this novel can elaborate many threats to the common good.

The story is well known: a family of Lithuanian immigrants settles in

---

[74] Ibid., 16.

[75] "But though they are of inexhaustible fascination and frequent beauty, the natural and mathematical sciences are only rarely of ultimate interest. I mean that they have added little to our knowledge or governance of human possibility, that there is demonstrably more of insight into the matter of man in Homer, Shakespeare, or Dostoevsky than in the entirety of neurology or statistics" (G. Steiner, *Language and Silence* [New York: Atheneum, 1986], 5).

[76] See L. C. Wade, "The Problem with Classroom Use of Upton Sinclair's *The Jungle*," *American Studies* 32, no. 3 (1991): 79–101.

Packingtown, the center of Chicago's meatpacking industry (as well as the center of Lithuanian immigration). They are exploited and deceived, beginning in the very first chapter, which describes the wedding feast of Jurgis and Ona in a bar. They expect the wedding guests to contribute to the cost of the meal, as is the custom, but they depart without paying, leaving the young couple with significant debts. Soon after that, the family signs an agreement to buy a house, only to learn when it is too late that the contract is full of hidden fees and the poorly maintained house overpriced. The novel describes the dangerous working conditions and the lack of solidarity in a climate of crime, exploitation, and corruption. With no employer liability regulations and no insurance, minor accidents can ruin entire families. Prostitution, drug addiction, and alcoholism are described as almost inevitable responses to the toxic stress and chronic deprivation. It is, indeed, a jungle, with a pecking order and a hierarchy among the immigrants: each member of the family has gotten his job "by the misfortune of some other person."[77] There was a clear social stratification: "The workers had all been Germans. . . . Afterward, a cheaper labor had come, these Germans had moved away. The next were the Irish. . . . The Bohemians had come then, and after them the Poles."[78]

The Jungle provides disturbingly vivid descriptions of broken families, downward spirals, disregard of safety as a common good, mistrust in institutions, and the lack of institutional support—as well as the specific vulnerabilities of women, children, and the elderly; exploitation; and the dynamics of using another person's vulnerability for one's own benefit and advantage. We see a failing state with corrupt government inspectors, and the collapse of families because of the level of the constant stress: "Jurgis had, alas, very little time to see his baby; he never felt the chains about him more than just then."[79] And then:

> Brother Jonas disappeared. One Saturday night he did not come home, and thereafter all their efforts to get trace of him were futile. . . . So with the spring time . . . the wild idea of escaping had come to him! Two years he had been yoked like a horse. . . . But now the income of the family was cut down more than one-third, and the food demand was cut only one-eleventh, so that they were worse off than ever.[80]

---
[77]Upton Sinclair, *The Jungle*, Signet Classic, 4th Printing (New York: New American Library of World Literature, 1963), 66.
[78]Ibid., 70.
[79]Ibid., 110.
[80]Ibid., 122–23.

The novel paints a gruesome picture of particular dynamics that are also described by David Hollenbach in his analysis of the common good in American inner cities.[81] The categories Hollenbach suggests are also helpful hermeneutical categories for *The Jungle*: "social isolation" (defined as "lack of contact or of sustained interaction with individuals and institutions that represent mainstream society"), "ghetto poverty" and "ghetto-related behaviour," the "multiplier effects" of social isolation, "lack of self-efficacy," the "aggregate effect of history," and "negative interaction" (in the sense that the suburbs relate to inner cities in a mode of institutional self-defense).

A careful analysis of the stakeholders in their agency and of the structural dynamics that shape and frame their interactions can provide helpful insights into the common good—or the "common bad." It is also remarkable from a common-good perspective that Sinclair's novel has had a significant impact on the American public and the perception of the meat industry even though—or precisely because—it was only partially accurate.[82] The novel has even led to a discussion of the role of context on agency (i.e., the effects of a slaughterhouse on the surroundings) through the so-called Sinclair effect.[83]

Obviously, this is just one example, but the use of fiction can definitely prove fruitful for a portrait of a principle, adding color, thickness, and depth. A second example that I would like to mention briefly is a dystopian text by Paul Auster.

Auster's *In the Country of Last Things* paints a picture of a world and society where the common good has been lost. The masses are homeless; there is no sense of safety and security, nor permanence and stability. The overall experience of life is struggle and decay, loss and death, crime and starvation. The narrator explains,

> When you live in the city, you learn to take nothing for granted. Close your eyes for a moment, turn around to look at something else, and the thing that was before you is suddenly gone. Nothing lasts, you see, not even the thoughts inside you. And you mustn't waste your time looking for them. Once a thing is gone, that is the end of it.[84]

---

[81] D. Hollenbach, *The Common Good and Christian Ethics* (Cambridge: Cambridge University Press, 2002), chap. 7, "Justice and the Good of the City."

[82] D. Moss and M. Campasano, "*The Jungle* and the Debate over Federal Meat Inspection in 1906," *Harvard Business School Papers* 9-716-045, Harvard Business School, 2016; R. I. Roots, "A Muckraker's Aftermath: The Jungle of Meatpacking Regulation after a Century," *William Mitchell Law Review* 27, no. 4 (2001): 2413–33.

[83] A. J. Fitzgerald, L. Kalof, and T. Dietz, "Slaughterhouses and Increased Crime Rates: An Empirical Analysis of the Spillover from 'The Jungle" into the Surrounding Community," *Organization and Environment* 22, no. 2 (2009): 158–84.

[84] P. Auster, *In the Country of Last Things* (New York: Penguin, 1987), 1–2.

Some people are so thin that they are blown away by the wind. One's goods can be confiscated anytime by the corrupt police or stolen by ruthless thieves. "There are many people who will sell anything just to turn a profit: eggs and oranges filled with sawdust, bottles of piss pretending to be beer. No, there is nothing people will not do."[85] There are scavengers who try to find whatever can be used in the remains of homes and the city infrastructure and "vultures," people who steal from scavengers. Some people—called "the runners"—will run until they drop from exhaustion; others climb to the highest place to jump. Euthanasia clinics offer a wide spectrum of services. You can only survive by letting go of all the things that remind you of your own humanity. Since plumbing does not exist any longer, the management of human waste has become a major issue that affects all persons. The loss of any kind of a social dimension of life, let alone social cohesion, leads to the total destruction of the common good. The narrator's situation is "more than lonely":

> I became dull inside, all instinct and selfishness.... I was nearly raped.... I stole food from an old man who tried to rob me one night ... snatched the porridge right out of his hand and didn't even feel sorry about it. I had no friends, no one to talk to, no one to share a meal with.[86]

The situation described is hell on earth, the total loss of a sense of community and any orientation to the common good.

Once again, we witness a negative approach to the common good in literature in this example; it would be similarly fruitful to take a deeper look at utopian fiction, beginning with the understanding of the common good and a flourishing community in Thomas More's *Utopia*. What is the notion of a flourishing community in More's famous text? He paints a picture of a community without private property, without locks on the doors, without permanent homes (there is a rotation system where people move homes every ten years); meals are taken in community dining halls, travel is restricted, and greed is curbed (gold and silver are treated as nonprecious materials); every person is required to engage in farming for two years, and everyone has to learn an essential trade. The workdays are short (six hours), and there is no unemployment. Is this a true vision of the common good? More describes slavery as a feature of this community with each household possessing two slaves (who are either criminals or people from other countries, especially prisoners of war). Is this a lesson about the (moral) cost of the common good of a particular community?

---

[85]Ibid., 5.
[86]Ibid., 43–44.

These questions can be sharpened and deepened in conversation with scenarios developed in fiction. Fiction provides thick accounts of (possible) social realities that can be used to think through principles and positions. An example that pursues the explicit intention to show the realization of principles is Steven Lukes's *The Curious Enlightenment of Professor Caritat*, in which Lukes describes a fictional journey through Western political philosophy: Professor Caritat explores Utilitaria, Communitaria, and Libertaria in a quest to find the best of all possible (political) worlds.[87] Fiction provides rich material for the portrayal of principles.

Measurement and Indicators

"Indicators" can be considered a second element in a portrait of the principle of the common good. One of the challenges of principles is "how to measure progress." If one takes the principle of the common good as an aspirational concept that provides a sense of direction, how will it be possible to measure or at least establish that we are moving in the right direction? Take a mayor, for example. She may want to pursue a common-good-oriented way of governance and politics. How would she know that she is on the right track?

A portrait of the concept of the common good could look into existing material, such as the Bristol Workplace Wellbeing Charter, the Canadian Index of Wellbeing, the Greater New Haven Community Index, the Jacksonville Quality of Life Progress Report, the Santa Monica Local Wellbeing Index, the UK National ONS Wellbeing Index, the Bertelsmann Social Justice Index, or Bhutan's conception of Gross National Happiness with its nine dimensions. In each case, there has to be a series of normative considerations approaching "a whole community" before designing approaches to assess and measure. There seems to be consensus that issues like health, safety, the environment, economics, governance, and relationality are key aspects of the well-being of a community. However, the idea of a "thriving city" or "vibrant community" is a normatively charged idea.

Cinzia Castiglione, Edoardo Lozza, and Andrea Bonanomi have introduced a Common Good Provision Scale (CGP).[88] They focus on two main dimensions: accessibility (making the common good accessible to everyone and covering people's basic needs) and personal gain (getting a return and some personal advantage in exchange for one's contribution).

---

[87] S. Lukes, *The Curious Enlightenment of Professor Caritat*, 2nd ed. (London: Verso, 2009).

[88] C. Castiglione, E. Lozza, and A. Bonanomi, "The Common Good Provision Scale (CGP): A Tool for Assessing People's Orientation towards Economic and Social Sustainability," *Sustainability* 11, no. 2 (2019): 10.3390/su11020370.

In her PhD dissertation Ana T. Badard offers a Common Good Index based on the capabilities approach, working with "a set of indicators that measure the presence of human functioning capabilities in society."[89] To develop criteria, she first identifies "meta-criteria" that satisfy the following requirements:

- They measure human functioning capabilities.
- They shed light on important aspects of human functioning capabilities.
- They are measured reliably and consistently over time by governments or recognized private research organizations.
- They have international resonance and can be compared to other nation's statistics.
- They capture how the most vulnerable members of society are affected.
- Their use causes neutral or positive impact on poor and vulnerable populations.
- The number of total indicators is manageable, so the index is a practical tool that is not unduly cumbersome to use.[90]

She arrives at a list of thirteen human functioning capabilities with corresponding indicators,[91] which could be used for the operationalization of the common good.

Catholic Social Teaching texts provide a deep, rich framework for un-

---

[89] A. T. Bedard, "Introducing the Common Good Index and a Common Good Immigration Ethic" (PhD dissertation, Loyola University Chicago, 2011), 93.

[90] Ibid., 95–96.

[91] In conversation with Martha Nussbaum's list of basic human capabilities (from M. Nussbaum, *Women and Human Development* [Cambridge: Cambridge University Press, 2000]), Bedard proposes,
- Life (infant mortality, uninsurance, poverty).
- Health (uninsurance, poverty, carbon dioxide emissions).
- Bodily integrity (homicide, poverty).
- Senses, imagination, and thought (high school dropout).
- Emotions (suicide).
- Practical reasoning (high school dropout).
- Affiliation (poverty, uninsurance).
- Other species and nature (carbon dioxide emissions).
- Play and recreation (no indicator listed).
- Control over environment (voter turnout, poverty).
- Relationship to the Transcendent (God very important).
- Raising children in a stable, supportive environment (teen pregnancy).
- Work (unemployment, high school dropout, poverty).

Lists like these leave us with three questions: What is considered and what is not considered? What is the definition or understanding of the terms mentioned? Are the chosen indicators adequate for their purposes?

derstanding the concept of the common good. Working with key sources we are able to identify a variety of indicators for the common good: the availability and accessibility of microcommunities,[92] a healthy pluralism,[93] a long-term perspective,[94] contributive justice,[95] the management of hidden privileges[96] and opportunities for redistribution to the benefit of the underprivileged,[97] full employment,[98] the existence of unions,[99] a proper fiscal culture,[100] care for the environment,[101] proper payment structures,[102] absence of unfair competition,[103] absence of favoritism,[104] fostering an inward sense of justice and kindliness,[105] fostering economic initiatives and diversity,[106] safeguarding the political framework of economics,[107] and the culture of life.[108]

Each of these indicators could be more carefully described. The project of "painting portraits of principles" invites an approach with broad and finer strokes with a conceptual brush. One could add structure, details, and finesse to different parts of the portrait. Let me provide an example of a theological deepening of one indicator, the concept of diversity. The term "diversity" has gained political prominence; diversity has been recognized as an institutional value. From the perspective of Catholic Social Tradition, one could offer a specific perspective on the meaning and weight of diversity as an important reference point for the common good. The *Compendium of the Social Doctrine of the Church* holds, "*The social nature of human beings is not uniform but is expressed in many different ways.* In fact, the common good depends on a healthy *social pluralism.*"[109] No pluralism without diversity—but what does "diversity" mean?

---

[92] *CSDC* 61.
[93] *CSDC* 151.
[94] *CSDC* 164.
[95] *CSDC* 167; Leo XIII, *Rerum Novarum*, "Rights and Duties of Capital and Labor" (1891) no. 34, hereinafter *RN*; *Octogesima Adveniens*, "Eightieth Anniversary [of *Rerum Novarum*]" (1971), no. 24, hereinafter *OA*.
[96] *CSDC* 189.
[97] *CSDC* 363; Pius XI, *Quadragesimo Anno*, "On Reconstruction of the Social Order" (1931), no. 57 (hereinafter *QA*).
[98] *CSDC* 288.
[99] *CSDC* 305; *GS* 68.
[100] *CSDC* 362.
[101] *CSDC* 466; *LS* 23.
[102] *QA* 74.
[103] John XXIII, *Mater et Magistra*, "On Christianity and Social Progress" (1961), no. 80, hereinafter *MM*.
[104] *PT* 56.
[105] *GS* 73; *CV* 71.
[106] *SRS* 115; *LS* 129.
[107] *CV* 36.
[108] John Paul II, *Evangelium Vitae*, "The Gospel of Life" (1995), no. 72, hereinafter *EV*.
[109] *CSDC* 151.

Brief Excursus:
Aspects of a Catholic Social Theology of Diversity

Let me offer a brief reflection on diversity in seven simple steps:

1. Biblically speaking, we could distinguish "created diversity" (reflected in the theology of creation; see Sir 42:24), "chosen diversity" (Jesus's election of disciples), and "spirit-filled diversity" (the Pentecost event in Acts 2). These three forms of diversity point to unity, complementarity, and beauty. We can find a number of metaphors in Scripture to express this "ordered and unifying diversity": "one spirit, many gifts"; "many members, one body" (1 Cor 12); "one house, many dwelling places" (Jn 14:2); "one vine, many branches" (Jn 15:5). These metaphors are powerful in their messages about diversity. However, there are also at least two further biblical motifs concerning diversity: "being different" as a sign of "being chosen" (see Esth 3:8 resonating with the idea of "the sacred as the separate"). Second, the myth of the tower of Babel in Genesis 11 points to a narrative of a sinful loss of unity leading into debilitating diversity. This is the idea of diversity that undermines order, as also expressed in Leviticus 19:19. There seems to be a diversity of discourses on diversity in the Bible, with one central organizing principle: unity and order.

2. Based on the belief that each person is created in God's likeness there is a belief in a fundamental equality and in the dignity of all,[110] an understanding of equality (and dignity) based on a transcendent foundation. This equality is deeper than diversity. However, this equality is also to be understood as "equality in uniqueness"—human persons are equal also in the sense that each person is unique. Negotiating uniqueness and equality in this context happens with reference to the dignity of the human person. There is danger in losing the sense of universality with an increasing diversity of cultural factors,[111] even though a false conformity and "false universalism" also undermine a sense of human dignity and uniqueness.[112] Hence, there is a need to reflect on the "transcendent unification" that brings about "harmony" and "communion," not in spite of, but because of diversity: "When properly understood, cultural diversity is not a threat to Church unity. The Holy Spirit, sent by the Father and the Son, transforms our hearts and enables us to enter into the perfect communion of the blessed Trinity, where all things find their unity. He builds up the communion and harmony of the people of God."[113] This harmony

---
[110] Paul VI, *Lumen Gentium*, "The Dogmatic Constitution on the Church" (1964), no. 29, hereinafter LG.
[111] *GS* 61.
[112] *FT* 100.
[113] *EG* 117.

and communion are built on "the diversity of peoples who experience the gift of God, each in accordance with its own culture."[114] The idea of "Christianity as monocultural and monotonous" does "not do justice to the logic of the incarnation."[115] The richness and beauty of evangelization are based on a diversity of approaches.[116] Diversity is a wealth.[117] A deep understanding of the transcendent foundation of unity and diversity can be developed in conversation with Aquinas's reflections on "difference" in the context of the most Holy Trinity.[118]

3. An important reference point for a theological understanding of diversity is the connection between integrity and diversity in creation.[119] Destroying (biological) diversity leads to corruption of the earth's integrity. The loss of biodiversity is grave, with severe consequences,[120] thus biodiversity must be protected.[121] Monocultures pose tremendous risks.[122] This discourse on "theology of creation and biodiversity" offers insights and language that are also relevant for other forms of diversity. Diversity is not only to be seen as a resource but also in terms of beauty beyond a cost-benefit analysis.[123]

4. Catholic Social Tradition also offers a connection between creativity, productivity, and diversity. A vibrant society is based on associations with a diversity of purposes.[124] There is a notion and experience of "fruitful diversity."[125] There are motifs of "division of labor" and "sharing of responsibility" within an order, exemplified in the cooperation within the church.[126] Pope Francis mentions that "it is imperative to promote an economy which favours productive diversity and business creativity."[127] Diversity is also linked in this context to small initiatives in the spirit of subsidiarity. The idea of "enriched newness based on diversity" can also be applied to the realm of ideas: "The combination of two different ways of thinking can lead to a synthesis that enriches both."[128] Communion

---

[114] *EG* 116.
[115] *EG* 117.
[116] Paul VI, *Evangelii* Nuntiandi, "In Proclaiming the Gospel" (1975), no. 66, hereinafter *EN*.
[117] *EG* 230.
[118] Thomas Aquinas, *Summa Theologiae* I-I, q.132, a.2, ad 2.
[119] See *LS* 8.
[120] *LS* 24, 35, 38.
[121] *LS* 37, 169.
[122] *LS* 39.
[123] See *LS* 190.
[124] See *QA* 87.
[125] See *GS* 75.
[126] See *LG* 28. 32.
[127] *LS* 129.
[128] Francis, *Amoris Laetitia*, The Joy of Love" (2016), no. 139, hereinafter *AL*.

is enriched by respect and appreciation for differences.[129] We could read this observation as an invitation to embrace principles of charity with regard to diversity; the default position is the desirability and positive value of diversity.

5. There is a particular type of "being different" that is of special theological importance, in the spirit of a preferential option for the poor. "No authentic, profound and enduring change is possible unless it starts from the different cultures, particularly those of the poor."[130] An argument resides here for a "standpoint epistemology," an approach to lift up less-privileged positions and to honor the particularity of persons and cultures. "The experience of being raised in a particular place and sharing in a particular culture gives us insight into aspects of reality that others cannot so easily perceive."[131]

6. The language Pope Francis offers with regard to "diversity" is "reconciliation" (*Evangelii Gaudium* 131: "Diversity must always be reconciled by the help of the Holy Spirit; he alone can raise up diversity, plurality and multiplicity while at the same time bringing about unity"). "Reconciled diversity" is the goal,[132] based on a process of reconciliation and a cultural covenant—under the guidance of the Holy Spirit.[133] Reconciled diversity is an expression of peace, not as a negotiated settlement, but as a result of a conversion of hearts and reconciliation.[134] The Church is called to be a sign of brotherhood and sisterhood and to model "honest dialogue" as part of unifying all human persons.[135]

7. Reconciled diversity is not possible without a commitment to the common good, which, in turn, is not compatible with an attitude of selfishness and maximizing one's own advantage.[136] There is a call to generosity and humility, an understanding of one's own limits and a recognition of the legitimacy of diverse approaches and ideas. There is an understanding of contributive justice inextricably linked to a spirit of generous sharing and a commitment to unity: "In virtue of this catholicity each individual part contributes through its special gifts to the good of the other parts and of the whole Church."[137]

In a nutshell: Diversity needs to be reconciled, especially through a commitment to a transcendent foundation and endpoint. A plausible

---
[129] *AL* 139.
[130] *FT* 220.
[131] *FT* 144.
[132] *EG* 230.
[133] *EG* 230.
[134] *EG* 230.
[135] See *GS* 92.
[136] See *FT* 10.
[137] Paul VI, *Lumen Gentium*, "The Dogmatic Constitution on the Church" (1964), no. 13.

means to nurture a culture of reconciled diversity is dialogue based on a commitment to the common good and informed by virtues such as generosity and humility. Diversity is not an end in itself, but serves communion and order. Its value, however, cannot be exhausted using a language of determining means and calculating benefits; there are also the categories of beauty and harmony. A plausible candidate for an understanding of reconciled diversity is the category of integrity (also understood as "being whole," "being healed").

***

I have tried to show that diversity as an indicator of the common good according to Catholic Social Tradition can be theologically deepened. This can be done for all of the common good indicators mentioned above. There is room for a theology of privileges, a theology of full employment, a theology of competition, and so on. All the indicators could be carefully described in more depth and then translated into action points, and progress toward the realization of these action points assessed. One could even construe a common good matrix making use of these reference points.

The Common Bad

In addition to "fiction" and "measurements and indicators," a third element I would suggest to round out a portrait of the common good is a deep knowledge of the "common bad." As we have seen, Hollenbach has described the loss of a culture of the common good in US cities. A short life expectancy for inner-city blacks, Hollenbach states, "is the result of the weak community relationships evident in low levels of neighborhood cohesion, physical security against violence, quality of education, and access to medical care that are commonly found in American core cities."[138] There is a moral dimension to the social isolation of the inner-city poor. If somebody is left behind, a "common bad" dynamic kicks in that is detrimental for all members of the community. "Poor people who are unemployed, inadequately housed, and undereducated in American inner cities are not part of a society that can be called a commonwealth."[139]

Certain responses to reviving urban neighborhoods exacerbate inequalities by introducing gentrification. The term "gentrification" (British English "gentry"—people of good social position) was introduced by Ruth Glass in 1964 in her book *London: Aspects of Change*. Glass described

---

[138] Hollenbach, *Common Good and Christian Ethics*, 175.
[139] Ibid., 202.

the changes happening in the borough of Islington, an area of London that working-class people had traditionally inhabited. Gradually, young professionals began to move in, transforming the neighborhood, taking over apartments and turning them into more elegant and expensive residences; because of this dynamic, the original occupiers are (again, gradually) displaced, and the character of the district is transformed. Eventually this dynamic is institutionalized and becomes an intentional change process. Neil Smith has described the "rent gap" as an important factor in this process. The rent gap is the disparity between how much a property is worth in its current state and how much it would be worth gentrified.[140] A great deal of profit can be made by those in a position to invest. The well-known Matthew effect ("those who have will be given more")[141] can be observed, which can undermine the community by increasing inequalities. Peter Moskowitz has written an angry book to show how gentrification means loss of community, is based on deeply rooted inequality, and has racist aspects.[142] It is, at the same time, understood that real estate developers are, generally, decent people who identify opportunities. The issue transcends the level of individual goodwill. It has to be addressed on the institutional level of policies.

We need major institutions to enhance the common good; they are the drivers of social justice. But it also takes a different way of thinking, a different kind of self-perception: "Successful middle-class suburbanites will significantly misunderstand themselves if they overlook all the ways the communities they live in have enabled them to become who they are,"[143] Hollenbach says, perhaps reflecting a case of "middle-class fragility" (the unwillingness of middle-class people to see their own complicity in societal inequality). This is where the plea of Catholic Social Teaching comes in to connect the notion of the common good to a sense of justice and kindliness.

A negative approach could entail an approximation of the principle from a minimum threshold. To seize upon an image by Stefano Zamagni, the common good works not like addition, but like multiplication. In addition, the total may still have a positive value, even if a zero value is included: 1 + 3 + 6 + 0 equals a positive number. This is not the case with

---

[140]N. Smith, "Toward a Theory of Gentrification: A Back to the City Movement by Capital, Not People," *Journal of the American Planning Association* 45, no. 4 (1979): 538–54.

[141]The term was introduced in an article by Robert Merton: "The Matthew Effect in Science," *Science* 159, no. 3810 (1968): 56–63.

[142]P. Moskowitz, *How to Kill a City: Gentrification, Inequality, and the Fight for the Neighborhood* (New York: Nation Books, 2017).

[143]Ibid., 210.

multiplication; if one of the factors is zero, the entire product is zero: 1 x 3 x 6 x 0 = 0.[144] Understood in this way, it is contrary to the idea of the common good to leave behind or write off even a single person. This does not sound very realistic since it involves a maximalist concept.

One fundamental challenge in applying Catholic Social Teaching is the negotiation between maximum and minimum. If we follow the model of using "humiliation" as a negative criterion to assess a violation of human dignity, we could ask if principles like solidarity or the common good are being violated. What minimum standards have to be respected under all circumstances? Sometimes it is easier to settle on a minimum than to discuss the issue of a maximum.

If you see the common good as a multiplication equation that equals zero, even if only one of the factors is zero, then the common good can also be negative if just one factor is negative. Multiplying 4 times –3 equals –12. The common good becomes negative if one factor is negative. Then the common good is "below zero," and it is not "the absence of flourishing" but the destruction of a community.[145]

In trying to provide a concrete illustration of a below-zero common good, I think of a situation in South Bend, Indiana, in January 2019. It was cold, well below freezing, and there were homeless people on the streets, living in thin tents or cardboard boxes. This is not a phenomenon that occurs only in the American Midwest. People can be found on the streets in subzero temperatures in London, Moscow, Vienna, New York, and many other places. Leilani Farha, the United Nations Special Rapporteur on Homelessness, wrote in 2015 that people often talk about homeless people in dehumanizing language, calling them "vermin" or "scum," and act as if homelessness was always the result of specific personal failures. However, she writes,

> We need to resist the urge to blame the victim. You see, if there were just several hundred homeless people worldwide we might reasonably conclude that homelessness is about the bad choices or bad luck of a few. But the millions of people worldwide sleeping rough, doubled up with family and friends in overcrowded housing, living with violent partners or in squalor with no legal rights to their homes, suggests that there is more at play than individual pathologies. It suggests

---

[144] S. Zamagni, "The Common Good and the Civil Economy," in M. Nebel and T. Collaud, eds., *Searching for the Common Good: Philosophical, Theological and Economic Approaches* (Baden-Baden: Nomos, 2018), 79–98, at 86.

[145] Let us put aside the mathematical law that two negatives result in a positive for the sake of the argument and the point that the common good can go beyond zero common good.

that governments are taking decisions, and creating societies that produce homelessness, that their policies and programs are failing vulnerable and marginalized groups.[146]

We have managed to create societies in which it is part of life that people are homeless, on the street, even when temperatures are below zero. What does this mean for our discourse on the common good? Avoiding the destruction of human beings may be the minimum standard we seek to maintain in the search for a culture of the common good.

The COVID-19 outbreak has been a powerful reminder of the moral necessity to reach out to those who are most disadvantaged, most at risk, and least privileged. The pandemic has clearly revealed the fragility not only of our care structures and safety nets but also of our entire economic system with its hidden assumption of "healthy workers and customers." The pandemic, with its painful debates about "essential" and "nonessential" workers, has brought the idea of the common good to the fore. Questions of identity and values have emerged as crucial: What kind of community do we want to become? Who do we want to be? The question of minimum standards to protect the dignity of each person has been negotiated in a new way, pointing to the politics of the common good. There have been suggestions that the elderly should sacrifice themselves for the economy. This is an explicit assault on persons and the idea of the common good.

I would like to designate the minimal level with a simple word: *hell*. The minimum common good is to avoid the creation of hell on earth. Why is speaking of hell socioethically relevant? When values are defined as "conceptions of the desirable,"[147] then concepts of hell express "conceptions of the undesirable," namely, what we really, really do not want. Concepts of hell are normatively relevant in that sense, because they indicate what we want to guard against, to prevent.

How could one describe hell in greater detail than as the epitome of the erosion of individual and communal flourishing? In the *Aphothegmata Patrum* of the fourth century, Abbas Makarius describes hell, which he has seen in a vision, as a place where people are tied back to back and cannot look each other in the eye. The key phrase is "It is not possible to see the face of another" (οὐκ ἔστιν πρόσωπον πρὸς πρόσωπον θεάσασθαί

---

[146]Leilani Farha, "Homeless People are Not Cockroaches or Vermin—They Are Human and Have Rights," *The Guardian*, December 21, 2015.

[147]See J. W. Van Deth and E. Scarbrough, "The Concept of Values," in Van Deth and Scarbrough, eds., *The Impact of Values* (Oxford: Oxford University Press, 1998), 21–47, at 27.

τινα).[148] Hell, according to this vision, is a situation of facelessness: the face (*prosopon*) of the other person is not visible.[149] The idea of facelessness as the opposite of the common good brings us back to our discourse on human dignity. Facelessness is a special form of contempt for human dignity.

Not to be seen, not to have a face is the definition of hell on earth. It is no coincidence that the Nazi concentration camps, which constituted systematic efforts to bring hell to earth, took from the prisoners their names and faces, reducing individuals to numbers and uniforms. We could systematically explore the common bad by looking at those who are invisible.

Making use of fiction, indicators, and a negative approach we could work toward a portrait of the principle of the common good; this effort inevitably reveals personal tastes and preferences, a personal style with specific examples and experiences. There is a clear link between the principle and the person trying to make sense of it, as this chapter has illustrated by offering the idea of the portrayal of principles.

---

[148] *The Sayings of the Desert Fathers*, trans. B. Ward, rev. ed. (Kalamazoo, MI: 1984), 136–37; see B. Müller, *Der Weg des Weinens. Die Tradition des 'Penthos' in den Apophthegmata Patrum* (Göttingen: Vandenhoeck und Ruprecht, 2000), 203f.

[149] In the thinking of Emmanuel Levinas, the category of the face plays a special role in describing the living presence of the other, the demanding presence of the other; the naked face, through the associated revelation of vulnerability, creates a form of closeness and a form of responsibility; see R. Burggraeve, "Violence and the Vulnerable Face of Others," *Journal of Social Philosophy* 30, no. 1 (1999): 29–45.

3

Raw Thinking

"I have a transgender son. I am a Catholic. Some who know me have said, 'How can you still be a Catholic? Your Church thinks your child is disordered.'" How do we react to this statement from the perspective of Catholic Social Tradition in a way that would encourage us to see matters of gender—and sexual morality—in relational terms, as matters also of social justice?

It will not do to repeat statements written elsewhere, nor to consider the question of a theology of transgender identities closed before it has even been opened. There is a need for a proper mapping of the semantic landscape and a proper clarification of the terms at stake.[1] There is a need for consulting a wide range of thinkers since new challenges call for new discourses: for example, Cardinal Willem Jacobus Eijk refers to feminist philosophers Judith Butler and Simone de Beauvoir in his 2015 address "Christian Anthropology and the Theory of Gender."[2] There is a need for an identification of key questions and for tentative rather than definitive claims, as shown in David Albert Jones's writings on gender identity and gender reassignment surgery.[3] These tentative claims can be expressed in a mode of thinking that is an experimental process, a way of raw deliberation not yet seeking the protection of the polishing of claims. *Raw thinking* experiments with issues and with ways to engage these issues. This kind of tentative thinking is especially important when dealing with new phenomena, such as public discourse on transgender identities.

---

[1] See J. A. DiCamillo, "Gender Transitioning and Catholic Health Care," *National Bioethics Catholic Quarterly* (Summer 2017): 213–23, esp. 214–17.

[2] Willem Jacobus Eijk, *L'antropologia cristiana e la teoria del genere*, address to the European Doctrinal Commissions, January 2015.

[3] D. A. Jones, "Gender Reassignment Surgery: A Catholic Bioethical Analysis," *Theological Studies* 79, no. 2 (2018): 314–28; D. A. Jones, "Truth in Transition? Gender Identity and Catholic Anthropology," *New Blackfriars* 99, no. 1084 (2018): 756–74.

The raw thinking on these matters has been restructured with the 2019 document "'Male and Female He Created Them': Towards a Path of Dialogue on the Question of Gender Theory in Education," issued by the Roman Curia's Congregation for Catholic Education. Here we find normative language that is relevant for any theological discussion of "(trans)gender" issues. However, even given this document, there is a need to engage with it, to ask questions; it is not enough only to repeat sections from it in pastoral contexts. An engagement with the document should also ask about its history and the discussions, deliberations, and thinking processes that led to its creation.

Behind well-ordered thoughts that give rise to polished papers and precise normative statements, there is, more often than not, a messy reality of surprises, disruptions, ambiguities, and confusion. The mother of a transgender child whose statement opened this chapter found herself thrown into a new existential situation from one hour to the next. She writes,

> My 17-year-old daughter asked to start seeing a counselor. One day she asked me to come to one of the appointments—she had a letter she wanted to read me. I went to the appointment and listened to her read the letter in front of the counselor. She said, "Mom, I am transgender, I am a boy, not a girl. I am your son." [Her mother comments]: "Suddenly, the 'path of life' felt scary, long, and lonely."

As mentioned earlier, quoting documents is not enough; deeper engagement is needed.

We have seen in the judicial debates about human dignity and its violation that there is no standard process for arriving at a definitive result. There are moments of tentative and experimental thinking, moments of epistemic risks and the exploration of potential judgments. When confronted with something new and something particular, we cannot repeat what has been said elsewhere. We have to make judgments honoring the uniqueness of a situation.

A famous case in medical ethics is the "Mary and Jodie" case from Manchester, England, here laid out by Paris and Elias-Jones:

> A 34-year-old white woman with no other children became pregnant. At four months of gestation ultrasound revealed conjoined twins. The treating physician on the Maltese island of Gozo recommended transfer to Saint Mary's Hospital, Manchester, where he had trained. Because of a long-standing agreement between Malta and Great Britain, the patient was transferred to the care of the

British National Health Service. On transfer magnetic resonance imaging revealed significant problems with the pregnancy. The smaller of twins was not expected to survive. The parents, because of their religious belief that "everyone has a right to life," declined the option to terminate the pregnancy. The pregnancy was allowed to continue for 42 weeks before delivery by caesarean section on 8 August 2000. The combined birth weight of the infants was 6000 g. Both infants were immediately intubated. They were ischiopagus tetrapus conjoined twins linked at the pelvis with fused spines and spinal cords, and with four legs. Jodie, the healthier of the two, had an anatomically normal brain, heart, lungs, and liver. She shared a common bladder and a common aorta with Mary. Mary was severely abnormal in three aspects: brain, heart, and lungs. She had a very poor "primitive" brain. Her heart was vastly enlarged, very dilated, and poorly functioning. There was a virtual absence of functional lung tissue. Mary was not capable of independent survival. She lived on borrowed time, all of which was borrowed from Jodie.[4]

The medical personnel were faced with three options: (a) no surgery (permanent union) until the death of both girls, probably within three to six months; (b) elective separation (leading to Mary's death, but increasing Jodie's chances to survive and have a good quality of life); or (c) emergency separation in the event of Mary's death, with a decreased probability of Jodie having a good quality of life.

Obviously, just the choice of language matters; the description of the situation reveals linguistic preferences, which carry value judgments. The parents could not give their consent to the surgery, so the medical staff turned to the courts for permission to perform the surgical separation. The archbishop of Westminster coordinated a submission to the Court of Appeal, based on a theological evaluation. The fact that there was a process of deliberation shows that there was not a ready-made and easily available response to the question about how to proceed. There had to be a deliberation, which required raw thinking prior to arriving at a clear result. The raw-thinking process could have used terms like "intentional killing" or "intentional mutilation,"[5] "doctrine of necessity,"[6] "best interest

---

[4] J. J. Paris and A. C. Elias-Jones, "'Do We Murder Mary to Save Jodie?' An Ethical Analysis of the Separation of the Manchester Conjoined Twins," *Postgraduate Medical Journal* 77 (2001): 593–98, at 593.

[5] See C. Kaczor, "The Tragic Case of Jodie and Mary: Questions about Separating Conjoined Twins," *Linacre Quarterly* 70, no. 2 (2003): 159–70.

[6] C. Dyer, "Doctrine of Necessity Could Allow Separation of Twins," *British Medical Journal* 321, no. 7262 (2000): 653.

of the child," "quality of life," "double effect," or the distinction between "ordinary" and "extraordinary" medical treatment.[7] The archbishop's submission chose to work with "five overarching moral considerations":

(a) Human life is sacred, that is inviolable, so that one should never aim to cause an innocent person's death by act or omission.

(b) A person's bodily integrity should not be invaded when the consequences of doing so are of no benefit to that person; this is most particularly the case if the consequences are foreseeably lethal.

(c) Though the duty to preserve life is a serious duty, no such duty exists when the only available means of preserving life involves a grave injustice. In this case, if what is envisaged is the killing of, or a deliberate lethal assault on, one of the twins, "Mary," in order to save the other, "Jodie," there is a grave injustice involved. . . .

(d) There is no duty to adopt particular therapeutic measures to preserve life when these are likely to impose excessive burdens on the patient and the patients' carers. . . .

(e) Respect for the natural authority of parents requires that the courts override the rights of parents only when there is clear evidence that they are acting contrary to what is strictly owing to their children.[8]

There is a "lived ethic of thinking" at work here, a decision to select relevant principles and apply them to a particular situation. Categories like "inviolability of life," "bodily integrity," "duty to preserve life," "excessive burdens," and "natural authority of parents" were chosen to guide the submission. Many other categories could have been selected and applied, or even created and coined. We also find some aspects of raw thinking in the court discussions.[9] One comment said, "By privileging rationality over emotion, the court made a moral choice. . . . The judges were acutely aware that the Attards loved both girls equally; indeed, they praised the parents for their devotion. . . . However, it is not self-evident that a dispassionate, disinterested observer is necessarily the most capable person to decide what is in a child's best interest."[10] There are

---

[7] See M. C. Kaveny, "Conjoined Twins and Catholic Moral Analysis: Extraordinary Means and Casuistical Consistency," *Kennedy Institute of Ethics Journal* 12, no. 2 (2002): 115–40.

[8] Cormac Murphy-O'Connor, "The Conjoint Twins: Submission to the Court of Appeal by the Archbishop of Westminster," *Catholic Medical Quarterly* (November 2000).

[9] See J. M. Appel, "Ethics: English High Court Orders Separation of Conjoined Twins," *Journal of Law, Medicine and Ethics* 28, no. 3 (2000): 312–13.

[10] "English Law. Court of Appeal Authorizes Surgical Separation of Conjoined Twins Although Procedure Will Kill One Twin. Re A (Children) (Conjoined Twins: Surgical Sepa-

hard questions about "how best to think about a case." Judge Johnson is quoted with these words:

> Mary's state is pitiable. . . . However pitiable her state now, it will never improve during the few months she would have to live if not separated. Mary cannot cry. She has not the lungs to cry with. . . . So I ask, what would happen as the weeks went by and Jodie moved, tried to crawl, to turn over in her sleep, to sit up. Would she not, I ask, be pulling Mary with her? Linked together as they are, not simply by bone but by tissue, flesh and muscle, would not Mary hurt and be in pain? In pain but not able to cry.[11]

This is a way to approach the topic, not yet a result, not yet the refined end of a process. In other words, here is raw thinking at work. Unprecedented cases require raw thinking. There is no automatic, easy, or cheap application of principles, since the very selection of categories, distinctions, and principles is part of the thinking process.

In situations where we cannot expect a clear answer based on existing categories and a clear process, there is a case for thinking afresh, for looking at a topic with different eyes and a new intellectual presence. In other words, this is a case for what could be termed "raw thinking." The art and challenge of raw thinking are frequently off stage, not part of the open discourse and its crafting. As a rule, the hard intellectual struggle, the wrestling with ideas behind academic research gets lost, buried by the results, which are somehow deemed to be the sole purpose of the exercise. The whole thinking, sourcing, and writing process is ignored, more often than not. This comes with missed opportunities and opportunity costs since so much can be learned from raw thinking.

Raw Thinking and Catholic Social Tradition

If one looks at the Catholic Social Teaching documents as sources of reference points to map the moral territory of social life, some areas are more clearly mapped and charted than others. There are blank spots on the moral map provided by Catholic Social Teaching. Catholic Social doctrine does not respond to certain socially significant questions, such

---

ration [2000]), 3 F.C.R. 577 (C.A.). *Harvard Law Review* 114, no. 66 (2001): 1800–1806, at 1805.

[11]In Re A (Children) (Conjoined Twins: Surgical Separation) [2001] Fam 147, *Mental Health Law Online*, https://www.mentalhealthlaw.co.uk/, 174–75.

as the moral status of vegetarianism,[12] an assessment of the idea of a basic income, or the political attractiveness of a monarchy. These are open questions, sometimes because the questions are new, sometimes because the respective authorities have never dealt with the questions. There is, for example, not much debate about research methods and Catholic Social Tradition. Are there research methods that come closer to a culture of respecting human dignity than others? From the perspective of a normative tradition that puts the dignity of the human person at the center, there is, for instance, a peculiar uneasiness with certain research methods and research results. How to avoid "epistemic injustice" and the exploitation of intellectual property such as "local knowledge"? For example, exploration geologists gather information from local miners that will eventually destroy their livelihood. What would the response be from the Catholic Social Thought perspective?

There is also the question of how theological field research deals with moral challenges. Todd Whitmore recounts an example of what Nora Berenstain calls "epistemic exploitation"[13] with this quote from a respondent from the community Whitmore was studying:

> "We know you have your research. But what are you going to do for us? . . . You come and steal our knowledge. You steal our culture. You come and talk to us about our knowledge and our culture and then take it all back with you. And we have nothing left. Look at us. You see how we live. What are you going to do for us?"[14]

The relationship between Catholic Social Teaching values and research methods are underexplored. One could also wonder, for instance, about aspects of some randomized controlled trials. Does it do justice to the dignity of the person to design experiments with human beings without full disclosure about the research design? Some raw thinking may be indicated on this issue.

In some areas raw thinking is imperative for theology more broadly or Catholic Social Thought more specifically, especially in areas where we enter uncharted territory and encounter blank spots on the map of Catholic Social Tradition. As an example, when I was at university, I

---

[12]See A. Tardiff, "A Catholic Case for Vegetarianism," *Faith and Philosophy* 15, no. 2 (1998): 210–21.

[13]See N. Berenstain, "Epistemic Exploitation," *Ergo: An Open Access Journal of Philosophy* 3, no. 22 (2016): 569–90.

[14]Todd Whitmore, "'If They Kill Us at Least the Others Will Have More Time to Get Away': The Ethics of Risk in Ethnographic Practice," *Practical Matters* 3 (Spring 2010): 1–28, at 4–5.

learned most of what I now know about cognition and language in those legendary seminars on the medieval theologian John Duns Scotus at the University of Innsbruck, taught each semester by the eminent professor Vladimir Richter. There was nothing particularly striking in the methods he used; we usually had to read Scotus's texts straight out of the original Latin, translating them as we went. Of course this meant that we had to be able to understand—really understand—the text we were reading; otherwise any discussion—lively or otherwise—would have been impossible. *Everything* counted! Richter was clearly in his element in these seminars as we fought and struggled our way through the texts in front of us, rather in the same way the biblical scholar Fridolin Stier, when preparing his famous translation of the New Testament, must have fought and struggled hour after hour, day after day, to find the best German word or phrase to convey the original meaning. He was partaking in the neverending quest to find "the right word," which Ludwig Wittgenstein described on numerous occasions as "Die Suche nach dem erlösenden Wort" (the task of philosophy is to find the redeeming word).[15] Stier and Wittgenstein both wrestled with the language in long and often painful processes.

This is what my teacher, Vladimir Richter, did: he struggled with meaning and word. The amazing thing about the Scotus seminars, and that which sticks most in my mind, is how deeply we were involved in the thinking process of the teacher before us: we could (for want of better words) see and hear him thinking out loud. This was inspiring, but the inspiration did not come from answers, let alone ready-made answers; it did not come from results or refined endpoints reached. The inspiration came from the hard work of asking honest questions in a sincere way. This was teaching in the deepest sense. As George Steiner observed,

> There is no craft more privileged. To awaken in another human being powers, dreams beyond one's own; to induce in others a love for that which one loves; to make of one's inward present their future ... It is a satisfaction beyond compare to be the servant, the courier of the essential—knowing perfectly well how very few can be creators or discoverers of the first rank.[16]

---

[15] Ludwig Wittgenstein, MS 105 (1929), 44; see A. Pichler, *Wittgenstein's Later Manuscripts: Some Remarks on Style and Writing*, Wittgenstein Archives Working Papers 5 (Bergen: University of Bergen, 1992); also I. Somavilla, "Wittgenstein's Coded Remarks in the Context of His Philosophizing," in N. Venturinha, ed., *Wittgenstein after His Nachlass* (Basingstoke: Palgrave Macmillan, 2010), 30–50, at 41.

[16] G. Steiner, *Lessons of the Masters* (Cambridge, MA: Harvard University Press, 2003), 183–84.

Richter helped us discover hidden layers of each text, sophisticated questions, and multiple ways of approaching a sentence or word. We didn't have some preprepared, prepackaged food for thought. We were given the raw ingredients and expected to roll up our sleeves and work out what those ingredients were and how to use them.

This was raw thinking, as opposed to the "cooked" thinking so aptly described by Claude Lévi-Strauss in differentiating between two very different kinds of cognitive mechanisms or processes. "Raw thinking" can be defined as tentative and exploratory, like a person cautiously trying to find her way in a dark room. One would move slowly and search for obstacles and dangerous objects. One would put fragments together in order to understand one's context. Raw thinking is not safe and housed and "protected." It takes place outside of the architecture of existing theories or the buildings of schools of thought. It is an activity that depends on agreement with no one other than oneself—a dialogue that does not have to worry about conventions, expectations, or frameworks. This kind of thinking is akin to carrying a burden up and down a staircase without using the banister. Hannah Arendt, who modeled her philosophy after Socrates, the master of the question, saw herself as engaged in the art of thinking without using the support or directive power of a banister.[17] Entering new and uncharted territory calls for raw thinking—a crafting of thoughts, a creation of epistemic pathways. Reading the signs of the times and engaging in the theological process of *aggiornamento* points to the need for tentative reflections. Clearly, the enactment of Catholic Social Tradition poses challenges that invite raw thinking.

Bringing raw thinking to the Catholic Social Tradition, however, is not without its own challenges. Documents play a major role in the shaping of Catholic Social Tradition as "Teaching" and "Doctrine." Documents are by their nature refined and cooked; they are endpoints and the results of deliberative processes. A document records and codifies a result—and going forward, this result can serve as a stable point of reference. The transition from raw to refined thinking can be compared to the transition from an oral culture to a culture of literacy, with its new possibilities of permanence and objectivity (and bureaucracy).[18]

However, even documents have a history, a story, a biography.[19] Docu-

---

[17] See "Hannah Arendt on Hannah Arendt," in H. Arendt, *Thinking without a Banister: Essays in Understanding, 1953–1975*, ed. Jerome Kohn (New York: Schocken Books, 2018), 443–75.

[18] See J. Goody and I. Watt, "The Consequences of Literacy," *Comparative Studies in Society and History* 5 (1963): 304–45; J. Goody, *The Interface between the Written and the Oral* (Cambridge: Cambridge University Press, 1987).

[19] Sylvia Sellers-García has provided a stellar example of this approach in her article

ments go through rough stages and many drafts before they reach their refined form. Conducting an archaeology of documents is an exercise that can be fruitful for texts as different as the Universal Declaration of Human Rights or the Second Vatican Council's Constitution on Revelation *Dei Verbum*.[20] And, of course, before there is a draft document, there raw thinking is at work.

If we claim the relevance of Catholic Social Tradition for our everyday lives, we need to be prepared to look at new issues as well as familiar ones with fresh eyes. For example, what does Catholic Social Teaching say about homelessness? If I ask a colleague to show me how she goes about tackling a particular issue with Catholic Social Tradition as her guide—when confronted by a homeless person forced to live on the streets, for example—what would I see or hear? Even though homelessness is not really addressed in official documents,[21] some insights can still be drawn from the available teachings. For instance, *Laudato Si'* offers some reference points for "home-building,"[22] and elsewhere establishes a link between home and identity: "Having a home has much to do with a sense of personal dignity and the growth of families. This is a major issue for human ecology."[23] These are building blocks for crafting thinking on homelessness—but just the beginning of an open-ended journey where the result (or destination) is not fixed at the time or point of departure.

And what does classical Catholic Social Teaching have to say about children? Not only do we have to admit that the history of sexual abuse of children and the politics of covering up the abuse challenge the credibility of Catholic Social Teaching. We also have to admit that the topic of children has not played any major role in Catholic Social Teaching

---

"Biography of a Colonial Document" (*Oxford Research Encyclopedia of Latin American History*, 2016 [https://oxfordre.com/latinamericanhistory]), exploring the creation, travel, and storage of colonial documents. Michael Buckland has published a helpful introduction to "document theory" (M. Buckland, "Document Theory: An Introduction," in M. Willer, A. J. Gilliland, and M. Tomić, eds., *Records, Archives and Memory: Selected Papers from the Conference and School on Records, Archives and Memory Studies* [Zadar: University of Zadar, 2015], 223–37); see also D. McKenzie, *Bibliography and the Sociology of Texts* (Cambridge: Cambridge University Press, 1999), which can be read as an eloquent plea for increased attention to the social aspects of document creation and use.

[20]See P. Tiedemann, *Was ist Menschenwürde? Eine Einführung* (Darmstadt: Wissenschaftliche Buchgesellschaft, 2006), chap. 2; H. Sauer, *Erfahrung und Glaube: Die Begründung des pastoralen Prinzips durch die Offenbarungskonstitution des II Vatikanischen Konzils*, Würzburger Studien zur Fundamentaltheologie, Band 12 (Frankfurt am Main: Peter Lang, 1993).

[21]An exception is "The Church and the Housing Problem," a document of the Pontifical Commission for Justice and Peace (1987).

[22]Francis, *Laudato Si'*, "On Care for Our Common Home" (2015), nos. 147–48, hereinafter *LS*.

[23]*LS* 151–52, at 152.

documents, where children are "barely visible."[24] Is it helpful to browse relevant documents and trace how children are mentioned? Today, the context within which children are described in the documents seems to be less than persuasive, because of the dominant image of the intact nuclear family and the tendency to assign caretaking responsibilities primarily to mothers. The family is described as the first school of life, preparing children for future citizenship.[25] Children are counted among the weakest members of society and, because of that, deserve special attention that can be read as a preferential option for children. *Quadragesimo Anno* talks about the "special concern for women and children";[26] *Mater et Magistra* establishes the state's duty "to protect the rights of all its people, and particularly of its weaker members, the workers, women and children."[27] *Evangelium Vitae* provides a list of "society's weakest members" that mentions children after "the elderly, the infirm, immigrants,"[28] and calls for special attention to children, particularly with regard to the consideration of violence.[29]

Unsurprisingly, children are characterized by a particular vulnerability that constitutes a need for protection: *Quadragesimo Anno* warns against work-related abuse and inhumane working conditions,[30] and thematizes the vulnerability of children with regard to (socialist) propaganda since children can be influenced and manipulated so easily.[31] In other documents, children's need for special care because of their special vulnerability is noted (with partly sexist undertones): "The children ... need the care of their mother at home";[32] and children need "care, love and affection."[33] Some Catholic Social Teaching documents see children as agents who contribute to the common good of the family as well as to their parents' well-being and development. This is especially explicit in *Gaudium et Spes*: "As living members of the family, children contribute in their own

---

[24]This is the result of an analysis by Ethna Regan, in "Barely Visible: The Child in Catholic Social Teaching," *Heythrop Journal* 60 (2014): 1021–32.

[25]Pontifical Council for Justice and Peace, *Compendium of the Social Doctrine of the Church* (2004), 210ff, hereinafter *CSDC*.

[26]Pius XI, *Quadragesimo Anno*, "On Reconstruction of the Social Order" (1931), no. 28, hereinafter *QA*.

[27]John XXIII, *Mater et Magistra*, "On Christianity and Social Progress" (1961), no. 20, hereinafter *MM*.

[28]John Paul II, *Evangelium Vitae*, "The Gospel of Life" (1995), no. 8, hereinafter *EV*.

[29]*EV* 10.

[30]*QA* 71. See also the same message in *MM* 13 and John Paul II, *Centesimus Annus*, "On the Hundredth Anniversary [of *Rerum Novarum*]" (1991), no. 8, hereinafter *CA*.

[31]*QA* 121.

[32]John XXIII, *Gaudium et Spes*, "Pastoral Constitution on the Church in the Modern World" (1965), no. 52, hereinafter *GS*.

[33]John Paul II, *Laborem Exercens*, "On Human Work" (1981), no. 19, hereinafter *LE*.

way to making their parents holy. For they will respond to the kindness of their parents with sentiments of gratitude, with love and trust";[34] children "contribute very substantially to the welfare of their parents."[35]

In this way, one could systematically explore the available documents and construct a reading of the status of children as vulnerable agents. This method of gathering relevant quotations is only a first step, which can guide but also inspire tentative thinking. It can sometimes be an advantage to see raw thinking at work, since those present—for example, students, listeners, or readers—get to observe not only the "final" results but the step-by-step process of getting there. Raw thinking *reveals*, while cooked thinking *presents*. In other words, here is a difference between showing and saying, a difference that Wittgenstein emphasized at the end of his *Tractatus*. In one famous passage, Wittgenstein wrote, "My propositions are elucidatory in this way: he who understands me finally recognizes them as senseless, when he has climbed out through them, on them, over them. (He must so to speak throw away the ladder, after he has climbed up on it.) He must surmount these propositions; then he sees the world rightly."[36] This statement, the penultimate entry of the *Tractatus*, sheds light on the status of all the previous propositions: they have a demonstrative value; they "show" something; they point to something beyond the propositions, beyond language. The statement does suggest that something else is at work here, something directing us toward a deeper, epistemological question.

Raw thinking is a kind of epistemic labor that shows the thinking process; that points to "thoughts in the making"; that asks, how are thoughts being crafted? We seldom read about a person's experience when reading a text or about a person's emotions when writing an academic article. There is not only the history of the text that a person writes but also the author's biography. Undeniably, some publications show raw emotions more clearly than others; Theresa Berger's reflections on the invisibility of women in the history of liturgy[37] demonstrate an explicitness of emotional

---

[34]GS 48.

[35]GS 50.

[36]Ludwig Wittgenstein, *Tractatus Logico-Philosophicus* (London: Routledge and Kegan Paul, 1961), 6.54.

[37]T. Berger, *Gender Differences and the Making of Liturgical History* (Surrey: Ashgate, 2011). Berger's project is not "dispassionate," but shows commitments and concerns: "Rendering visible the complex ways in which liturgy has always been shaped by changing gender constructions will I hope open a space for nuanced reflections in a world where gender differences continue to be alive and well in worship. Among the more publicly visible issues are continuing questions about women's ministries, questions surrounding the full ecclesial life of queer Christians, and popular discussions of the need for a more 'muscular' Christianity in an otherwise 'impotent' because 'feminized' church" (33).

involvement that differs from the "Instruction on Certain Aspects of the 'Theology of Liberation,'" a 1984 document by the Congregation of the Doctrine of Faith. But in neither case are we dealing with a disinterested observer's perspective. The "Instruction" is a well-designed text. We see refined thinking but not the thinking process; we see the text but not the preceding struggle with the words and thoughts. Such a struggle can be seen or felt "before" and "underneath" most texts. There may be emotions—even strong ones—at work, informed by lives and experiences. The same applies to the texts we count as belonging to the Catholic Social Tradition. Pope Paul VI refers to his own experience that shaped his thinking about development in *Populorum Progressio*: "We made trips to Palestine and India, gaining first-hand knowledge of the difficulties that these age-old civilizations must face in their struggle for further development."[38]

The thesis put forward in this book challenges the notion that Catholic Social Tradition is a collection or hierarchy of principles and instead advocates that it is something supremely spiritual. However, we need to remember that spirituality does not mean to hide away or shun discussion, as will be familiar to those of you who are acquainted with discussion and debate. Teaching aids can play an important role, acting as valuable starting points and providing assistance in finding one's way through a maze of beliefs and practices—but that is what they basically are: aids and assistance in starting or branching out.

Disciplined Raw Thinking

Text types like the *Catechism of the Church*[39] or the *Compendium of the Social Doctrine of the Church* convey cooked thinking in its most refined form; it has been carefully worded and composed, arranged and laid out. These texts are "epistemically safe" in the sense that proper research has been done, proper discussions have been held, proper words have been found, and proper justifications have been provided. The text—indispensable as a means of orientation—can thus serve as a reference point in debates and be presented as a product with clear boundaries and a clear message. The text, then, is the end of a discussion—but also, probably more importantly so, the beginning of another one. Raw thinking was brought to bear in the generation of the text in its refined form. But of

---

[38] Paul VI, *Populorum Progressio*, "On the Development of Peoples" (1967), no. 4, hereinafter *PP*.
[39] *Catechism of the Catholic Church* (Libreria Editrice Vaticana, 1997), hereinafter CCC.

course, even that process of thought started from a normatively relevant point of departure. We know that Pope John Paul II convened an Extraordinary Synod of Bishops in January 1985 to commemorate the Second Vatican Council in light of new signs of the times. The synod provided the opportunity to request the use of a catechism as a tool for orientation:

> The idea of a universal catechism had been put to the Synod earlier by Cardinal Law of Boston; and Cardinal Wetter of Munich had spoken of the new German catechism for adults as an aid to the overcoming of religious ignorance today. As for the many ecclesiological, pastoral, and missionary themes mentioned in the reports, they harmonized quite well with what Cardinal Arinze, president of the Secretariat for Non-Christians and reporter for English-language Group A, called the "key concept of communion."[40]

This communication of a concern was part of the background story inviting raw thinking about how to design a new catechism for the universal Church, and in 1986 the pope appointed a commission to draft a text. The group's work would require what could be called "disciplined raw thinking" or "guarded and guided raw thinking," informed by normative reference points.

The same process of disciplined raw thinking can be observed on other occasions. For instance, Pope Pius XII prepared for the Apostolic Constitution *Munificentissimus Deus*[41] with his short encyclical *Deiparae Virginis Mariae*[42] addressed to "the Patriarchs, Primates, Archbishops, and other Ordinaries at peace and in communion with the Apostolic See." In this encyclical the pontiff asks for episcopal input into a grave deliberation process:

> We earnestly beg you to inform us about the devotion of your clergy and people (taking into account their faith and piety) toward the Assumption of the most Blessed Virgin Mary. More especially We

---

[40]S. O'Riordan, "The Synod of Bishops, 1985," *The Furrow* 37, no. 3 (March 1986): 139–58, at 152.

[41]Pius XII, *Munificentissimus Deus*, "Defining the Dogma of the Assumption" (1950), hereinafter *MD*.

[42]Pius XII, *Deiparae Virginis Mariae*, "Virgin Mother Mary" (1946), hereinafter *DVM*. To be precise, the pope had sent this letter *in forma del tutto reservata*, dated May 1, 1946, to all the bishops of the world asking what their clergy and people thought about the Assumption and whether they themselves judged it "wise and prudent" that the dogma should be defined. The document was originally printed in *Il Monitore Ecclesiastico* (fasc. 7–12, 1946; pp. 97–98) as a letter.

wish to know if you, Venerable Brethren, with your learning and prudence consider that the bodily Assumption of the Immaculate Blessed Virgin can be proposed and defined as a dogma of faith, and whether in addition to your own wishes this is desired by your clergy and people.[43]

The months and years after that May 1, 1946, were dedicated to disciplined raw thinking that in a refined form would be communicated to the pope. Clearly *most but not all* bishops in those years were in favor of a dogma declaring the bodily Assumption into heaven of the Blessed Virgin. *Munificentissimus Deus* mentions an "almost unanimous affirmative response."[44] (I do not want to make too much of this, but it is of theological interest that a bishop was free to argue for a "no dogma" option in spring 1946 but not in fall 1950. The Apostolic Constitution is the final [and definitive] result of a process that also involved disciplined raw thinking.)

Even if we accept the idea that raw thinking in the context of Catholic theology is well advised to be disciplined and guided, there is a need and a place for this kind of open processing. When Pope Francis is talking about a "bruised" Church or the danger of "ostentatious preoccupation with liturgy," which can turn "the life of the Church" into a "museum piece or something which is the property of a select few,"[45] we might understand this to mean that the people of and in the Church need the courage to take that step beyond the comfort zone of "controlled test conditions" with their predictable results and answers: "Evangelical fervor is replaced by the empty pleasure of complacency and self-indulgence," says *Evangelii Gaudium*,[46] while *Amoris Laetitia* encourages us to shift our focus from "what" to "how."[47] In this regard, mercy is a core principle, not on account of any propositional content but on account of it being the expression of

---

[43]*DVM* 4. This call for input had been motivated by undeniable hopes for a further Marian dogma since "for a long time past, numerous petitions (those received from 1849 to 1940 have been gathered in two volumes which, accompanied with suitable comments, have been recently printed), from cardinals, patriarchs, archbishops, bishops, priests, religious of both sexes, associations, universities and innumerable private persons have reached the Holy See, all begging that the bodily Assumption into heaven of the Blessed Virgin should be defined and proclaimed as a dogma of faith. And certainly no one is unaware of the fact that this was fervently requested by almost two hundred fathers in the Vatican Council" (*DVM* 2).

[44]*MD* 12.

[45]Francis, *Evangelii Gaudium*, "The Joy of the Gospel" (2013), nos. 49, 95, hereinafter *EG*.

[46]*EG* 95.

[47]See Francis, *Amoris Laetitia*, "The Joy of Love" (2016), nos. 6, 49, 296, hereinafter *AL*.

how we should act and behave. Thinking in the spirit of mercy requires an openness well in line with raw thinking.

Raw thinking is the opposite of following a script. Even if the script is official and well justified and coherent, it is not enough to simply repeat the official lines in a pastoral situation, where the Church is committed to considering each case in its uniqueness. This is what a young woman once told me:

> I am a lesbian woman. I have felt extremely ostracized from my hometown parish. I have gone to confession a couple times just to speak candidly with a priest as well as speaking to our pastor individually. They just followed their script, told me that homosexuals are called to a life of chastity and friendship. Now, of course this is the official teaching of the Church, so I was not surprised. However, there was no sense of support. I felt the sense that it was an uncomfortable topic that they didn't want to talk about or engage with, so they followed the prewritten script.

Raw thinking, in this case, is a struggle to find the right words beyond the prewritten script, the right words that honor the particularity of the situation and the uniqueness of the person—especially since one important aspect of honoring the dignity of the person is recognizing her uniqueness. The kind of raw thinking I am mentioning here is not arbitrary or random, or utterly untamed. Raw thinking within a tradition and in communion with a community of people committed to discipleship is guided and guarded, disciplined and deliberate. There are always reference points available and sources of normativity. But even that is not enough. These sources have to be "inhabited," they have to be appropriated. Reading is an act, not the passive reception of rigid content.[48] To take up Claude Lévi-Strauss's metaphor once again, reading is closer to cooking than to eating. Raw thinking about the blank spots on the Catholic Social Tradition map does not happen without the guidance of normative sources, but these sources have to be properly adopted. In addition, reading documents requires some raw thinking as well.

When the encyclical *Laudato Si'* was published in 2015, for example, I was particularly interested in the footnotes, which say so much about a text. If a book is an invitation into a home, footnotes point to the places from which someone obtained the furniture for that home. In the case of the encyclical it is remarkable that Pope Francis did not just go to the

---

[48]See W. Iser, *The Act of Reading: A Theory of Aesthetic Response* (Baltimore, MD: Johns Hopkins University Press, 1978).

Vatican Archives to furnish the text. The culture of footnotes developed in *Laudato Si'* points to new sources of normativity. The encyclical:

- Makes references to the Ecumenical Patriarch Bartholomew[49] and to many local Bishops' Conferences, thus underlining the idea of a regional if not even an ecumenical magisterium.[50]
- Contains references to global discourses (Rio Declaration and Earth Charter).[51]
- Mentions theologians and philosophers beyond a safe body of classical texts (such as Augustine, Aquinas, and Bonventure), including John Chryssavgis, Pierre Teilhard de Chardin, Juan Carlos Scannone, Paul Ricoeur, and the spiritual Sufi writer Ali al-Khawas.[52]

The text also makes ample reference to texts by Pope Francis's predecessors Paul VI, John Paul II, and Benedict XVI. One of the main concerns of the encyclical, the notion of and call for an "ecological conversion," is found in a quotation from John Paul II.[53] These are interesting gleanings from the act of reading the encyclical in an attempt to make the text one's own, to explore and draw insights from its language and sources rather than just passively absorbing its main points.

The footnotes in *Laudato Si'* also point to an ever-higher level of accepted epistemic risk than previous social encyclicals. A safe theological document has a certain self-referentiality in the sense that it refers to other documents, thus developing a culture of discursive commitments as described by philosopher Robert Brandom.[54] The dynamics can be reconstructed like this: a statement with a truth claim limits the possibilities of future statements with truth claims, and given standards of consistency and coherence, this narrowing structures the discursive space. With their normative status, magisterial documents structure possible moves in future magisterial documents. Pope John Paul II's 1994 Apostolic Letter to

---

[49]*LS* footnotes 15–18.

[50]See *LS* footnotes 22 (South Africa), 24 and 32 (Latin America and Caribbean), 25 (Philippines), 26 and 127 (Bolivia), 27 and 42 (Germany), 30 (Argentina), 55 (Canada), 56 (Japan), 65 (Brazil), 70 (Santo Domingo), 77 (Paraguay), 78 (New Zealand), 124 (Portugal), 133 (Mexico), 153 (Australia)—even a regional Bishops' Conference from Argentina (Patagonia-Comahue Region) is mentioned in footnote 30; a particular commission of a Bishops' Conference in footnotes 55, 113, and 133; and a declaration from a colloquium sponsored by the Federation of Asian Bishops in footnote 94. This points to a more regionally and diversely layered magisterium, operating in different regions and on different levels.

[51]*LS* footnotes 114, 126, 132, and 148.

[52]*LS* footnotes 15, 53, 59, 117, and 159.

[53]*LS* footnote 5.

[54]R. Brandom, *Making It Explicit: Reasoning, Representing, Discursive Commitment* (Cambridge, MA: Harvard University Press, 1994), esp. chap. 3.

Catholic bishops, *Ordinatio Sacerdotalis* (On Reserving Priestly Ordination to Men Alone), ends with the teaching, "I declare that the Church has no authority whatsoever to confer priestly ordination on women and that this judgment is to be definitively held by all the Church's faithful" (section 4). This is an expression of a discursive commitment that structures the space for any future discussion on this topic. Quoting documents—and working with a limited set of documents—is epistemically safe.

By bringing in references to science, contemporary authors, and his personal theological preferences (the references to Romano Guardini in section 203 and footnotes 83, 87, 92, 144, and 154, for example), Pope Francis in *Laudato Si'* shows a high level of epistemic risk taking—including the risk of being proven wrong. Epistemic risks have been part of Catholic Social Tradition since the very beginning. Once the canon of the New Testament had been finalized, references to the Bible were references to a closed set of texts (however much development we see in hermeneutics and exegesis). References to social conditions, on the other hand, are references to open realities that change during the time of processing (and also because of) the description.

Catholic Social Teaching, as mentioned earlier, was officially introduced by an encyclical that took considerable epistemic risks: *Rerum Novarum*,[55] in its move toward the contingent sphere of social conditions that change over time, put the pope in a situation of epistemic vulnerability with the text's departure from a *philosophia perennis*[56] or a theology based on revelation. That Leo XIII decided to write about aspects of a contemporary social situation opened a new chapter in the history of inculturation. The first social encyclical could be read as a step toward a culture of "non-ideal" theories.[57] Here we find a shift in the emphasis of the language games under discussion, a shift with emphasis not on "unchanging supernatural realities" such as doctrinal questions of Christology or the Trinity but on trade unions and climate change. The notion of social teaching being an architecture of open-ended judgments[58] is perhaps a good one to consider in the struggle to come to grips with raw thinking.

We now could ask ourselves what it would be like to view a question through the lens of Catholic Social Tradition. What does raw thinking

---

[55] Leo XIII, *Rerum Novarum*, "Rights and Duties of Capital and Labor" (1891), hereinafter *RN*.

[56] A body of philosophical truths said to exist outside of time or place.

[57] Laura Valentini argues that non-ideal theories, unlike their counterparts, ideal theories, refuse to take unrealistic assumptions on board and are more interested in the actual transfer and application of a theory; see L. Valentini, "Ideal vs. Non-Ideal Theory: A Conceptual Map," *Philosophy Compass* 7, no. 9 (2012): 654–64.

[58] "Ein Gefüge von offenen Sätzen" [A structure of open sentences], as German Jesuit theologian Oswald von Nell-Breuning puts it.

look like? Or how could it be realized? We take a detailed look now at two further examples, namely a general discussion with regard to fiscal ethics and the question of a just wage.

Example 1:
The Ethics of Taxation

In a seminar on Catholic Social Teaching, a student asked me whether the tradition would support the idea of replacing compulsory taxes with voluntary donations since Catholic Social Teaching emphasizes human freedom so much and since we can also find warnings against a powerful state at the expense of individual responsibility and individual initiative. Would the social tradition of the Church agree to such an idea or would it be skeptical?

Of course, like all questions, this one had a particular rationale behind it: the student operated under the assumption that a good state was a minimal state and that a minimal state would be one with low levels of taxation. This question is reminiscent of the proposal put forward in 2009 by German philosopher Peter Sloterdijk that taxes (a leftover practice from some obsolete feudal system) should gradually be replaced by unsolicited donations.[59] In fact, the question is both valid and valuable in our discussion, particularly if considered in the light of Sloterdijk's proposal, which has come in for some fierce criticism.[60] Notwithstanding, here is what we might ask in line with our current investigation: how should we view the whole question of taxation in the light of Catholic Social Teaching?

I would like to make my own train of thought visible here, my raw thinking. It is understood that the description of one's own thinking process constitutes epistemic vulnerability because of the absence of justificatory defense mechanisms, caveats, and the polished patina of refined language—all devices that create distance between author and text, the thinker and her product.

My first reaction to the student's question was a sense of irritation not so much related to the "what" of the question, but to the "who," a privileged white male student preparing for a career in the financial industry. He clearly had no idea that the structures of a tax-based European welfare state based on solidarity were the result of many struggles and a remedy for many social ills, such as extreme poverty and destitution.

As a second step in my thinking process, I decided to engage in a con-

---

[59]P. Sloterdijk, *Die nehmende Hand und die gebende Seite* (Berlin: Suhrkamp, 2010).
[60]See A. Honneth, "Fataler Tiefsinn aus Karlsruhe," *Die Zeit*, September 24, 2020.

ceptual exercise. Relevant terms would have to be defined; for instance, "taxes" are a compulsory payment levied via systems of rules and regulations intended for public purposes in the public sector and for which, characteristically, no clearly defined return service can be expected (in other words, taxation is not a transaction with precisely defined terms of reciprocity). The notion of taxation embraces the concept of some form of commonweal that we tend to call "the state," and at the same time assumes the existence of some kind of relationship between individual human beings and their possessions—their "private property"—within this state. The whole idea of taxation, viewed in this way, signals (1) coercion and obligation, (2) public purpose, (3) rigid rules and regulation, (4) a public authority that enforces, levies, and administers.

In making sure that the foundations of our normative discussion were sound, I also reflected on the ethical foundations involved in the actual process of taxation and on the ethics of issues that arise as a result of laws enforced. Taxation ethics revolve around the core principle of the common good: taxation enables and secures the material basis of a *bonum commune* by redistributing resources. By means of taxation, the state can iron out socioeconomic differences and put networks of safeguards and safety measures in place for the needy. In ethical language, taxes serve a fiscal purpose by procuring revenue for the state; taxes encourage, direct, and drive desirable habits or behavior patterns and redistribute wealth, thus reducing the gaps between low- and high-wage earners and the disparity of assets. Three fundamental ethical concerns are to be raised in this regard:

- The justification for and reasoning behind taxation, whereby we need to differentiate between reasons for taxes in general and specific taxes due to certain circumstances (e.g., an inheritance tax or entertainment tax).
- Tax implementation and administration.
- Compliance management, including responding to disruptive conduct related to tax avoidance and tax evasion.

I decided in a third step to turn to Thomas Aquinas (always a good idea in theological labor), who of course would not have experienced democracy or the notion of a monumental state and who certainly had no idea what global politics might mean, but who had something important to say about taxes: he regarded systems of taxation as forms of legitimized theft. Money is extracted from the subject by a ruler—thus there is an element of theft. But it is within the rights of the sovereign to levy taxes from his subjects (even with force if need be), in order to secure the commonweal—the good of the community.⁶¹ The normative foundation stone Aquinas falls back on is Romans 13 and Augustine's *De Civitate Dei* (IV.4): taxes become criminal—even sinful—if the sovereign demands more than his subjects can give, thereby breaching the "ability to pay" principle and violating his commonweal obligations. Aquinas defends the right of ownership—by pointing to the goods that can derive from it, such as greater and more scrupulous care in dealings, improved social structures, and satisfied citizens—not only according to traditional thinking but also to what is ethically relevant—but not absolute—from a fiscal point of view. If A has a surplus and B is in need, then A has an obligation to share that surplus with B.⁶² Aquinas is thus explicitly acknowledging that taxation can be justified if founded on the well-being of the community. John Finnis argues that Aquinas could justify the redistribution of wealth via taxation quite simply because it was the sovereign duty of any ruler to protect the peace in his own realm. Doing so was only feasible if each individual citizen contributed to peaceful community life by making sure that he (or she) had enough to survive according to one's means.⁶³ Fiscal laws must also be seen in the light of what Aquinas understood to be a "just legal system," that is, publicly promulgated and reasonably justified directives for the good of the community⁶⁴ and the highest good.⁶⁵ Any breach of the law may in exceptional circumstances be justified, with the onus of proof lying with the person who has violated the law only insofar as the law serves to reflect the divine higher order (Rom 13:1).⁶⁶ Only when the law is clearly in violation of divine law does Acts 5:29 apply: "We must obey God rather than any human authority."⁶⁷ Hence, we can conclude from this common-good tradition a clear justification of redistribution through taxes and the unambiguous declaration of duties and obligations pertaining to fair taxation practices and conditions.

The Christian tradition offers many other sources of inspiration, such as the seventeenth-century theologian John DeLugo, who taught that paying taxes requires a just cause determined by the common good, that a tax's level must be proportional to its purpose as well as a proportion

---

⁶¹Thomas Aquinas, *Summa Theologiae* II-II, q.66, a.8, resp, hereinafter *ST*. See C. T. Meredith, "The Ethical Basis for Taxation in the Thought of Thomas Aquinas," *Journal of Markets and Morality* 11, no. 1 (2008): 41–57.

⁶²*ST* II-II, q.66, a.1, resp.

⁶³J. Finnis, *Aquinas: Moral, Political and Legal Theory* (Oxford: Oxford University Press, 1998), 191–95; cf., Thomas Aquinas, *De Regno* 2,2; *ST* II-II, q.77, a.4.

⁶⁴*ST* I-II, q.90, a.3, resp; *ST* I-II, q.96,.4, resp.

⁶⁵*ST* I-II, 90.2, resp.

⁶⁶*ST* I-II, 92.3, ad 2.

⁶⁷*ST* I-II, 96.4, resp.

between the level of contributions and the significance and size of the groups of beneficiaries, that fiscal ethics follow an ability-to-pay principle, and that no taxes should be imposed on common necessities of life such as bread and oil.[68]

A fourth element in my raw thinking process was the study of specific texts and documents. Texts having to do with social teaching directly address taxation, and the Catholic Church's compendium of social teaching considers taxation to be fundamentally legitimate,[69] based on the traditional interpretation of the question of taxes as found in the Synoptic Gospels.[70] The thirteenth chapter of Paul's Letter to the Romans—particularly verse 7: "Pay to all what is due to them, taxes to whom taxes are due, revenue where revenue is due, respect . . . and honor to whom [it] is due"—is regarded as being relevant for fiscal ethics.[71] Taxes are seen as being part and parcel of the common welfare principle and are thus an essential part of the obligation of solidarity. Fairness and reasonableness are categories to be considered in determining degrees of taxation, as are the meticulous concern and honesty with which taxes are administered and executed. Any necessary redistribution is to be based on the principles of solidarity, equality, and commitment to the family. An ability-to-pay principle is accepted: "It grows increasingly true that the obligations of justice and love are fulfilled only if each person, contributing to the common good, according to his own abilities and the needs of others, also promotes and assists the public and private institutions dedicated to bettering the conditions of human life."[72]

In *Rerum Novarum* we can already discern a moderate and fair system of taxation as being the basis for a state to run smoothly[73]—but in reference to this same document, *Quadragesimo Anno* warns against violating the principle of ability to pay:

> The wise Pontiff [Leo XIII] declared that it is grossly unjust for a State to exhaust private wealth through the weight of imposts and taxes. For since the right of possessing goods privately has been conferred

---

[68] See John DeLugo, *Disputationes Scholasticae et Morales* (1651), disputatio 36. Also see C. Curran, "Just Taxation in the Roman Catholic Tradition," *Journal of Religious Ethics* 13, no. 1 (1985): 113–33, at 114; for the context, see G. Brinkman, *The Social Thought of John de Lugo* (Washington, DC: Catholic University of America Press, 1957).

[69] Pontifical Council for Justice and Peace, *Compendium of the Social Doctrine of the Church* (2004), 379, hereinafter *CSDC*.

[70] Mk 12:13–17; Mt 22:15–22; Lk 20:20–26.

[71] *CSDC* 380.

[72] *GS* 30.

[73] *RN* 32.

not by man's law, but by nature, public authority cannot abolish it, but can only control its exercise and bring it into conformity with the common weal.[74]

This in turn is supported by an argument in *Mater et Magistra*: "But the justification of all government action is the common good. Public authority, therefore, must bear in mind the interests of the state as a whole; which means that it must promote ... agriculture, industry and services—simultaneously and evenly."[75] Thus, taxes are an integral part of fiscal policymaking to ensure a healthy economy.

We find normatively precise propositions in having to overcome individualistic tendencies, as in *Gaudium et Spes*: "Many ... do not hesitate to resort to various frauds and deceptions in avoiding just taxes or others debts due to society."[76] In *Populorum Progressio*, in which the very idea of tax avoidance or tax reductions is deemed to be so obnoxious as to be ethically scandalous, a world of free persons "involves building a human community where men can live truly human lives, free from discrimination on account of race, religion or nationality, free from servitude to other men or to natural forces which they cannot yet control satisfactorily";[77] and "On the part of the rich man, it calls for great generosity, willing sacrifice and diligent effort. Each man must examine his conscience, which sounds a new call in our present times."[78]

We each need to ask ourselves if we are prepared to assist and support the poorest in our society out of our own pocket and by our own hand. We need to ask ourselves if we are willing to pay additional taxes, to be invested in development aid in the public sphere.[79] The question is, "Is he prepared to pay higher taxes so that public authorities may expand their efforts in the work of development?"[80] This invitation is not to an ethical decision-making process, but to spiritual discernment.

We find similar sentiments in *Economic Justice for All*, written in 1986;

---

[74] *QA* 49.
[75] *MM* 150.
[76] *GS* 30.
[77] *PP* 47. Cf. Lk 16:19–31.
[78] *PP* 47.
[79] See *PP* 84: "Government leaders, your task is to draw your communities into closer ties of solidarity with all men, and to convince them that they must accept the necessary taxes on their luxuries and their wasteful expenditures in order to promote the development of nations and the preservation of peace ... [and] mutual collaboration between nations, (...) that is friendly, peace oriented, and divested of self-interest, a collaboration that contributes greatly to the common development of mankind and allows the individual to find fulfilment."
[80] *PP* 47.

here the US bishops linked taxation with an option for the poor with the proviso that taxes be redistributed where and when necessary.[81] Of course, we could say that any option for the poor must always be embedded in the framework of social teachings and linked in some way to the principle of common welfare, bearing in mind that assisting the most disadvantaged will ultimately be of benefit to the whole community. *Caritas in Veritate* introduces subsidiarity into the fiscal policy discussion for the first time, linking subsidiarity directly to taxation.[82]

On to step five: finding inspiration in contemporary discussions on fiscal ethics. In 1944 Martin Crowe published a book on the moral obligation to pay taxes, and Charles Curran followed with a study some forty years later, emphasizing

> the following aspects in arriving at a just distribution of the tax burden: the universal destiny of the goods of creation to serve the needs of all God's people; the role of the state in working for the common good, with a recognition of the growing complexity of social relations calling for an increased role of the state; distributive justice with emphasis on the criterion of need as the principle to govern the tax burden; the need for the state to promote the right of the poor to share properly in the goods of creation.[83]

Key issues at stake are the idea of the state and the relationship between the right to private property and the teaching on the universal destination of goods.[84]

Taking the texts mentioned here into consideration, I saw an idea emerge that does not suggest a "more minimal the state, the better" approach, especially if the purpose of redistribution of taxes is emphasized. The popular notion of "tax compliance" then expresses an obligation of solidarity that can only be reasonably implemented and taken seriously if enforced by some central legislative power with the necessary authority to

---

[81] United States Catholic Bishops, *Economic Justice for All: Pastoral Letter on Catholic Social Teaching and the U.S. Economy* (1986): "Government may levy the taxes necessary to meet these responsibilities, and citizens have a moral obligation to pay those taxes. The way society responds to the needs of the poor through its public policies is the litmus test of its justice or injustice" (123).

[82] Benedict XVI, *Caritas in Veritate*, "Charity and Truth" (2009), no. 60, hereinafter, *CV*.

[83] M. T. Crowe, *The Moral Obligations of Paying Just Taxes* (Washington, DC: Catholic University of America Press, 1944); Curran, "Just Taxation in the Roman Catholic Tradition," 129.

[84] For a reading that nuances these matters differently than Curran, see a commentary by the Acton Institute: R. G. Kennedy, "Catholic Social Teaching and Tax Justice," *Acton Commentary* (March 2018), https://www.acton.org/pub.

do so. Furthermore, social teaching acknowledges an anthropology that recognizes that in society some social structures and the vulnerability of certain of its citizens are dependent on each other, and that this is the natural result of human nature. This seems to be close to Thomas Nagel and Liam Murphy's concept of "ownership," in which they advance the thesis that it is an illusion to imagine that *we* earn our money and then *we* give some back to the state for its use. Taxation is legally and contractually binding, and without it there would be no ownership or right of ownership. In other words, ownership and right of ownership would not exist without the state, since the state makes the laws that make ownership possible in the first place—no state, no ownership.[85]

The foundation for taxation, one could argue, is a commitment to enabling people to live dignified lives without lack or loss of safety and without extreme poverty. Taxes ensure the common good–oriented practices of the government. Since not every aspect of the handling of fiscal expectations can be strictly monitored, there has to be some basic solidarity and buy-in into the system.

Step six: a central concept that emerges, then, is trust. Trust is the implicit cornerstone of the explicit fiscal contract between individuals and the state administration and also among individual taxpayers (so that all can trust that each is contributing according to his or her possibilities). Trust ensures peace[86] and is one of the most precious goods of any public welfare system. In a certain way, the role of the state within the fiscal culture can be described as "facilitating trust" or "establishing trust-conducive structures." Trust has to be a rational attitude leading to well-justified fiscal practices.[87] A well-functioning fiscal system makes it rational to trust in the tax system and its agency and agents.

This concept of trust was a key element in my response to the student. Replacing compulsory taxes with voluntary donations seems to ask for a tremendous level of trust: trust in a commitment to the common good, trust in people's abilities to judge social and political priorities, and trust in the willingness to share resources without maximizing one's own advantage. This level of trust, one could argue, is not realistic; it is not realistic

---

[85] T. Nagel and L. Murphy, *The Myth of Ownership* (Oxford: Oxford University Press, 2004); see also L. Murphy, "Taxes, Property, Justice," *NYU Journal of Law and Liberty* 1, no. 3 (2005): 983–86; for further discussion on a "pre-tax world," see F. Maultzsch, "Morals and Markets: The Significance of Pre-Tax Ownership," *Modern Law Review* 67, no. 3 (2004): 508–23; and L. Zelenak, "The Myth of Pretax Income," *Michigan Law Review* 101, no. 6 (2003): 2261–74.

[86] *CSDC* 499.

[87] This is a key idea brought forward by Martin Hartmann: *Die Praxis des Vertrauens* (Berlin: Suhrkamp, 2011); see also "On the Concept of Basic Trust," *Behemoth: A Journal on Civilisation* 8, no. 1 (2015): 5–23.

that the perspective of individual taxpayers can replace an institutional perspective of policy priorities. However, one could also say that if this level of trust were realized, people would not have any issues with a properly institutionalized tax system. The very point of the tax system is the pursuit of the common good. We have to grow into this commitment; one important means of personal growth is development of habits, as we see in the next chapter. A habitual culture of taxpaying serves not only the practical purposes of state functionality and redistribution, it also serves the educational purpose of fostering a sense of citizenship through the habit of paying taxes. Then, together with the proper administrative mechanisms and democratic structures, it becomes rational to trust in the moral division of labor between institutions and individuals attempting to realize the common good.

These points about fiscal trust as a key concept can be developed, of course, into a refined account. But if I were to publish an account of fiscal trust I would, as a general rule, not be able to publish this description of the raw thinking process, but only the results—not the emotions felt, but the appropriately justified conclusions reached.

Example 2:
A Just Wage

What is a just wage in the light of Catholic Social Tradition? How do we arrive at an answer to this important element of the labor question? What would I have to consider to give an appropriate, clear, and practical answer? How would I go about exploring those considerations?

Personal Remarks

My first step in the thinking process, before actually moving into a close analysis of Catholic Social Tradition, would be a search for experiential reference points. One particular colleague comes to mind; I remember him telling me, "I am overpaid." He meant what he said. He would consider his own remuneration as nonjust, as excessive. He is the only colleague I ever met who would say something like this. I am much more familiar with these phrases: "I am underpaid," or "My salary is too low." I can also add a personal experience. When working in Bhutan I witnessed the effect of a "salary leak"—the salary of the Canadian co-manager of the project was made public by mistake (he made 150 times as much as the project's average employee). The effect was twofold: On the one hand, people felt demotivated and wondered why they should bother working hard. On the other hand, there was a visible wave of mistrust: "If I need to work 150 hours to make as much as this person does in one single hour, this person must be perfect and superhuman and as an overpaid employee cannot make the slightest mistake or cannot show the slightest trace of carelessness." The ripple effects of this disclosure were significant.

Wage matters are important; they touch upon issues of identity and recognition, hierarchies and criteria of success, and emotions like envy and greed. Emotions tend to be honest indicators of what we value. In any institution I have worked in, access to the salary information has been a crucial and delicate matter. Then, of course, what do you do with this knowledge? Does it create a "wound of knowledge"—that is to say, a painful and burdening knowledge? I once, for instance, through a communication mistake where a whole email chain was forwarded to colleagues, saw that the offer made to a job candidate was 25 percent more for a junior position than I was making in a senior position. It took an intentional effort *not* to compare: matters of just remuneration carry deep emotional weight.

Reflecting on the Framework

A second step in this raw thinking exercise would be to reflect upon the framework of the actual discussion and upon the significance of the general normative conditions regarding fair pay as laid down in the Catholic Social Tradition. If I assume that the principles of Catholic Social Teaching—rooted in human dignity, the common good, an option for the poor, and protecting, guarding, and furthering creation—are all relevant for our question about a fair wage, then I would also be able to pinpoint five framework criteria (FC):

FC 1 *Integrity.* Remuneration and reward need to accommodate the dignity of the individual and enable that individual to live a life worthy of a human being: that is, to enable and empower his or her integrity. A life of integrity in all its aspects and dimensions—objective and subjective, material and immaterial, moral and spiritual—should be within the reach of each and every human being. With this benchmark in mind, a just wage becomes a means to the integrity of the person, to a life in accordance with human dignity.

FC 2 *Common good.* Remuneration should enable the person to take part and be actively involved in building and maintaining the common good, in an expression of contributive justice. A just wage needs to enable a person to become a contributive agent toward the *bonum commune.*

FC 3 *Option for the poor.* Catholic Social Tradition obliges us to seek out the most disadvantaged or most discriminated against: does remuneration policy ensure that those at a disadvantage are not disadvantaged still further by the wage structure?

FC 4 *Participation.* Catholic Social Teaching encourages participation and co-ownership: in other words, the possibility of sharing in any assets at the source. A just wage reflects not only the procedure of paying wages as a result of negotiations and agreements reached, but also patterns of shared ownership.

FC 5 *Care for creation.* The means and mechanisms used to pay out wages—no matter how fair they may seem—can never be justified if creation is put at risk, trampled upon rather than protected. While institutional measures may be fulfilled, that is, Catholic Social Teaching criteria followed within a business, institutional measures can only pass the litmus wage test if the wages paid would be acceptable in the wider context of the world beyond the company's fringes.

In a nutshell, here are questions that arise for the criteria:

FC 1 *Integrity.* Does the wage allow the preservation of a person's integrity, respecting the dignity of the human person?[88]

FC 2 *Common good.* Does the wage structure contribute to the common good? Does the wage structure contribute to community building?[89]

FC 3 *Option for the poor.* Does the wage structure contribute to the inclusion of the most disadvantaged members of society?

FC 4 *Participation.* Has the wage structure been built in a way that fosters cultures of participation and the possibly of co-ownership?[90]

FC 5 *Care for creation.* Does the wage structure contribute to the preservation of the environment (e.g., by incentivizing certain choices of goods and types of behavior)?

The overarching principle in Catholic Social Tradition is the dignity of each human person—a wage is just if it enables a person to live a life in correspondence to one's dignity, that is, a decent, dignified life. A just wage, then, enables frugal but comfortable living, meeting "ordinary family needs"[91] with "decent comfort."[92]

Looking for Insights from the Tradition

A third step might be to look back over the tradition of Christian social thinking to gain inspiration for our project. John Ryan, SJ, is undoubtedly a central source on the question of a just wage. In Ryan's view, a "living

---
[88] See *CSDC* 279; *RN* 20; *LE* 19; *CV* 63.
[89] See *QA* 74; *GS* 71.
[90] See *QA* 65.
[91] *QA* 71.
[92] *RN* 45, 46; *QA* 63, 75.

wage" is a core value of natural justice, an indestructible right founded on the fundamental principle of the universal destination of goods.[93] Every human being has a "God-given" right to a decent livelihood, dignity being vitally inherent in the broader meaning of "decent."

In his groundbreaking work from 1912, *A Living Wage*, John Ryan systematically develops the idea that a "just wage" is a "living wage"—and that a living wage is a natural right: "The thesis to be maintained in this volume is that the laborer's claim to a Living Wage is of the nature of a *right*. This right is personal, not merely social: that is to say, it belongs to the individual as individual, and not as member of society. . . . It is a natural, not a positive right."[94] Natural rights protect a certain minimum of goods to cover the reasonable needs of the human person. Of importance here is the idea of a decent life, a life in accordance with the dignity of the person.[95] In order for a person to live a dignified life, she needs to be able to access the goods necessary to maintain her life. Within the system of a wage structure, this right has to be translated into the right to a just wage, Ryan says. This right

> is not an original and universal right; for the receiving of wages supposes that form of industrial organization known as the wage system, which has not always existed and is not essential to human welfare. . . . The right to a Living Wage is evidently a derived right which is measured and determined by existing social and industrial institutions. . . . The primary natural right from which the right to a Living Wage is deduced is the right to subsist upon the bounty of the earth.[96]

The goods of the earth are meant for all, pointing to the well-established limit on private property: "Private ownership of the earth's resources is right and reasonable not for its own sake—which would be absurd—but

---

[93] L. Murphy, "An 'Indestructible Right': John Ryan and the Catholic Origins of the U.S. Living Wage Movement, 1906–1938," *Labor Studies in Working Class History of the Americas* 6, no. 1 (2006): 57–86.

[94] J. Ryan, *A Living Wage* (London: Macmillan, 1912), 43.

[95] "The laborer has a right to a family Living Wage because this is the only way in which he can exercise his right to the means of maintaining a family, and he has a right to these means because they are an essential condition of normal life" (ibid., 118). And later in the text: "A decent livelihood for the adult male laborer means a wage capable of maintaining himself, his wife, and those of his children who are too young to be selfsupporting, in a condition of reasonable comfort" (123). Similarly, "The question that we are concerned with is not what a man must have in order to be a profitable producer, but what he ought to have as a human being" (132).

[96] Ibid., 68. Given the wage structure there is an obligation to pay a just wage (100–101).

because it enables men to supply their wants more satisfactorily than would be possible in a regime of common property."[97] Private ownership can be justified and so can certain wage differentials: "It is true that society will do well to pay exceptional rewards in order to obtain exceptional services."[98] The community may be interested in certain types of services and will be prepared to pay more for these services. Living-wage demands address the same community.[99]

In his principal work, *Distributive Justice,* Ryan argues that a living wage is the basic minimum requirement of any just system: "The State is obliged to enact laws which will enable the laborer to obtain a living wage; but the duty of actually providing this measure of remuneration rests upon that class which has assumed the wage-paying function."[100] Ryan goes beyond this basic premise of the universal destination of goods by incorporating two further principles. The first reads, "The inherent right of access to the earth is conditional upon, and becomes actually valid through, the expenditure of useful labor." And the second, the social principle: "The men who are in present control of the opportunities of the earth are obliged to permit reasonable access to these opportunities."[101] A worker—in working or having worked—has a claim to those goods: "Every man who is willing to work has, therefore, an inborn right to sustenance from the earth on reasonable terms or conditions."[102] This right is to more than enough to merely "exist"; it envisages a wage that enables self-improvement and growth. Indeed, this idea of self-improvement cannot be divorced from the idea of human dignity. Thus we see emerging a close connection between a tangible aspect of life (a just wage, a living wage) and intangible aspects (growth, development, justice). We can distinguish here another vital aspect of "wage" that comes out more clearly in Kenneth Himes on Ryan, in which any discussion of minimum wage becomes a discussion about maximum wage: "The more interesting ethical question, to my mind, when addressing inequality, is not whether there is a floor beneath which none should fall (that is widely acknowledged among Christian ethicists), but is there a ceiling above which none should rise?"[103]

---

[97]Ibid., 71; see also 106. "Private property is morally legitimate because it is the method that best enables man to realize his natural right to use the gifts of material nature for the development of his personality. . . . The private right of any and every individual must be interpreted consistently with the common rights of all" (72).
[98]Ibid., 76.
[99]Ibid., 101.
[100]J. A. Ryan, *Distributive Justice* (New York: Macmillan, 1916), 365.
[101]Ibid., 359–60.
[102]Ibid., 360.
[103]K. Himes, "Catholic Social Teaching on Building a Just Society," *Religions* 8 (2017): 2–11, at 5.

This is obviously only one example representing many, but it speaks to an important debate in the Christian Social Tradition.

Identification of Key Texts

Our fourth point might well be termed "rooting around in source texts." For example, what do key texts of social teaching have to say on the question of wages? How are they viewed in social encyclicals and in the *Compendium of the Social Doctrine of the Church*?[104]

Rerum Novarum links earnings with facilitating private property or savings,[105] establishes wage fraud as a serious crime,[106] and calls for special protection of vulnerable wage earners, those who rely on wages and not assets for their livelihoods.[107] It also presents the core idea about a just wage in the language of the time: "Wages ought not to be insufficient to support a frugal and well-behaved wage-earner."[108] In other words, a worker's wages should be "sufficient to enable him comfortably to support himself, his wife, and his children."[109]

An especially long section on remuneration can be found in *Quadragesimo Anno*,[110] which reaffirming the claim that the justice of a contract cannot be based on agreement alone and calling for a partnership contract that includes the possibility of participation. It also teaches, "The just amount of pay, however, must be calculated not on a single basis but on several,"[111] and reiterates the key idea of a just wage: "The worker must be paid a wage sufficient to support him and his family."[112] This claim is strengthened by the aspect of the protection of childhood and the prevention of the abuse of children through child labor. *Quadragesimo Anno* introduces a new criterion in the question of just wage, namely the condition of the business: "In determining the amount of the wage, the condition of a business and of the one carrying it on must also be taken into account; for it would be unjust to demand excessive wages which a business cannot stand without its ruin and consequent calamity to the workers."[113] It also establishes an explicit link to the

---

[104] An initial finding provides the following list of key passages: *RN* 5, 20, 37, 44–46; *QA* 63–75; *GS* 67; *LE* 19; *CA* 8; *CV* 63; *CSDC* 301–302.
[105] *RN* 5.
[106] *RN* 20.
[107] *RN* 37.
[108] *RN* 45.
[109] *RN* 46.
[110] *QA* 63–75.
[111] *QA* 66.
[112] *QA* 71.
[113] *QA* 72.

common good: "The amount of the pay must be adjusted to the public economic good."[114]

Laborem Exercens describes remuneration for work as the most important way of securing a just relationship between the worker and the employer and a key criterion with which to judge the justice of a social structure according to its commitment to the common good: "A just wage is the concrete means of *verifying the justice* of the whole socioeconomic system."[115] Then the well-known concept of a family wage is restated: "Just remuneration for the work of an adult who is responsible for a family means remuneration which will suffice for establishing and properly maintaining a family and for providing security for its future."[116] The role of women is mentioned, social benefits are listed, and in that context the "right to rest"[117] is reconfirmed.

Centesimus Annus confirms all of the above and criticizes "unbridled capitalism," stating that the state has a duty to protect earning levels.[118] On the question of fair pair for fair work in the twenty-first century, *Caritas in Veritate* points out the direct link between poverty and unemployment and the connection between work and human dignity, making use of the concept of "decent work."[119] The sixth chapter of the *Compendium of the Social Doctrine of the Church* takes up this same point, warning of the dangers of exploiting weaker members of society and those people in greater need[120] and underlining the idea of a family wage.[121] At the same time, it sets the question of a fair wage in the context of theological reasoning, for example, Luke 10:7: "for the labourer deserves to be paid." It also talks about the right to a just wage,[122] characterizing it as the legitimate fruit of work done and "the instrument that permits the labourer to gain access to the goods of the earth."[123]

Working in Depth with One Crucial Text

Part of a raw-thinking exercise could be a deeper look at a selected key passage. The highest-ranked document to talk about a just wage is the Pastoral Constitution of the Second Vatican Council, *Gaudium et Spes*.

---

[114] *QA* 74.
[115] *LE* 19.
[116] *LE* 19.
[117] Already known from *RN* 41–42.
[118] *CA* 8.
[119] *CV* 63.
[120] *CSDC* 148.
[121] *CSDC* 250.
[122] *CSDC* 301.
[123] *CSDC* 302.

Its key passage on just wage encapsulates precisely the simple message of what fair earnings are: "Remuneration for labor is to be such that man may be furnished the means to cultivate worthily his own material, social, cultural, and spiritual life and that of his dependents, in view of the function and productiveness of each one, the conditions of the factory or workshop, and the common good."[124] This passage alone gives us five criteria for a just remuneration (R):

1. If R enables the laborer L (and his or her dependents) to lead a (four-dimensional) decent life.
2. If R properly considers the function of L.
3. If R properly considers the productivity (performance) of L.
4. If R properly considers the situation of the employer E.
5. If R properly considers the common good.

We can make a number of observations from an analysis of this passage, paying special attention to its original Latin text:

The context of the passage is chapter 3 of Gaudium et Spes *with the following messages.*

- Human labor is superior to the other elements of economic life.
- Human labor comes immediately from the person who transforms things of nature ("subdues" the "things of nature" and "stamps them with his/her seal").
- Labor serves the purposes of self-support and support of family, fellowship, service, charity, divine partnership in creation, and the redemptive work of Jesus Christ who worked in Nazareth with his own hands—in other words, labor is discipleship.
- People have both duty to work faithfully and a right to work.
- It is the contextual duty of society to create conditions so that citizens are able to find sufficient opportunity to work.

Remuneration for work in the specified way is obligatory. The addressee of this claim is not specified, and the question of who carries this obligation (perhaps both employer and state together?) is left open, even though *Gaudium et Spes* 67 earlier mentions the duties of society.

Remuneration and the obligation to ensure this remuneration serve a

---

[124]*GS* 67. The Latin text reads, "Denique ita remunerandus est labor ut homini facultates praebeantur suam suorumque vitam materialem, socialem, culturalem spiritualemque digne excolendi, spectatis uniuscuiusque munere et productivitate necnon officinae condicionibus et bono communi."

purpose. The justice of remuneration is measured by the fulfillment of the defined purpose, which means there have to be indicators for the level and degree of this fulfillment.

The purpose of remuneration is to offer (Latin praebere*) X*. There is a certain optionality implied in *praebere*, as if it was something offered and left to the discretion of the recipient whether to take and use it.

The object of the offer—that is, X—is "facultates," meaning power, means, capacity, opportunities, ability, while "to offer" can be understood as "to enable," "to give access to," "to make available." In a nutshell, the purpose of remuneration is to offer facultates, which can be understood in multiple ways, including means or capacity or opportunity; in addition, the different ways matter, but in each case the underpinning key notion seems to be freedom—the freedom to pursue ends, the freedom to realize possibilities. One could argue that there is an epistemic closeness to a version of the "capability approach" with its central value of freedom ("remuneration as freedom").[125]

*The object of the "facultates"—that is, the "aims of the freedoms"—is the cultivation of a dignified and decent life (*vitam digne excolendi*) in its material, social, cultural, and spiritual dimensions*. Even though "political" is not explicitly mentioned, we could assume that it is part of the social dimension, given the societal context mentioned before and after the passage. "*Excolere*" (cultivate) points to the active effort necessary; the term "*digne*" seems weak, given the key importance of human dignity in Catholic Social Tradition, and qualifies "*vitam excolere*." Rather than to cultivate the decent life, the official Italian translation suggests: "permettere . . . una vita dignitosa": The suggestion seems to be that the remuneration of labor should enable a person to cultivate a four-dimensional life "worthily"—that a proper consideration of the four dimensions, properly cultivated, leads to a decent life).

The statement about the purpose of remuneration is relativized and contextualized by pointing to four factors

- "*Munus*": gift, service, office, function, duty—there are many ways to translate the term. Since the second term ("*productivitas*") points to the person's input into the job, one could find grounds to argue that "*munus*" is "function," that is, the status of the person given the status of the work (the official Italian translation is "*tipo di attività*" or [type of activity].
- "*Productivitas*": not an ancient term, this reflects the efforts to adapt the official Church Latin to changing conditions; the Ital-

---

[125]Cf. A. Sen, *Development as Freedom* (New York: Anchor Books, 1999).

ian translation (*rendimento economico*) points in the direction of "return on investment," and the German translation ("*Leistungsfähigkeit*") in the direction of "performance capability" rather than "performance" ("*Leistung*"). Given the meaning of *productivitas* as "faculty to produce," the performance- and achievement-related reading of this second term seems justified. Together, *munus* and *productivitas* can be seen to balance person and work, considering the first aspect through an emphasis on "function," the second aspect through the emphasis on "performance."

- "*Conditiones officinae*": an "*officina*" (etymologically connected to "opus") is a shop where goods are manufactured, and just remuneration has to consider the situation and conditions of the workplace. If it is meant to refer to the institutional context of work, the term "*officina*" seems too narrow. There may be a slightly one-sided "best example" of a factory worker in the background, echoing some of the underlying images in *Rerum Novarum*; in any case, the third term as well as the fourth both refer to contextual aspects. "*Officina*" may be understood to express the idea of an "ability to pay," but this necessitates going beyond the text itself.
- "*Bonum commune*": the well-established term "common good" (or the sum total of conditions that ensure the flourishing of each person and the entire community) expresses the social and political aspects of the institutional context of work ("*officina*"). With the recognition of a global common good in Catholic Social Teaching,[126] the context of the work to be considered for questions of a just wage becomes a global one.

The Construction of Criteria

In the light of these text-bound observations, we can reconstruct eight key criteria for a just wage and pair them with particular passages from normative texts:

C 1: *Decent life*: Wage structure enables decent life and family life.[127]
C 2: *Assets*: Wage enables asset building.[128]
C 3: *Security*: Wage offers basic social security, for example, pension

---

[126] John Paul II, *Sollicitudo Rei Socialis*, "On Social Concerns" (1987), nos. 10, 22, 35, 36, hereinafter *SRS*; *LE* 23.
[127] *CSDC* 250; *RN* 45, 46; *QA* 71; *MM* 71; *GS* 67; *LE* 19; *CA* 8, 15, 34; *CV* 63.
[128] *CSDC* 250; *RN* 5, 46; *QA* 63, 74; *LE* 19; *CA* 15; *CV* 63.

provision, accident insurance, paternity/maternity leave.[129]

C 4: Equality: Wage structure is nondiscriminatory.[130]

C 5: Temperance: Wage structure does not allow for excessiveness.[131]

C 6: Participation: Wage structure has been built in a participatory way and encourages participation.[132]

C 7: Work: Wage considers performance, qualification, and type of work.[133]

C 8: Employer: Wage structure considers situation of the employer.[134]

Indicators

For each of the eight listed criteria we need to identify indicators in conversation with the documents:

Ad C 1 (Decent life): living wage level / scheduling powers;[135] leisure and cultural-spiritual "otium."[136]

Ad C 2 (Assets): private ownership;[137] disposable income / possibility for wage growth;[138] savings.[139]

Ad C 3 (Security): vulnerability levels / worst-case scenarios.

Ad C 4 (Equality): gender equality;[140] no traces of racism / inequitable working conditions for people with disabilities;[141] transparency of wage structure.

Ad C 5 (Temperance): Moderate ratio of the highest to lowest wage;[142] justifiable ratio to average wage in society.

Ad C 6 (Participation): Collective bargaining and role of trade unions;[143] co-ownership options / decision latitude;[144] lean bureaucracy.[145]

Ad C 7 (Work): Incentive, raise, and bonus structure / appropriate classification of types of work.

---

[129] *CSDC* 279, 301; *LE* 19; *CA* 34.
[130] *CSDC* 295, 536; *GS* 66; *CV* 63.
[131] *QA* 72, 74; *GS* 71; *LE* 19; *CA* 15.
[132] *QA* 65; *MM* 32; *LE* 15.
[133] *GS* 67; *MM* 71.
[134] *GS* 67.
[135] See *MM* 112.
[136] *RN* 20; *GS* 67; *LE* 19.
[137] *GS* 71.
[138] *RN* 5; *MM* 112; *CA* 15.
[139] *RN* 46; *CA* 15; *CSDC* 250.
[140] *CSDC* 295.
[141] *LE* 19; *CSDC* 148.
[142] *QA* 75; *MM* 139.
[143] *CA* 15; *CSDC* 292.
[144] *MM* 112; *GS* 71.
[145] *LE* 15.

Ad C 8 (Employer): "Industry proportionality";[146] long-term perspective reflected in contracts and sustainability of business.[147]

Deepening the Criteria

A next step in thinking about just wages from a Catholic ethics perspective could be a deep analysis of the criteria. Let me offer a case study about the one on "excessiveness." A reflection on "nonexcessiveness" criterion could look like this:

A particular way of justifying high wages is "merit" or "desert." The desert principle can be expressed as: A deserves B because of C, which means that A has a moral claim to B because of C.

A stands for "the individual wage earner," B for "a high wage," C for "meritorious status (either ex ante: qualification, type of position, market situation; or ex post: performance), and the "because of" establishes a causal connection ("A is fully responsible for C").

How, we could ask, can one evaluate "merit" in a theological framework that accepts 1 Corinthians 4:7: "What do you have that you did not receive? And if you received it, why do you boast as if it were not a gift?" Catholic Social Tradition is clearly not in favor of wage egalitarianism in a strict sense or a leveling of wages; it recognizes the justifiability of differentiated remuneration schemes and expresses the idea of natural inequality that is also reflected in the wage structure.[148] An appropriate wage considers performance, qualification, and type of work.[149] Wages definitely have a personal dimension in which the principle of "desert" (effort, performance) can be accepted as a key criterion. But how can "desert" be defined and how can one principle of desert—the more deserving should receive more—be applied?

A highly remunerated CEO told me, "We are normal human beings," and my response was, "Then I wonder how you can justify your salary." There is a moment of "skill basis" or "merit basis" when we consider whether a particular wage is excessive.

X is excessive if

(1) there is a norm N defining the appropriate quantity $Q(x)$;
(2) x equals more than $Q(x)$, leading to a difference $D(N,x)$; and
(3) $D(N,x)$ is significant.

---

[146] *MM* 70, 79, 111.
[147] *CV* 40.
[148] See *RN* 17, 34.
[149] See *MM* 71; *GS* 67.

Such an analysis can generate two concepts of "excessiveness": A wage is first compensation or remuneration for work and second an instrument to secure a livelihood. A particular wage, then, is "excessive" if the wage goes significantly above the norm defining an appropriate wage level. An important normative question is the question whether an "excessive x" has reached or violated N. If the Israelites in the book of Exodus (5:7–9) are asked to produce a particular number of bricks per day, and they exceed this target, they have met the target. Let us call this the "surplus understanding of excess"; there is a right amount that defines a target as a minimum that can be surpassed. This scenario is different from the limit of the maximum amount of decibels to assess acceptable noise levels; once this limit of, let us say, an average noise level of 85 decibels a day has been exceeded, the target has been violated. Let us call this the "violation understanding of excess."

One particular way of using the word "excess" is in an excessiveness of meaning. "A shoe is not the meaning of a shoe; the meaning of a shoe permits the shoe to show itself both as meaningful and as exceeding meaning."[150] We could argue that the very idea of an excess wage undermines the meaning of "wage." An excessive wage has lost the purpose of a wage. The virtue of temperance is not meant to cultivate an attitude of modesty but to foster a morally and spiritually good life.

Having an excess of something means "having too much" of something[151]—related terms would be "superabundant" or "in abundance"—but how much is enough and how much is too much? This question cannot be separated from the question of a good life. A just wage is connected to a just life. Catholic Social Teaching offers a normative perspective that calls for not only a floor but a ceiling.[152] Ever since the promulgation of *Quadragesimo Anno* in 1931, there has been a normative understanding that the wage structure is not to allow for excessiveness; the encyclical states: "In determining the amount of the wage, the condition of a business and of the one carrying it on must also be taken into account; for it would be unjust to demand excessive wages which a business cannot stand without its ruin and consequent calamity to the workers."[153] later, *Quadragesimo Anno* asserts,

> The amount of the pay must be adjusted to the public economic good, ... everyone knows that an excessive lowering of wages, or

---

[150]R. Polt, "Meaning, Excess, and Event," *Gatherings: The Heidegger Circle Annual* 1 (2011): 26–53, at 32.
[151]A. Abbott, "The Problem of Excess," *Sociological Theory* 32, no. 1 (2014): 1–26, at 2.
[152]Himes, "Catholic Social Teaching on Building a Just Society."
[153]*QA* 72.

their increase beyond due measure, causes unemployment. . . . Hence it is contrary to social justice when, for the sake of personal gain and without regard for the common good, wages and salaries are excessively lowered or raised; and this same social justice demands that wages and salaries be so managed, through agreement of plans and wills, in so far as can be done, as to offer to the greatest possible number the opportunity of getting work and obtaining suitable means of livelihood.[154]

This gives us two arguments—an argument "ad intra," looking to the business's long-term prospects, and an argument "ad extra," looking to the common good, with its demands for contributive justice and participation. The first has been explicitly linked with the discourse on sustainability,[155] which is by no means a new insight. Bishop Wilhelm Emmanuel Ketteler, an important social theologian who had a major influence on the first social encyclical *Rerum Novarum* (Leo XIII, 1891), warned against excessive expectations in the nineteenth century. He was speaking to workers and not CEOs, but the logic of the argument is compelling in any case: wage increases must be tempered by a long-term perspective for a sustainable business.[156] Excessive wages can put the very existence of the business at risk.[157]

Catholic Social Tradition uses excess in many different ways—documents talk about "an excessive affirmation of equality," an "excessive presence of the State in public mechanisms," an "excessive growth in public agencies," and an "excessive bureaucracy."[158] There are warnings against "excessive exploitation of the environment," "excessive demands of work that make family life unstable and sometimes impossible," and "excessive profits of individual businesses" that have to be moderated.[159] John Paul II introduces the term "superdevelopment" and defines it as "an excessive availability of every kind of material goods for the benefit of certain social groups."[160]

---

[154]QA 74.
[155]CV 40.
[156]W. E. Ketteler, *Die Arbeiterbewegung und ihr Streben im Verhältniß zu Religion und Sittlichkeit—Eine Ansprache, gehalten auf der Liebfrauen-Haide am 25. Juli 1869* (Mainz: Verlag Franz Kirchheim, 1869), 10.
[157]See D. Eissrich, "An Economist's View of the Work of Wilhelm Emmanuel von Ketteler and Its Influence on the Encyclical *Rerum Novarum*," in J. Backhaus et al., eds., *On the Economic Significance of the Catholic Social Doctrine* (Wiesbaden: Springer, 2017), 11–25, at 21.
[158]CSDC 158, 187, 354, and 412, respectively.
[159]CSDC 482, 280, and 347, respectively.
[160]SRS 28.

In all these cases the term "excess" is used to express a lack or loss of temperance, appropriateness, and a sense of proportionality and adequacy. In all these cases the term is used to describe a hindrance to the good life, both in individual and in communal terms. What seems to be at stake, then, is the normative concept of the good life. The two arguments against excessive wages—the company-based one and the society-based one—can be complemented by two further arguments, well in line with Catholic Social Tradition: one that is based on the person and one that is based on the environment. The former points to the question of the appropriate wage for the spiritual health and moral integrity of a person, the latter the destructive effects of superdevelopment for the environment. Remuneration in excess of a moderate living wage is not necessarily a "better living wage." There seems to be a tipping point where the wage may increase but the moral, spiritual, and even overall quality of life does not increase. Excessiveness threatens the spiritual integrity of a person since excess includes excess of desires and excess of things.[161] We may be tempted to talk about "spiritual rights," that is, the right to integrity-building growth, including the right to have access to humbling moments (one particularly relevant entry point for humbling moments is not having a vast excess of resources). "Moral and spiritual integrity" emerges as a key concept in reflecting on the excessiveness of compensation from the perspective of Catholic Social Tradition.

Looking for Examples

The raw thinking above could be complemented by the search for examples—let me offer one that allows us to see the reality of a just wage: an analysis of the remuneration structure of the Archdiocese of Vienna, which is the result of collective bargaining.[162] The document laying out the remuneration structure expresses moral expectations ("sentire cum ecclesia" and a sense of responsibility for representing the Church); it states regular working hours (Monday to Thursday, 8 a.m. to 4:30 p.m.; Friday, 8 a.m. to 2 p.m.) and the possibility for "agreed flexibility"; and it regulates breaks and holidays in addition to state holidays as well as special paid days off, irrespective of holidays: three days in the case of marriage or death of spouse; two days for the death of a parent or child, or a household move; one day for the marriage of a sibling or child. The policy grants continuing education (five working days per year); as per the Austrian law it guarantees paid holidays (twenty-five working days

---

[161] Abbott, "Problem of Excess," 6.
[162] See www.zentralbetriebsrat.at/site/.

per year, if employed for less than twenty-five years; thirty working days per year, if employed for more than twenty-five years). The remuneration takes into consideration "relevant previous Church work experience," and compensation is based on a particular "level" according to years of employment and type of work determined by the job description. An employee automatically moves up the remuneration levels every two years but there is also the possibility of merit pay. Social benefits added to the basic salary include a family benefit (only on the basis of a Catholic marriage), which is increased if the employee is the "sole breadwinner." There are also benefits for each child, with three times the base amount for a disabled child. There are extra payments for a Catholic wedding, the birth of a child, and loyalty payments after ten, twenty-five, and forty years of employment. This is the Archdiocese's basic remuneration structure.

Observations to be made on the above contract are as follows:

- Base salaries are comparatively low.
- Salary differentials are also low—for example, comparing the lowest level (G 1) with the highest level (A 25) results in a ratio of 1:3.56.
- Time served seems to be the main prime factor in salary increases—it seems to take primacy over the salary scale, particularly if we remember the breaks, weekends, annual holidays, special or compassionate leave, and in-service training.
- In general, provisions are designed to support families and family life (both in working hours and remuneration).
- Some provisions, such as taking into account ("Catholic") work experience, suggest an "inside reward system," underpinned still further by preferencing married Catholic couples and rewarding loyalty with an automatic biennial pay rise
- The contract supports a Catholic way of life (Sunday as a day of rest and Church holidays which also ensure a day of rest)
- Moral expectations cannot be left out (e.g., the explicit expectation that employees shoulder the responsibility of representing the Church in public
- Provisions leave room for exceptions judged on an individual case basis, for example, in assessing salary scaling or one-off payments (which risks lack of transparency).

Some questions remain unanswered: Can the comparatively low level of wages be justified at a trans-contextual level? Does the whole system of salary scaling sufficiently take into account levels of responsibility? And how can this criterion justify seniority according to Catholic Social

Tradition? Just how much diversity can such a system allow or encourage? Do not too many special payments at irregular intervals promote a loss of transparency?

Still-Open Questions

There are open questions beyond those from this example. After this process of raw thinking, we still have a great deal of work to do. We could ask questions such as: Is there an underlying one-sided diet of examples (best examples) for "workers" and "work situations"? How can the documents be reconciled with the value of gender equality? Is there a ranking and an order of the criteria? Are the criteria mentioned competitive in the sense that one can be used to weaken the other? Does the description do justice to the political context? With these questions, the process can be continued.

Raw Thinking as Thinking as Pilgrims

The examples I've used of taxation and a just wage hopefully convey a sense of what raw thinking in connection to Catholic Social Tradition could mean; raw thinking shows us what it is like, it invites us to ponder. It is understood that Catholic Social Teaching as one expression of the tradition, is part of the magisterium and not another voice in the theological discourse. These teaching documents have to be placed on a different level in their normative status. But even here, raw thinking (in the appropriate framework) can be taken to be an expression of intellectual and spiritual honesty, of a commitment to engaging with a text. I remember a dinner with an Opus Dei priest. The two of us shared a meal, and we also talked about homosexuality and the Church's teaching. In the protected atmosphere of the dinner the priest told me that he would be open to the Church changing its teaching on the subject and explored some of the challenges he found in his ministry with the official teaching. My point here is not doctrinal or moral, but epistemological: it will not do from either an intellectual or a pastoral point of view to repeat existing statements. There has to be personal and existential engagement, one expression of which is raw thinking. Raw thinking has its place and its limits. There is an undeniable value in refined texts and the definitive results of a deliberation. These safe texts can offer a kind of protection that the raw thinking in an epistemic wilderness cannot. My priest friend was willing to explore some issues in an informal, trust-based space, off the record. It was actually moving for me to see his sincere struggle.

Raw thinking reveals the person doing the thinking. That person in her entirety, with her history and theological background, adds yet another facet to raw thinking, one that goes beyond ethics and moves into spirituality, the primary concern of social teaching. Raw thinking in this sense honors the idea that Catholic Social Tradition is, first and foremost, discipleship and a way of life and not primarily a set of documents, principles, or propositions. There has to be a place for the existential drama beyond the polished words and thoughts.

We find a contrast between raw thinking and polished thought in the book of Job in the Hebrew Bible. While Job is deep in the abyss, grappling with God's will, his friends take a comfortable backseat-driver approach, with tried and tested theological reasoning and advice. They use polished theological language, while Job uses existential speech. Job acts with honesty and rawness in a second-person encounter with God. This perspective is different from a discourse in the third-person, talking "about" God as an object rather than "to God" as a subject.[163] In the final chapter of the book of Job we read,

> After the LORD had spoken these words to Job, the LORD said to Eliphaz the Temanite: "My wrath is kindled against you and against your two friends; for you have not spoken of me what is right, as my servant Job has.... My servant Job shall pray for you, for I will accept his prayer not to deal with you according to your folly." (42:7–8)

One can read this through a lens of raw authenticity versus cooked professional performance. Existential outcry meets textbook phrases. Job's thinking process is rough and jagged, raw. The wise thoughts of his friends seem prefabricated and processed.

Another example that shows the difference between raw and cooked thinking and the importance of that difference comes from two works by C. S. Lewis, which are, like Job, also connected to human suffering. In 1940 he was preoccupied with the woes of the world and wrote down his insights in the perfectly phrased language we would expect from a university don. The book was titled *The Problem of Pain*, a brilliant book with a simple message: pain is God speaking through a megaphone to a deaf world. Twenty years later he would publish another book on pain, this time a private diary written upon the death of his beloved wife. *A Grief Observed* is Lewis trying to come to grips with the exact same problem he had struggled with twenty years before, except this time he

---

[163]See E. Stump, "Second-Person Accounts and the Problem of Evil," *Revista Portuguesa de Filosofia* 57, no. 4 (2001): 745–71.

had been personally hit, and his loss is so painful as to be all-consuming. He is in a state of existential shock. His language is pared down to its raw roots; gone are sophisticated constructs. He stammers, stutters, stumbles around in the dark; his grief paralyzes him, chilling him to the bone. Gone are any expectations he may have had, replaced by frustration, untamed anger, and rage but also by hesitance and a reluctance to look and to see. Literary norms of expression are replaced by a rough-and-ready sketch of God: God as iconoclast. This work represents an entirely different way of thinking, one that is raw and filled with emotion.

Raw thinking has to do with showing things in a plain and honest way, bluntly and directly. It underpins the human journey of not having yet arrived, of being in the midst of a struggle. Archbishop Bruno Forte developed ideas along these lines in his 2006 Walgrave lecture; we are all on a pilgrimage, he says, expressing it beautifully and bluntly:

> When human beings ask the deepest questions about their inevitable vulnerability to pain and death, they do this not as people who have already arrived, but as searchers for the distant homeland, who let themselves be permanently called into question, provoked and seduced by the furthest horizon. Human beings who stop, who feel they have mastered the truth, for whom the truth is no longer Someone who possesses you more and more, but rather something to be possessed, such persons have not only rejected God, but also their own dignity as human beings.[164]

The spirituality of the pilgrim cannot be reduced to acquired truths or notions that now need to be taken somewhere safe. No, the spirituality of the pilgrim is rooted in the Christian tradition of *human-beingness*: truth is the person we meet along the way who shapes and molds the experiences we have. These raw human encounters move and impact us in a way words cannot. Theological thinking, like the pilgrim, needs to "rough it" to grow, needs a tent rather than a temple. The tent is an expression of roughing it; being in the raw, it is part of the longer journey, as is raw thinking. The deep practice of human dignity entails an openness to ever-changing circumstances and challenges that call for the gift of raw thinking—like judges handing down court decisions, as we have seen. Human dignity is a concept that never finishes saying what it has to say.

---

[164] B. Forte, "Theological Foundations of Dialogue within the Framework of Cultures Marked by Unbelief and Religious Indifference," *Louvain Studies* 31 (2006): 3–18, at 13.

4

Experiments with Truth

In her book on devotion to Our Lady of Guadalupe among Mexican women in the United States, Maria Del Socorro Castañeda-Liles describes how Mexican women carry medals and pictures of *La Virgen*, pray to her, and ask her to bless their children. The women were introduced to these devotions in their early childhood and have developed a relationship with *La Virgen de Guadalupe* that shapes their everyday lives. For good reason, Castañeda-Liles titles her book *Our Lady of Everyday Life*.[1]

Since faith reflects a fundamental attitude towards life as such and towards the world as a whole, it cannot be limited to certain segments of life; it needs to inform and shape the everyday. This is a question of spiritual creativity (or the creative workings of the Holy Spirit). Enacting the Catholic Social Tradition is more than a mechanical translation of principles into practice. We have discussed both the importance of raw thinking and of personally "inhabiting" principles. Enacting human dignity is a matter of navigating the challenges of particular situations and especially of adverse conditions. Living the social dimension of the faith is an expression of discipleship with the imperative of being recognized as a disciple ("'By this everyone will know that you are my disciples, if you have love for one another'" [Jn 13:35]), and this love translates into practices and attitudes.

What does it mean to enact Catholic Social Tradition concerns in the everyday life of a medical doctor or teacher or lawyer? This is a question of truth, the truth of particular ways of living life, particular habits. As the social dimension of faith, Catholic Social Tradition is social spirituality, a way of life that needs to be practiced—lived out—more in the habits that we acquire or that are ingrained in us than in any propositions we may

---

[1] M. Del Socorro Castañeda-Liles, *Our Lady of Everyday Life: La Virgen de Guadalupe and the Catholic Imagination of Mexican Women in America* (Oxford: Oxford University Press, 2018).

care to discuss. It is exactly this notion of "having habits" and how we acquire and develop them that interests us here; habits are what enable us to perceive the Catholic Social Tradition as "*regula*," a rule of life. Faith is a gift that oscillates between the habitual and the creative, between "the established" and "the new." Faith is not only the mountaintop experience, famously alluded to by Martin Luther King Jr. in his last speech on April 3, 1968. Faith is also the experience of the ordinary and even of the desert, where it takes habit to get through spiritually arid times.

The challenge of translating faith into habits, belief systems into daily lives, has been part of the spiritual struggle of individuals and communities throughout the centuries. L'Arche founder Jean Vanier spoke in the Canadian Parliament on June 7, 1967, about his father, Georges Vanier, the governor general of Canada, who had died three months earlier in office. He mentioned his father's daily habit of spending half an hour in the chapel, "with strict regularity . . . just thinking, and reflecting before his much-loved God."[2] Georges Vanier believed in the necessity of feeding one's soul through the habits of prayer, spiritual reading, and reflection. Prayer, as the *Catechism of the Catholic Church* teaches, is "the habit of being in the presence of the thrice-holy God and in communion with him";[3] a life of discipleship is a prayerful life, and a prayerful life expresses itself in regularity and rhythm, in habitual structures. A particularly touching account of this "journey into habits for the journey" is the spiritual classic *The Way of the Pilgrim*, whose narrator seeks to understand the meaning of the exhortation to pray continuously, without ceasing (1 Thess 5:17).[4] After a tiring journey he receives a life-changing answer from a hermit:

> "The ceaseless Jesus Prayer is a continuous, uninterrupted call on the holy name of Jesus Christ with the lips, mind, and heart; and in the awareness of His abiding presence it is a plea for His blessing in all undertakings, in all places, at all times, even in sleep. The words of the Prayer are: 'Lord Jesus Christ, have mercy on me!'"[5]

The pilgrim grows into the habit of reciting the Jesus prayer day and night, beginning with three thousand times a day and then moving to twelve thousand times a day and beyond. With the Jesus prayer ever on

---

[2] J. Vanier, "Integrity in Public Life," in J. Vanier, *Eruption to Hope* (New York: Paulist Press, 1971), 62–70, at 63.

[3] *Catechism of the Catholic Church* (Libreria Editrice Vaticana, 1997), 2565, hereinafter CCC.

[4] Anonymous, *The Way of the Pilgrim and The Pilgrim Continues His Way*, trans. H. Bacovcin (New York: Image Books, 1978), 4.

[5] Ibid., 9.

his lips, the pilgrim embarks on his journey toward growth in integrity and truth.

We can read this book as the sincere and honest struggle of a man who engaged in experimenting with truth. It brings us to another witness of the art of proper habits: Mahatma Gandhi. The project of identifying truth in the different areas of his life was his motivation to "experiment with truth," as the title of his autobiography would have it,[6] even going as far as to say, "My life consists of nothing but those experiments."[7] He distinguishes his political experiments from his experiments in the spiritual or moral field, which he notes are "known only to myself."[8] Over the years, he experimented with nonviolence, celibacy, education, hygiene and medication, food and fasting. While in London, he tested—for both economic and moral reasons—different dietary regimes, "giving up starchy food at one time, living on bread and fruit alone at another, and once living on cheese, milk and eggs."[9] While in South Africa, he experimented with methods for doing washing and laundry, and with household remedies to treat illness, with the education of his children thereby accepting some considerable risks. Gandhi adopted a scientific attitude both in conducting and in narrating the experiments. "I claim for them nothing more than does a scientist who, though he conducts his experiments with the utmost accuracy, forethought and minuteness, never claims any finality about his conclusions."[10] Gandhi was clear that his experiments were not mere satisfaction of curiosity, but an expression of the deep humility of a truth-seeker, a person trusting in the promise and possibility of truth. In some instances, his experiments with truth were nourished by external pressures; a particularly telling story is his experiment with washing his own collars:

> I shall never forget the first collar that I washed myself. I had used more starch than necessary, the iron had not been made hot enough, and for fear of burning the collar I had not pressed it sufficiently. The result was that, though the collar was fairly stiff, the superfluous starch continually dropped off it. I went to court with the collar on, thus inviting the ridicule of brother barristers, but even in those days I could be impervious to ridicule. "Well," said I, "this is my first experiment at washing my own collars and hence the loose starch. But it does not trouble me, and then there is the advantage

---

[6]M. Gandhi, *An Autobiography: or The Story of My Experiments with Truth*, trans. from the Gujarati by M. Desai (Ahmedabad: Navajivan Publishing, 1927 [reprint 1996]).
[7]Ibid., ix.
[8]Ibid., x.
[9]Ibid., 48.
[10]Ibid., x.

of providing you with so much fun." "But surely there is no lack of laundries here?" asked a friend. "The laundry bill is very heavy," said I. "The charge for washing a collar is almost as much as its price, and even then there is the eternal dependence on the washerman. I prefer by far to wash my things myself." But I could not make my friends appreciate the beauty of self-help.[11]

Experiments with truth can be motivated by internal as well as external forces; they are a matter of decision and decisiveness. They may lead to some embarrassment and moments of failure (that is why they are experiments); they may require repetition and modification; they may reach an (however provisional) endpoint that can serve as a basis and point of reference for future action.

Experiments with truth, understood as an earnest search for truth, can be seen as a response to a moral imperative. "Obedience to the truth" (1 Pet 1:22) is a motif that John Paul II chooses for the opening of his 1993 encyclical *Veritatis Splendor*. Five years later, in his encyclical *Fides et Ratio*, John Paul II characterizes human beings as those who "know themselves."[12] "Know yourself" has been characterized as a necessary condition for personal growth, giving insight into the truth of one's fallibility, mortality, woundedness, fragility, and responsibility.[13] The desire for truth is part of who we are, part of human nature, even though the search for ultimate truth seems sometimes neglected.[14] There is truth to be sought and found in questions of practical reason and in questions of pure reason. There is the question of truth in teaching and also in the application of the teaching.

Enacting Catholic Social Tradition is an invitation to strive to weave a seamless garment, a consistent form of life. In the midst of compromises and contradictions, brokenness and failures, the idea stands out of an intentional effort to serve the one Master in the big discernments and the small decisions. How can we translate the principles of Catholic Social Tradition into habits?

A possible model comes from the Kroc Institute of International Peace Studies at the University of Notre Dame, which, in close cooperation with the National Secretariat of the Social Pastorate–Caritas Colombia,

---

[11]Ibid., 177–78.

[12]John Paul II, *Fides et Ratio*, "Faith and Reason" (1998), no. 1, hereinafter *FR*.

[13]Margarita Mauri has elaborated on the connection between self-respect and honesty as a commitment to find the truth and to live according to it, and has established the claim that honesty can be considered the most remarkable expression of self-respect without any concessions to self-deception or other types of deception (M. Mauri, "Self-Respect and Honesty" *Filozofia* 66, no. 1 (2011): 74–82).

[14]*FR* 3 and 5, respectively.

has coordinated the Colombian Peace Accords Matrix since the historic Colombia peace agreement was signed on November 24, 2016. The point of the project is to monitor progress toward the implementation of the peace accord. The project has translated the text of the accord into action points and tracks the implementation of fifty-one different types of provisions, including ceasefires, constitutional reform, military reform, decentralization and federalism, media reform, and so on.

Similarly, we could translate Catholic Social Tradition documents into action points. The 2018 document *Oeconomicae et pecuniariae quaestiones*, published by the Congregation for the Doctrine of Faith and the Dicastery for Promoting Integral Human Development, could similarly be translated into action points.[15] For example, the following passage could be read as inviting Catholics into the habit of justifying profits: "No profit is in fact legitimate when it falls short of the objective of the integral promotion of the human person, the universal destination of goods, and the preferential option for the poor."[16] This could be enacted through the habitual monitoring of profit-increasing strategies. A later statement in the document can be translated into an evaluation and assessment tool: "Well-being must therefore be measured by criteria far more comprehensive than the Gross Domestic Product of a nation (GDP), and must take into account instead other standards, for example, safety and security, the growth of 'human capital,' the quality of human relationships and of work."[17] These criteria are "actionable items" that can shape decisions about the workplace and about decision-making processes.

Translating principles into habits is one challenge of the project of this book: enacting Catholic Social Tradition. The principle of the common good is abstract and can be used on even the highest macro level as a global common good. But one way to translate the principle into habits is to translate the common good into the habits and practices of neighborliness. The invitation to become a good neighbor is an important aspect of building the common good.[18] By definition, a "neighbor" is a person who

---

[15]Congregation for the Doctrine of Faith and the Dicastery for Promoting Integral Human Development, *Oeconomicae et pecuniariae quaestiones*, "Considerations for an Ethical Discernment regarding Some Aspects of the Present Economic-Financial System" (2018), hereinafter *OPQ*.

[16]*OPQ* 10.

[17]*OPQ* 11.

[18]In her book *Good Neighbors*, Nancy Rosenblum explores how encounters among neighbors create a democracy of everyday life. In times of disaster, neighbors become resources for rescue and care, and vibrant democracies need everyday practices that express a spirit of respect and consideration as well as practices of conversation and collaboration. Rosenblum's book project was triggered by a noncooperative (and inconsiderate) neighbor in an apartment building. See N. Rosenblum, *Good Neighbors: The Democracy of Everyday*

lives near another person, who is near another person. Being neighborly means cooperation,[19] fraternity,[20] and an intentional effort to overcome isolation.[21] Neighborliness can be translated into a culture of gift[22] and a culture of responsiveness, responding to the needs of the nearby other.[23] Being a neighbor is as much a matter of habits as it is a matter of attitude and perception. Good neighbors enter conversations and share aspects of everyday life, and thus build familiarity and a sense of mutual availability. Hence, the abstract principle of the common good becomes tangible and a matter of knowledge through acquaintance.

Catholic Social Tradition habits are those deep-set attitudes of mind and that basic inner poise that impress us, leave their mark on us, and make us who we are. Catholic Social Tradition focuses on the way we look at and interact with the world around us, and helps us regulate our perceptions of that world and its effect on our day-to-day dealings with others.

On the Concept and Dynamics of Habits

Habits are sets of dispositions ruling and regulating the way we act and the way we go toward making life easier for us to accomplish. Habits are commonplace. Terms like "self-evident," "familiar," and "regular" come to mind here, as opposed to "spontaneous," "unique," or "new." Habits structure a day. Habits make possible the transition from "day" to "everyday," since when certain habits become established, one day can become "everyday." In *Evangelium Vitae,* Pope John Paul II observes the very basis of a culture of life, namely "an everyday heroism, made up of gestures of sharing, big or small, which build up an authentic culture of life."[24] Here the commitment to life penetrates and shapes the everyday, and the everyday supports a culture of life. That is why John Paul II refers to the "need to promote a serious and in-depth exchange about basic issues of human life with everyone, including non-believers, in intellectual circles, in the various professional spheres and at the level of people's everyday life."[25]

Life in America (Princeton, NJ: Princeton University Press, 2016).

[19]Leo XIII, *Rerum Novarum,* "Rights and Duties of Capital and Labor" (1891), no. 50, hereinafter *RN.*

[20]Paul VI, *Octogesima Adveniens,* "Eightieth Anniversary [of *Rerum Novarum*]" (1971), no. 37, hereinafter *OA.*

[21]Francis, *Evangelii Gaudium,* "The Joy of the Gospel" (2013), no.75, hereinafter *EG.*

[22]Benedict XVI, *Caritas in Veritate,* "Charity and Truth" (2009), no. 6, hereinafter, *CV.*

[23]*CV* 7.

[24]John Paul II, *Evangelium Vitae,* "The Gospel of Life" (1995), no. 86, hereinafter *EV.*

[25]*EV* 95.

Everyday life is what gives life structure and support; everyday life is the sum of repetitive daily processes and the epitome of what we consider "ordinary." Thus, the concept of everyday life is contradictory—on the one hand, it stands for the familiar, the continuous, and on the other hand, for that routinely repeated, the "gray" of always the same. Hungarian sociologist Agnes Heller stressed the connection between everyday life and creativity and progress.[26] Heller was guided in her thinking by the conviction that the great achievements of a culture stem from the challenges, problems, conflicts, and needs of daily life. In human society, we attempt to create an everyday life, a "lifeworld" of everyday-life practice, as described by Edmund Husserl in his later work and made popular by Alfred Schütz.[27] Coping with everyday life structures our lives—it has to do with normality, predictability, and reliable repetition. The ability to cope with life's needs, in turn, says a lot about our mental and social health. There is a reciprocal dynamic at work here; a well-established everyday life enables spiritual growth, while spiritual depth leads to a rhythm and the art of living life in the ordinary.

A very simple habit can structure everyday life and lead to a change in one's attitude. Siberian priest Mikhail Chevalkov, a missionary of the Russian Orthodox Church, tells how, at the age of three, he was moved by his friend Yakov to reflect on such a simple habit. Yakov always prayed before and after eating, asking for a blessing and thanking God for the meal. When Chevalkov saw this, he thought to himself how holy this habit was, and it made him dissatisfied with his own manners.[28] Seeing his friend's habit give him the impetus to change his own life—beginning with just that one small step. And that little step was the beginning of a long journey that took Mikhail Chevalkov from a shamanistic home to the priesthood. The habit of a mealtime prayer can lead to further changes in attitude, igniting a "longing for more." This idea of changing one habit and thus impacting other structures of one's way of life was described by John Cassian in the early fifth century in *Institutes* and in

---

[26] A. Heller, *Everyday Life* (London: Routledge and Kegan Paul, 1994); see R. Wolin, "Agnes Heller on Everyday Life," *Theory and Society* 16 (1987): 295–304.

[27] A. Schütz and T. Luckmann, *The Structures of the Life World* (Evanston, IL: Northwestern University Press, 1973).

[28] M. Chevalkov, *Testament of Memory: A Siberian Life* (Jordanville, NY: Holy Trinity Publications, 2011), 3–4. See also see Francis, *Laudato Si'*, "On Care for Our Common Home" (2015), no. 227, hereinafter *LS*: "One expression of this attitude is when we stop and give thanks to God before and after meals. I ask all believers to return to this beautiful and meaningful custom." Francis writes about "the attitude of the heart, one which approaches life with serene attentiveness, which is capable of being fully present to someone without thinking of what comes next, which accepts each moment as a gift from God to be lived to the full" (*LS* 226). Attitudes lead to customs, and customs reconfirm attitudes.

Conferences, where he set out to describe good spiritual practices and a stable spiritual life within the framework of a monastic culture. The very idea of a monastery connotes a place that enables a rise of the ordinary, the establishment of rhythm, and the translation of discipleship into communal habits. Monasteries create and protect the spirit of an everyday life with their predictability and repetition.

Everyday life is precious and threatened. Especially in an arrhythmic time, which demands high speed and great flexibility, the experience of a rhythm of life can become a scarce resource. When everyday life is lost, the security of the recognizable and reliable performance of life disappears. The disruption of everyday routines can even be used as a strategy of suppression—occupying forces can erode the possibility of stable everyday life through arbitrary actions, unpredictable procedures, and unclear regulations. This leads to enormous collective stress and to the decline of normalcy. It is not surprising that Robert and Edward Skidelsky described "security" as a necessary element of a good life;[29] "security" is understood here as the legitimate expectation of a person that his or her own life will continue to go more or less on its usual course without interference from war, crime, revolution, or major social and economic upheavals. We could also say security is the ability to establish and maintain habits—and this ability is a basic element of a good life.

A habit is an established form of action; it is an acquired behavioral disposition. In John Dewey's words, "The essence of habit is an acquired predisposition to *ways* or modes of response."[30] Habits are kept alive by repetition and are characterized by a certain effortlessness. That is what makes habits so attractive; they make life easier. One does not have to design new actions in every situation, but can resort to familiar patterns. It thus becomes tiring to act against a habit that, after a certain frequency of execution, is also automated, that is, becomes a behavior that one does not think about. In 1799, the French Academy of Sciences announced an essay contest on "Habits." Pierre Maine de Biran, the winner, noted how difficult this task was, since habits, as familiar matters of course, are hidden from view. In short, they do not catch our eye. It is a paradox that the establishment of a habit leads to its evanescence: it loses "perceptibility."

Some habits sneak in, while other habits are the result of explicit decisions and efforts. The latter interests us here. Habits can diminish responsibility for an action, as stated by the *Catechism of the Catholic*

---

[29] R. Skidelsky and E. Skidelsky, *How Much Is Enough?* (New York: Other Press, 2012).
[30] J. Dewey, *Human Nature and Conduct: An Introduction to Social Psychology* (New York: Henry Holt, 1922), 42.

Church.[31] Enacting Catholic Social Tradition in and through habits is not to be left to random experiences. If one refers to the character of a human being as his second nature, then it must not be forgotten that we are partly responsible for how our second nature, our character, develops. "We are ourselves somehow partly responsible for our states of character," as Aristotle said.[32] Through habits, someone settles into life, inhabits her life. Habits are like a second skin that we adopt, like clothes. The Latin word "*habitus*" and the English "habit," meaning a religious garment, indicate this relationship; a habit is a behavior that follows a form, a "uniform" is standard clothing. The German word "*Kostüm*" and the English words "custom" and "costume" are as closely related to one another, as are the French words *coutume* and *couture*. "*Habitus*" is also associated with the Latin "*habere*," meaning to hold or to have something. Semantics and etymology are telling here. A habit has been appropriated, made one's own, made part of one's own, part of the self. A course of action becomes a habit when I need to make an effort to act differently.

This may be the place to insert the caveat that human life, if reduced to the predictability and repetitiveness of the ordinary and the everyday, could also become heavy with ennui. The tension between the ordinary and the extraordinary is part of a full and flourishing human life. A life without structure would lack commitments; a life without freedom would preclude growth. Catholic Social Tradition can be seen as both a thorn in the flesh and a basis for habits. The point of this chapter is to focus on the latter since we manage our everyday lives through habits, habitual routines, and little rituals that guide us through the day.

Mason Currey has put together a book of the daily routines of more than 160 famous people: writers and artists, musicians and philosophers, scientists and politicians.[33] He shows that such routines can help increase one's productivity and creativity. Here, experiments are necessary to find one's own working rhythm—when and where and how can I work best? Is music helpful? Do I work better when I see cows, as was the case with Gertrude Stein, for whom cows had to be driven into her field of vision for purposes of inspiration? Sylvia Plath struggled until her death to find a fertile daily structure for her work; she was aware that, paradoxically, regular routines open doors to creativity. The design of an everyday life that promotes creativity is an art. Many artists experiment with everyday routines until they find those that promote creativity and turn away dis-

---

[31] CCC 1735; cf. 2352.
[32] Aristotle, *Nicomachean Ethics* III.5, 1114b22.
[33] M. Currey, *Daily Rituals: How Great Minds Make Time, Find Inspiration, and Get to Work* (New York: Pan Macmillan, 2013).

traction. American writer Philip Roth's workspace was a guest cottage, where he worked after breakfast from 10 a.m. to 6 p.m., with a one-hour lunch break. He recognized this place and this rhythm as supportive.[34] Marcel Proust, on the other hand, wrote exclusively in bed, with his head supported by two pillows, which repeatedly led to pain and discomfort.[35] Viktor Frankl, after waking up and drinking a cup of strong coffee, brought to him by his wife, Elly, also remained in bed to write, to deal with correspondence, or to take notes, the dictating machine on a chair next to his bed.[36] William Faulkner worked best in the morning; Sigmund Freud preferred to write at night.[37] Somerset Maugham published seventy-eight books, mainly because he followed a clear routine, writing three to four hours each morning, and imposing on himself the obligation to write at least a thousand to fifteen hundred words each day.[38] Such routines create everyday life as the basis for a quiet life with a sense of security. Security is the ability to instill and practice habits, acquired through certain routines. The established routine is then less a habit that creates conduct than a habit that provides a framework.[39] This framework should be such that productive and creative work without exhaustion is possible.

The same idea—namely, providing space for freedom and fruitfulness—can be applied to the spiritual life. Spiritual growth can happen through the dynamics of external circumstances shaping the inner life and the inner life shaping the external structures. Indeed, inner stability can be fostered through habits. An important rule in spiritual life is the idea of "holding on to habits," of minimizing entry points for temptations. The *Catechism of the Catholic Church* describes prayer in these terms: "Prayer presupposes an effort, a fight against ourselves and the wiles of the Tempter. The battle of prayer is inseparable from the necessary 'spiritual battle' to act habitually according to the Spirit of Christ: we pray as we live, because

---

[34] Ibid., 145.

[35] Ibid., 89.

[36] H. Klingberg Jr., *Das Leben wartet auf dich. Elly und Viktor Frankl* (Wien: Deuticke, 2002), 366–69.

[37] Currey, *Daily Rituals*, 55 and 38–39, respectively.

[38] Ibid., 105.

[39] "Another variant of practice is the adoption of a daily routine or timetable in order to maximize productivity or creativity. In this case, the self-imposed habit does not aim to cultivate a particular disposition, skill or virtue. Its purpose is to provide a framework that effaces effort and decision about everyday matters: when to get up, what to wear, how to wash, when to eat, and so on. So a writer or an artist, for example, might adopt such a schedule in order to write or paint with a clear mind. Such habits may be idiosyncratic, for they are usually solitary. But they have a similar effect to the communal routines followed by monks and nuns, who live by a rule designed to free their attention for prayer" (C. Carlisle, *On Habit* [London: Routledge, 2014], 108).

we live as we pray."[40] Habits of thought as well as habits of action are ambivalent: they can be a helpful support, and they can be a prison.

Conversion as *metanoia* is an invitation to a new habit of thinking. Deep change in a person is equated with a change in thinking habits; Roger Bacon, at the very beginning of his *Opus Maius*, named "the long duration of habit" as one of the four main stumbling blocks and obstacles to truth. Certain habits have to be broken for the sake of truth. As John Paul II noted, "The depth of revealed wisdom disrupts the cycle of our habitual patterns of thought."[41] For instance, it is revealed to us that the human person is created in the image and likeness of God. In the spirit of enacting human dignity, therefore, we should be particularly interested in dignity-conducive habits of action and perception. A young volunteer in a homeless shelter, for example, spoke of learning "to see" with new eyes when participating in the Eucharist at the shelter:

> The Sign of Peace was the most memorable part of mass, when all gathered there would embrace one another, rather than the impersonal hand-shaking that would take place at my local parish. This was quite a contrast with what my parents have always taught me when encountering the homeless whenever we go into Chicago: walk by quickly and avoid eye contact. I've had it ingrained in me for a very long time to ignore the dignity of the homeless, so I look forward to change my perceptions of these people throughout my time here.

A deep way to change one's life is to change perceptions, to change the "seeing-as" structure, the structure of perceptually categorizing something *as* something. Enacting Catholic Social Tradition cannot be left to understanding; it has to be translated into habits of action, patterns of thought, and modes of perception. Respecting the dignity of the person is a way of seeing the person and the world. Justice, as a virtue, is primarily an attitude, a habit, a disposition; the *Catechism of the Catholic Church* talks about the just person as "distinguished by habitual right thinking and the uprightness of his [her] conduct toward his [her] neighbor."[42] Habitual doing, thinking, and perceiving are expressions of internalizing the key concerns of the Catholic Social Tradition in the spirit of the Sermon on the Mount, which translates external and observable norms into habits of perception: "I say to you that everyone who looks at a woman with lust has already committed adultery with her in his heart" (Mt 5:28).

---

[40] CCC 2752.
[41] *FR* 23.
[42] CCC 1807.

Experimenting with Habits

There is no manual describing how to translate principles of Catholic Social Teaching into practices and habits. A proven way of changing or creating habits is to try things out, engaging in what Roger Bacon calls *scientia experimentalis* (experimental science): learning not by reading or listening, but by doing, by experience. This experiential learning can also be applied to oneself, as Gandhi's example has shown.

Personal experimentation has a long tradition, particularly in the realm of medicine. In the early nineteenth century, American doctor Stubbins Firth (1784–1820) carried out some pretty drastic experiments on his own person to discover the causes of yellow fever, and we know that the Italian doctor Santorio Santori (1561–1636) was perhaps the first physician to undertake controlled experiments on himself as a human guinea pig. At the end of the nineteenth century this practice of self-experimentation resulted in a martyr to the cause: a Peruvian student doctor, Daniel Alcides Carrión (1857–1885), died as a direct result of experimenting with Oroya fever, now known as Carrion's disease. Alexander von Humboldt (1769–1859) was a compulsive researcher with unbridled curiosity who seemed to stop at nothing to find out what he wanted to know. He took extreme risks in his experiments with methane gas and poisoned arrows. It hardly needs to be pointed out that any form of experiment with the unknown always involves a high degree of risk, together with a real sense of responsibility for the test subjects, whoever they are.

What exactly can or do we learn through self-experimentation? And how do we categorize this sort of knowledge? It is personal and direct knowledge with one particular epistemological challenge: the small number of test subjects involved (with one being the absolute minimum), which ensures that any results will be biased. Katrin Soldhju has researched extensively on the epistemological dimension of self-experimentation, mainly in the field of pharmacology, exploring the neurological experiments carried out by Henry Heads on his own person, the psychiatric tests performed (with cannabis) by Jacques-Joseph Moreau de Tours on himself, and the laughing gas experiments done by Benjamin Paul Blood.[43] Self-experiments, seen in this way, are pathways toward self-knowledge.

The early Christians—in monastic cultures, ordinary life, or rather extreme forms of solitude—can be understood as engaging in spiritually motivated self-experiments. The different versions of monastic rules are one result of these experiments. Many Christians have engaged in spiritual

---

[43]K. Soldhju, *Selbstexperimente: Die Suche nach der Innenperspektive und ihre epistemologischen Folgen* (Munich: Fink, 2011).

self-experiments with self-mortification or asceticism. Even the annual Lenten sacrifices can be seen as spiritual self-experiments. There may be an advantage in such self-experimental approaches since the epistemic quality of a situation increases if the actual background and contextual factors are also taken into account. For instance, psychologist Seth Roberts, well-known for his experiments on himself, describes the privileged position and role of "the experts" involved in scientific research as epistemologically important because they "know" what they are doing and are prepared to take the risk; they are moving in familiar territory; and they have their "expertise" on their side. Roberts focuses in his work on "useful ways to improve sleep, mood, health, and weight." Of his fight against insomnia he says, "I was in an unusually good position to make progress. I had the subject-matter knowledge of an insider, the freedom of an outsider, and the motivation of someone with the problem."[44]

There is also the additional factor that tests carried out on oneself are simpler and "deeper" than conventional laboratory tests. American psychologist Allen Neuringer experienced similar findings: "If experimental psychologists applied the scientific method to their own lives, they would learn more of importance to everyone and assist more in the solutions of problems, than if they continue to relegate science exclusively to the study of others."[45] When you yourself are the guinea pig *and* the scientist, the experience and the results are likely to have a more profound effect and impact behavior that much more, because empirical learning has an immediacy and irrefutability all of its own. Let's take an example:

> Marie Price sought to prove that she was not dependent upon caffeine by having a friend place caffeinated instant coffee in a jar marked "A" and non-caffeinated instant coffee, identical in appearance, in another jar marked "B." Marie drank only coffee from jar "A" for two days, then from jar "B" for two days and so forth. She writes, "The results were staggering." She found that on decaffeinated days she slept longer at night and was more tired during the day, occasionally falling asleep while studying (something she rarely did prior to the experiment). . . . Marie's conclusion: "My unfounded reasons for drinking coffee as a pleasurable sensation might have continued if I had not tried this brief experiment. I now realize the

---

[44] S. Roberts, "The Unreasonable Effectiveness of My Self-Experimentation," *Medical Hypotheses* 75, no. 6 (2010): 482–89, at 483. S. Roberts, "Self-Experimentation as a Source of New Ideas: Ten Examples about Sleep, Mood, Health and Weight," *Behavioral and Brain Sciences* 27 (2004): 262–87.

[45] A. Neuringer, "Self-Experimentation: A Call for Change," *Behaviorism* 9, no. 1 (1981): 79–94, at 79.

effects of coffee and with that knowledge I am willing ... to (try to) make changes in my diet that will better my health. And that's what (self-) science is all about, bringing it into one's life on a more personal level for greater self-understanding."[46]

Self-science leads to greater self-understanding and is likely to leave a lasting memory, an "imprint." Self-science has its own rules and dynamics:

- There must be a motivational trigger of some kind or background knowledge.
- The test needs to have a clear structure with all the necessary rules in place at the outset, along with a realistic plan of implementation, including all possible ramifications.
- A good measure of self-discipline and honesty are necessary so that the results recorded are truthful and sincere.

These three conditions (motivation, clarity, and discipline) can also be applied to spiritual self-experiments like a Lenten sacrifice. The Rule of Saint Benedict requires the abbot's permission for Lenten offerings: "Let each one however confide to his abbot exactly what it is he is offering.... What is done without the consent of one's spiritual father will not be accounted meritorious, but presumptuous and vain-glorious. Therefore it is with the abbot's consent that all things are to be done."[47] Self-experiments demand prudent judgment. They can lead to new insights as well as a rethinking of existing habits.[48]

The idea is timeless: American journalist Judith Levine, for example, decided to spend one year buying only the things she really needed (with no cheating). In her book *Not Buying It* she describes the harsh reality of resisting the temptation to buy what she wants and only buy what she really needs.[49] It was her ultimate test, because in the sociocultural world in which she worked she was used to seeing and talking about such temptations. She was equipped, "armed" even, for the fight with her "robust identity," meaning that she was motivated and driven by inner conviction—suggesting that she should be less likely to fall into traps set

---

[46]Ibid., 83.

[47]"The Rule of Saint Benedict," trans. into English in *A Pax Book*, preface by W. K. Lowther Clarke (London: S.P.C.K., 1931), chap. 49.

[48]In chapter 49 the Rule of Saint Benedict also clarifies the point of the Lenten season: "Although the life of a monk ought always to have a Lenten character, yet because few have the degree of strength requisite for that, we therefore exhort that at least during Lent he live his life with scrupulous care and that likewise during this holy season he do away with any departures from strictness that may have been permitted at other time."

[49]J. Levine, *Not Buying It: My Year without Shopping* (New York: Free Press, 2006).

by her surroundings. She knew the rules of the game; she knew she could be her own worst enemy, only overcome and kept in check with rigorous self-discipline. This approach or mind-set is vital in trying to authentically live out the social dimension of the Christian faith. Let us now turn to another example of intentional self-experimenting and experimenting with truth. There is a great deal to be learned from experimenting with values.

Experimenting with Lifestyle

American writer Eve Schaub set out to live a sugar-free year with her family of four.[50] Her findings are singular and revealing, ones only she and her family could have experienced in the context of their own lives. At the same time, the things they experienced are as typical as they are unique, suggesting a wider universality than at first seems the case. If we reconstruct Schaub's experiences into three sections, we have basic rules, challenges and costs involved, and ethical aspects.

Basic Rules

Schaub's decision was triggered by a YouTube video on the truth about sugar. Her perception of sugar was abruptly turned upside down, and she found herself having to reclassify her understanding of the word "sugar," basically equating it with "poison." This realization led her to rethink the sugar culture she had grown up with and in which she now lived. For the theologically minded reader, one might at this juncture be reminded of the third chapter of John's Gospel in which Nicodemus finds himself having to take a deep look at the conventional thinking he had grown up with, and asking himself some serious questions if he is to take the road of conversion. Schaub's new take on sugar suddenly made her rethink other taken-for-granted categories in her life. Trying to order a meal in a restaurant became a nightmare, since it turned out that sugar was in just about everything on the menu. She was confronted with sugar in places she would not formerly have given any thought to; even in places like restaurants where she had assumed personnel were there to advise and inform, it turned out that this was not the case at all. There was an overall lack of knowledge at any level that in turn made Schaub doubt her entire worldview. So intense was the experience that the other members of the family were caught up in her newfound thinking; her eleven-year-old daughter, Greta, noted in her diary: "Now some people think sugar

---

[50]E. O. Schaub, *Year of No Sugar: A Memoir* (Naperville: Sourcebooks, 2014).

is simply sugar. But that unfortunately isn't the case. To trick shoppers into thinking there isn't sugar, they put in other things. But there is also simply sugar in different forms. Like evaporated cane juice—that's sugar. It's only a matter of being raw and evaporated."[51]

Thus the experiment took on a dimension not conceivable at the outset: it changed the basic perception and attitude of mind of the entire family to one of doubt and suspicion of a seemingly familiar social given. It comes as no surprise that Schaub began to rethink basic concepts and explore alternative lifestyles, reading books such as Jon Krakauer's *Into the Wild*, which vividly depicts the dilemmas and traumas of a young man, Chris McCandless, choosing a life in the wilds of Alaska, completely beyond civilization—a self-experiment that went tragically wrong, ending in Chris's death.[52] The narrative underlines the connections arising in the dynamics of literary quotations. Chris reads Thoreau's famous *Walden* and marks certain passages of particular importance, which Schaub in turn reads and quotes:

> It is hard to provide and cook so simple and clean a diet as will not offend the imagination; but this, I think, is to be fed when we feed the body; they should both sit down at the same table. Yet perhaps this may be done. The fruits eaten temperately need not make us ashamed of our appetites, nor interrupt the worthiest pursuits. But put an extra condiment on your dish, and it will poison you.[53]

The fruits and the value of those fruits are those of integrity.

This experiment, triggered by a video and snowballing into a complete retake on the meaning of life, turns Schaub's experiment into a life project with the home-field advantage of there being a clear beginning and end. A spirit of curiosity was central to her approach, along with sufficient research to enable the citizen-scientist (here Schaub) to work out a reliable framework on which to base her premise and methodology.[54] There was of course also the social factor that she was not doing this on her own but with her family, and the vital factor of a commitment to honesty both in performance and the noting down of results (no cheating) in diaries that

---

[51] Ibid., 89.
[52] Jon Krakauer, *Into the Wild* (New York: Anchor Books, 1997).
[53] Schaub, *Year of No Sugar*, 231. The quotation can be found in Henry David Thoreau, *Walden* (Boston: Houghton Mifflin, 2004), 171.
[54] Schaub allowed herself three exceptions to the "no-sugar" rule: once a month, one member of the family could choose a dessert of their choice; each family member was allowed one item of food that had low sugar content; and at birthday parties, the children could eat the same dessert as the other children at the party. These three exceptions served to maintain a degree of familial harmony.

each of them began during the test. A side effect of that commitment was the creation of a habit of honest observation and recording.

Challenges and Costs

Unexpected challenges cropped up in new situations; in uncontrolled or unknown environments—as in a trip to Italy; and the biggest obstacles tended to be social ones, which family members described as "temptations" and "tests." These included birthday celebrations, but the biggest proved to be Christmas, as Greta noted in her diary: "I'm totally bailing on the sugar project at Christmas. [I] mean you can't avoid Great Grandma Schaub's mincemeat cookies. Nor can you avoid Grandma Sharon's chocolate cookies and also Christmas cookies. I feel so helpless, like I have no will or say in anything. Like my mom's and dad's say and will comes first and overpowers mine."[55] One of the challenges of the experiment was that it required its participants to break with family traditions.

This experiment is a personal witness's account of what is means to step outside of the mainstream box of social standards, and it is clear that this kind of civil science brings its own social challenges, sometimes at the cost of community and friendships. When food and eating habits are on the agenda, they rattle the cage of deeply rooted nutritional norms and traditional eating habits. One example of this happens on a romantic evening out:

> "We can't go home without at least eating," I objected. "*Well, there's nowhere for us to eat!*" He was exasperated and losing it, and truthfully, so was I. We were both long past hungry. It was cold and dark, and we were driving around in circles trying to figure out what to do. The movie we had been hoping to make had already started. Fast food restaurants, chain restaurants were *everywhere*, but because we were not eating sugar, there was no place we could eat. This was turning out to be one big bummer of a date night.[56]

The experiment turned out to be a strain on relationships. Greta complains to her diary that the whole project is downright "unfair,"[57] and fairness is an interesting factor here—things that are felt or perceived to be overly and unduly demanding cannot really be measured or, therefore, recorded.

Then there was the cost of the time and effort invested: shopping took twice as long, and Schaub had to keep coming up with bright ideas on

---

[55] Schaub, *Year of No Sugar*, 236.
[56] Ibid., 41.
[57] Ibid., 52.

how to make meals interesting and tasty for the family. A great deal of cognitive energy was suddenly required for the routines of simple everyday life. On the positive side, a new world of hitherto unknown possibilities opened up, and creativity was sparked and nurtured; for example, Schaub faced the challenge of how to make sugar-free ice cream.[58] Interestingly, there is also the health issue of the venture because sugar-free does not automatically mean healthier: "Ironically, we sometimes found ourselves in the position of having to choose the French fries or the potato chips over the whole-grain bread basket."[59] Sugar-free *and* healthy eating requires a special approach.

As Schaub notes, the project also demanded fundamental life adjustments: "Pretty soon we found ourselves missing the myriad little things that sweeten up one's day—that little spark in your cereal, that spoonful of something in your afternoon tea, that bit of chocolate you might have after dinner for no particular reason. I couldn't shake that feeling after a meal that something was . . . missing."[60] Some surprising side effects were those linked with digestion and the dynamics of the digestive system, and included a change in taste—having sugar on the days it was allowed turned out to be strangely disappointing. Sugar was found to play a huge part in showing care and expressing affection in little ways. For example, "It was really, *really* nice to be able to put a cookie in each of our kids' lunches in the morning."[61] Schaub notes that her abstention from sugar was infinitely less painful than witnessing how her daughters suffered;[62] the girls' lives became clearly more difficult under the experimental conditions, and depriving her girls of many types of food was hard since "food is an expression of love."[63]

The social burden of it all began to show, as Schaub felt restricted in the ways she had traditionally shown her daughters love and affection: in the food she gave them. When they went out for a meal, Schaub was compelled to ask difficult questions of the serving staff who were obviously out of their depth, and ordering food became more of an ordeal than a treat, with Schaub gaining a reputation for being complicated in her food choices. She was aware that she had to make a point of being overly grateful, to show her profound thanks for the superhuman effort staff members felt was being asked of them.

The experiment had a social cost as well, which was particularly painful and apparent in relation to neighborhood fundraisers. The Schaubs had

---

[58]Ibid., 98.
[59]Ibid., 79.
[60]Ibid., 55.
[61]Ibid., 62.
[62]Ibid., 137.
[63]Ibid., 243.

to avoid such events because of the food involved, and this "antisocial" conduct was not conducive to enhancing neighborly relationships.[64] Even an attempt at patching up community relations with a potluck dinner could hardly be successful, considering the restraints on the food they could "honestly" serve.

Ethical Aspects

This experiment also had moral aspects that could lead to uncertainty and even anxiety. For instance, on the one hand, there is the challenge and perhaps necessity of finding out for yourself how it feels to do something outside of the box, and then being able to speak from experience rather than hearsay. On the other hand, there is the dilemma of just how far one can realistically (and tolerably) go in asking for "special treatment" without putting undue pressures on others (and making oneself very unpopular in the process). When do my "personal needs" begin to override the needs of and for the common good? The experiment raised moral questions that stretch the imagination and push the boundaries of possibility and opportunity. Schaub put it this way: "In the face of obvious suffering and illness of every variety, it was certainly tempting to feel like our family's little project was so . . . so . . . self-centered. Irrelevant. Egotistical, even. *Why* was I torturing our family again, anyway? *Who* cared what we had to eat every day?"[65] The whole moral status of the experiment is placed in the balance. Schaub wrote, "I took offense when a friend termed our project an 'intellectual exercise,' as if that characterization somehow minimized our efforts—but *did* it?"[66] Of course, one key aspect of self-experimentation is questioning the relevance of the actual experiment, and the longer the experiment lasts, the more one begins to doubt and question its purpose. As Schaub reflected on the point of the experiment, she wrote, "We felt like good people who cared about what our family ate."[67] But the Schaub family experiment also poses an ethical question in terms of its applicability—one could argue that it addressed a "first-world problem" to which few can relate.[68]

The project's sustainability is another important point in such experiments. Schaub tried to do things in "moderation," but she discovered that sugar is like an unwelcome guest, constantly trying to get in through the

---

[64]Ibid., 138.
[65]Ibid., 71.
[66]Ibid., 249.
[67]Ibid., 23.
[68]Ibid., 43.

back door: "creeping its way back like a virus."[69] Moreover, "moderation" can turn nasty when there is a danger of it turning into scrupulosity,[70] which brings us back to the larger questions of how far and how much is good and justified: How far can we go in building community before it turns in on itself and begins to fall apart? Where and how does humility fit in? How do you measure respect and regard for others?

Schaub pinpoints the crux of the matter:

> I honestly had no desire to be the dietary freaks of our community who carry their own marinated sawdust or whatever in a pouch with them so they can eat separately but equally everywhere they go—no. Yes, I admire [conscious-living advocates] like Scott and Helen Nearing or Tasha Tudor for being so passionate about their unique ways of life—they are fascinating to me. But their sacrifices were huge: these are folks who had to remove themselves from society to follow their ideals—which, above all, sounds pretty lonely.[71]

Self-experiments inevitably open the door to self-scrutiny with regard to self and the wider social fabric. They may well be able to provocatively contribute toward the cross- (or contra-) cultural discussion that tests the limits of any teaching, including social teaching.

Schaub's experience shows a culturally challenging negotiation of convenience, convention, community, and consistency. There is a deep motivation to live a more conscious life and to reduce thoughtlessness, which has been identified as a major force in the erosion and undermining of morally acceptable ways of life. Pope Francis's encyclical *Laudato Si'* ("On Care for Our Common Home") can be read as an exhortation to move away from thoughtlessness into a more intentional and more justifiable form of life. An undeniably worthwhile goal is to make sustainable changes to one's life by transforming habits. Habits are by their very nature sustainable, and modifying them contributes immensely to taking life-changing steps. In fact, the single most important element in sustainable change may be a change in habits, because such a change brings with it a change in one's way of life. It becomes a kind of exodus from an old way of being in the world to a new one. I report next on an experiment designed around the practice of "Catholic Social Teaching habits," in the spirit of *Laudato Si'*.

---

[69]Ibid., 254.
[70]Ibid., 258.
[71]Ibid.

A Case Study: *Laudato Si'*

In this 2015 encyclical, Pope Francis makes an appeal for "a change in lifestyle."[72] He notes that such a change requires "an awareness of the gravity of today's cultural and ecological crisis [that] must be translated into new habits."[73] The appeal is also an invitation for us to put the thoughts of *Laudato Si'* into everyday practice.

In the light of *Laudato Si'* I like to ask students a few questions, in the spirit of an examination of conscience. This sustainability questionnaire includes questions such as: Would you be in favor of the introduction of ecological taxes? Would you be in favor of rethinking national sovereignty in light of ecological challenges (i.e., ecologically irresponsible action from a state could justify an international, even military intervention)? Would you be in favor of introducing fines for flying, thus significantly increasing airfare? Would you be in favor of a rationing of air miles per person? Would you be ready to make personal sacrifices for the environment? Do you care about what state the planet will be in by the year 2100?

Discussion of these questions regularly invites deep conversations and fruitful reflections that have led to some change in practices—very much in the spirit of the encyclical.

Francis calls upon us to inspect our ways of life like never before, "to become painfully aware, [of] what is happening to the world"[74]: to our "pace of life and work";[75] to "pollution, waste and the throwaway culture";[76] to "the depletion of natural resources."[77] The text invites us to approach nature and to stop to contemplate the beauty of the world,[78] to invest more deeply in "interpersonal relations,"[79] and to become aware of "harmful habits of consumption" and "dominant lifestyle."[80] He encourages openness to awe and wonder[81] and an attitude of being aware of ecological change and "the harm done to nature and the environmental impact."[82] The text calls for a thorough reflection on the ecology of daily

---

[72] *LS* 206.
[73] *LS* 209.
[74] *LS* 19; see also *LS* 66.
[75] *LS* 18.
[76] *LS* 21, 123.
[77] *LS* 27; *LS* 55, 211.
[78] *LS* 34, 53, 97, 103, 112, 150, 215, and 235.
[79] *LS* 47.
[80] *LS* 55, 145, 203, 204.
[81] *LS* 11.
[82] *LS* 59, 117.

life,[83] on transportation,[84] and on our "environmental responsibility" in, for example, the "use of plastic and paper."[85] The encyclical exhorts us to be open to an education in "simplicity of life"[86] and to abstinence,[87] while promoting the common good.[88] Such aspects and attitudes pave the way for social experiments to be tried out, as shown by studies conducted by the Chicago school of sociology.[89]

We can break down this general invitation to inspect our lives into four main categories, in order to find out how and if it works:

- *C 1 Consumption*: foodstuffs, nonfood consumption, waste.
- *C 2 Resources*: energy consumption, use of specific resources.
- *C 3 Perception*: levels of awareness and experience of environmental damage, all that is beautiful, nature in all its shapes and forms.
- *C 4 Lifestyle:* downsizing, decluttering, working on personal relationships, slowing down.

This structure makes it easier to experiment more systematically, which is what I tried to do together with a group of committed students at the University of Notre Dame in 2016: I gave twelve students the task of carrying out a self-experiment for one month, based on an aspect of *Laudato Si'*.[90] Students were invited to choose a category (and a particular area within that category) that interested them, do all the necessary research, and collect the background information required. They were asked to define their own rules and make entries on a daily basis in their diaries. I've arranged the results in four groups: perception and categorization, habits and behaviors, social aspects, and ethically relevant insights.

Perception and Categorization

One central theme that occurs again and again throughout *Laudato Si'* is that of "taking things for granted," a goes-without-saying attitude about everything. Social teaching "dares" the moral power of the imagination; we can interpret this invitation as being asked to look more closely at

---

[83]*LS* 147, 152.
[84]*LS* 153.
[85]*LS* 211.
[86]*LS* 214, 222.
[87]*LS* 9.
[88]*LS* 232.
[89]M. Gross and W. Krohn, "Society as Experiment: Sociological Foundations for a Self-Experimental Society," *History of the Human Sciences* 18, no. 2 (2005): 63–86.
[90]Quotes refer to student (S) and day of entry (D), by number.

the tendency to take things for granted, putting our everyday "so-whats" under the microscope. As one student wrote,

> It is strange how you can fail to notice what is in front of you every day. Until deciding to avoid disposable plastic for November, I had never considered how widely it is used. It has become such a large part of the culture of convenient consumption that is so prevalent in America that I had never really thought to question it before. (S1, D1)

This is the observation of a student who tries to live one month without using throwaway plastic. Suddenly her life is full of obstacles:

> I don't understand the purpose of a straw. While I can understand why kids may use them—to keep their drinks from spilling (really to blow bubbles as loudly as possible), they were probably originally intended to prevent drinks from being spilled)—it seems bizarre and wasteful for them to always be given. I went out to eat today and asked for a water, not expecting that it would come out with a straw in it (although I probably should have). Straws seem like one of the most wasteful ways to use plastic (and the paper that they are usually individually wrapped in) because very few people need straws and they are given without being requested. It does not take much more effort to raise your glass a little more to drink regularly instead of with a straw, and, although one straw is not very much, the number of straws that are used in a day is undoubtedly tremendous and eliminating them could probably save a lot of plastic without majorly inconveniencing anyone (but maybe that's just because the presence of a straw caught me off-guard). (S1, D11)

Culturally established practices and habits offer us a window through which to look more deeply into those cultures. One participant wanted to take a closer look at the question of trash, which reveals a lot about the way we live.[91] The throwaway culture mentioned by Pope Francis on several occasions, beginning with *Evangelii Gaudium*,[92] is evident in the everyday life of students; they found that looking into their waste habits and garbage heaps was like entering uncharted waters:

---

[91] See W. Dowell, "Throwing the Sociological Imagination into the Garbage: Using Students' Waste Disposal Habits to Illustrate C. Wright Mills's Concept," *Teaching Sociology* 34, no. 2 (2006): 150–55; M. O'Brien, "Rubbish Values: Reflections on the Political Economy of Waste," *Science as Culture* 8, no. 3 (1999): 269–95.
[92] *EG* 53; see also *LS* 16, 22, 43, and 123.

I have the job of student custodian in my dorm. There is a trash room on each floor of my Hall, and my job is to collect the trash and throw it in the dumpsters outside the dorm on Saturdays evenings and Sundays when the normal cleaning staff is off of work. I never thought that the job would give me insights into the life of the students around me. First, the amount of trash (and recycling) produced is ridiculous. I probably collect about 5 recycling bins and 6 trash cans from each of the 4 floors each weekend. That's about 40 bins of waste for 240 students. That's a bin of waste produced for every 6 students **in just 2 days.** Maybe a lot of the trash is accumulated from earlier in the week, but this is a lot of waste. Perhaps the most common objects are cans and bottles of alcohol. We talk often about the effect of excessive alcohol consumption on our bodies and social behavior, but there is an immense environmental impact as well. Luckily, a lot of this material is recyclable, but many students throw this material in the trash cans because the recycling bins overflow. (S2, D13)

There is a theological significance in what is not used, as Stephen De Beer has pointed out in an article on dumping sites as homes; dumping sites have literally become home for a significant group of people who live off the discards of the throwaway culture. De Beer quotes 1 Corinthians 1:28 ("God chose what is low and despised in the world"), inviting us to discover the rich treasures hidden away in layers of garbage, and asks: what kind of world have we made and allowed, as theologians and Christian practitioners, if dumping sites become home, if they are the only safe spaces in the city?[93] It says a lot about a community to look at what is not being used. It says a lot about a person's way of life to look at what the person throws away. In this sense, garbage is a window into practices and attitudes.

Another window is coffee as a commodity. One student noticed the huge amount of "coffee-to-go" sold and served in throwaway cups:

Today I started thinking about my coffee-drinking habits in light of *Laudato Si'*. It started with an observation of coffee purchases while working at the Law School café and continued later with a conversation I had with a friend who works at Starbucks. While working at the café, I noticed the incredible amounts of coffee that

---

[93] S. de Beer, "Jesus in the Dumping Sites: Doing Theology in the Overlaps of Human and Material Waste," *HTS Teologiese Studies / Theological Studies* 70, no. 3 (2014): art. 2724.

is consumed by the students and that most do not use reusable mugs. Some people will buy multiple coffees every day and use a different cup each time. I do not know if they recycle the cups, but this creates a lot of waste. (S2, D16)

He soon realized that he had to rethink his own coffee-drinking habits, and in doing so remembered his time studying in Puebla, Mexico: "My host mom there would always make coffee with a French press. This method was cheap, it allowed her to use local coffee ground by the neighborhood coffee shop, and it created very high-quality coffee" (S2, D17). Experiencing alternative ways of doing things encourages us to expand our horizons of possibility but also makes us more keenly aware of the issues involved in maintaining the status quo.

The following passage is striking in that it shows just how all aspects of everyday life can be seen through the window of the encyclical; an expression of conscious living is the sincere attempt to make explicit what is implicit. One student tried to reduce the amount of trash he used, and in the normal procedure of placing an order at a fast-food chain he began to wonder about the mountain of waste being produced:

I was struck by the waste inherent in this system of fast food and how I had never really thought about it today. For my burger and fries, my burger was wrapped in paper, my fries were in a paper cup. I received 5 napkins, 3 ketchup packets, and 2 copies of my receipt. All of this was in my paper to-go bag. In 30 seconds, after I started eating my food, all this waste was in the trash. I didn't ask for these things, it's just how the system works for the sake of efficiency and sanitation. (S2, D7)

Another student reflected on the size of portions served, with some "ridiculously" and "irresponsibly" large—too large, which also means that we must assume that many such oversized portions land in the trashcan and not in our stomachs (S12, D13). Some intentional efforts are taking place within the hospitality industry to reduce portion size, as a case can be made for a correlation between portion size and food waste.[94]

Experiments like this open windows onto new landscapes of life experience that in turn impact a wider sphere of perception. One student suddenly realized how much food she was throwing away (S12, D8), and another student noted, "I didn't realize until today how heavily based the

---

[94] See M. R. Freedman and C. Brochado, "Reducing Portion Size Reduces Food Intake and Plate Waste," *Obesity* 18, no. 9 (2010): 1864–66.

American breakfast is on animal-based substances" (S5, D1). We begin to see things that have always been there but which we just hadn't "seen":

> My sister and I went shopping today. . . . We both got iced teas and a couple of purchases. The packaging for the iced tea included the cup, lid, straw, and straw wrapper. The purchases included tags, paper bags, and cardboard boxes, all of which were recycled. Again, I am reminded that this consumer society that we live in is very hard to combat. I could not have purchased a tea, but then I am not supporting a small business. I can send a letter and encourage them to use reusable containers for customers who are there, but then how could we take our drinks to go? Do we need to bring our drinks to go? Or is it an unnecessary convenience? (S4, D27)

The category of "convenience" emerges as a key to the hermeneutics of the experiment. Trying to avoid plastic creates many inconvenient situations (S1, D15). "Tissues are another product that are easily disposed of. I use tissues and paper towels frequently here at school, and before, I never gave them a thought when I was throwing them away. Convenience is a theme that I see in everything disposable" (S4, D3). Paper tissues, like plastic drinking straws, reflect the "thoughtless" habits of a culture.

One interesting theme running through the entries was that of making a sacrifice, not only theologically but ethically also. Pope Francis talks about personal sacrifice in *Laudato Si'*;[95] this notion of sacrifice stands in contrast to and even challenges our notion of all that is convenient (S2, D25). What am I truly willing to give up, to do without, to sacrifice? One student summed up the idea behind this dilemma thus: "Inconveniences that we face should be viewed as opportunities to grow in virtue" (S1, D21). "Convenience" comes under pressure when "efficiency" takes over, and as one student noted, "Convenience and efficiency are not always necessarily good" (S2, D7), but both aptly sum up a way of life we have become used to and take for granted. It is convenient to buy things online, but at what ecological and moral cost (S3, D5)? It comes as no surprise that Pope Francis picks up on this aspect of doing everything in a rush.[96] As one student realizes, mindfulness takes time:

> Another thing I have noticed is that I tend to take more food or excessive amounts of it when I am moving quickly through my day or in a rush. When I have to eat really quickly, I tend to take a lot

---
[95] *LS* 9, 200.
[96] *LS* 18, 225.

of food, often not pay as much attention to what I am putting on my plate, and I am more likely to eat something I wouldn't usually without time deliberating. (S3, D11)

The key category that seems to emerge here is "convenience"—something is convenient if it does not require extra effort or additional planning. According to marketing experts,

> An early application of the notion of convenience can be found in the term "convenience goods," where convenience relates to savings in time and effort by consumers in the purchase of a product.... Time and effort, as dimensions of convenience, remain consistent in convenience research, and developing this focus on these consumer resources, which are expended in buying goods and services, led to the notion of convenience as an attribute of a product or good that reduces its non-monetary price.[97]

Convenience is an expression of a lifestyle that values "comfort" and low levels of investment in order to obtain a good. Comfort is a category for a way of life that seeks to establish itself for the long run; "efficiency" and "feasibility" are both heuristic categories that can shed light on the meaning of convenience and comfort.

There is a certain refusal to accept the high cost of convenience. Pope Francis uses the term to talk about the importance of starting with the literal sense of a sacred text; otherwise the text becomes "too pliable." He writes, "Otherwise we can easily make the text say what we think is convenient, useful for confirming us in our previous decisions, suited to our own patterns of thought."[98] A convenience-based lifestyle does not encourage a sober look at one's ecological footprint, large-scale implications, or the big picture. It can be compared to the idea of "white fragility,"[99] a term coined by Robin DiAngelo to bring to light inconvenient truths: the tendency to create comfort zones without race-based stress, allowing for a positive self-image; the tendency to operate within polite contexts without looking into matters of complicity; and the reality of a system that privileges white people. It is convenient not to know and to uphold the illusion of noncomplicity—in ecological as well as racial matters. This

---

[97] J. Dawes Farquhar and J. Rowley, "Convenience: A Services Perspective," *Marketing Theory* 9, no. 4 (2009): 425–38, at 426.
[98] *EG* 152.
[99] Robin DiAngelo, *White Fragility: Why It's So Hard for White People to Talk About Racism* (Boston: Beacon Press, 2018).

ecological fragility is a challenge for the self-image of the good citizen and the belief that one's lifestyle is *not* a major moral issue.

Habits and Behaviors

As French philosopher Félix Ravaisson accurately pointed out, habits may be a curse or a blessing. They liberate and limit; they liberate in that they reduce moral and cognitive effort, and limit in that they can lead to thoughtlessness and wrongheadedness. In a study he carried out on habits ("De l'habitude") in 1838, Ravaisson provided evidence to support his theory that habits are like bridges, joining a state of necessity with one of freedom. He focused particularly on the double-edged nature of habits,[100] which he illustrates with an example involving wine. Contrasting drinking habits, with the alcoholic on one side and the wine connoisseur on the other, he observes that while the former loses all sense of taste and needs to constantly "up" the amount he consumes to achieve the desired effect, the latter refines and sensitizes his taste for wine with the merest mouthful. It is a clear example of the double-edged sword of habits that Saint Augustine describes as iron chains making us slaves to ourselves, to our own habits.[101]

The self-experiments carried out by my students in light of *Laudato Si'* also made them stop and think about their own habits, hitherto unnoticed and unquestioned. One student, who committed herself to practicing the Ignatian *Examen* to attain a deeper awareness of her own life, noted, "The examen is about taking yourself out of your own context to examine what happens" (S9, D21). This entails looking at an everyday given from another context—a different, more distanced point of view—with the aim of reducing that taking-it-for-granted element. A further aspect of the self-experiments was making an active effort to fight thoughtlessness, which involved taking an honest look at one's lifestyle. Closely observing one's own thoughtlessness is a meaningful exercise in itself (S2, D6). One student though about the amount of water he used for his morning

---

[100] See C. Carlisle, "Between Freedom and Necessity: Félix Ravaisson on Habit and the Moral Life," *Inquiry: An Interdisciplinary Journal of Philosophy* 53, no. 2 (2010): 123–45.

[101] Augustine, *Confessions* 8.5. Similarly, English writer Elizabeth Gaskell, who died in 1865, compared habits to chains that emerge in early domestic life without a child being able to resist them. In her view, only very few have the strength to free themselves from these chains: "The daily life into which people are born, and into which they are absorbed before they are well aware, forms chains which only one in a hundred has moral strength enough to despise and to break when the right time comes" (*Ruth* [London: Penguin, 2013], 8). Resisting the chains of habit requires conscious actions based on clear decisions. Here, experimentation with your own way of life is also necessary.

shower (S6, D1); another looked at collective habits and the resulting cumulative effect (S6, D19).

Experiments such as these underline the role habits play in our social culture. "We have so many disposable products integrated into our society" (S4, D1). Experiments put habits to the test; they question aspects of "automatism" (S2, D5) and habits of "busyness":

> This week has been very busy for me, and the biggest impact of this busyness on my eating habits is that I have been eating a lot of prepackaged food. I have already expressed discomfort in past entries about eating so much pre-packaged food, but I am beginning to realize that it is very much a way of life, especially in countries like America where busyness is seen as a good thing and efficiency is paramount. Compared to changing this lifestyle, giving up meat has been extremely easy. Today I realized two main concerns about eating so much pre-packaged food. First, this food produces a lot of waste because I have to throw away the wrappers and containers. Secondly, I just realized that the production of this food, especially food like granola bars that are in sealed wrappers, have to be produced and packaged in factories which use energy and likely contribute to the degradation of nature. (S2, D10)

A rushed and busy lifestyle takes its toll on the environment. When the pressure is on, there is often no time to think things through ethically; students need to keep their energy levels up, and the waste industry often has the last say and makes the biggest profit. Students buy quick, high-protein bars and drinks (S2, D14); tiredness can be dealt with in a similar fashion, conveniently, when there is no time to "waste" on hours of sleep (S3, D6). One of these students also observed that the busier she was, the more her private life and relationships suffered, since she didn't have time for her friends (S2, D12), an aspect that *Laudato Si'* also recognizes.[102] Tim Kasser, a psychologist working on issues of materialism, came to similar conclusions in his research on the impact of busyness on the environment:[103] living a busy life with many work hours and projects has a more negative effect on the environment than a more relaxed and less overburdened lifestyle.

Establishing "healthy habits" are the goal and objective (S3, D1). One student focused on what Pope Francis calls "the beauty of nature" and tied it in with his nightly run:

---

[102] *LS* 47, 119, 148.
[103] T. Kasser, *The High Price of Materialism* (Cambridge, MA: MIT Press, 2002).

> I went for a night run in the cold, and today what I noticed was how close you can feel to nature when alone on a wooded trail at night with no artificial buzz or sounds kind of just constantly in the background. I noticed how rather than air conditioners, refrigerators, electrical hums, and the like in the woods there is more of this calming nature to the sounds you hear. It's interesting how readily our minds let us know of these differences and how much more enjoyable the natural setting is. (S7, D9)

The same student tested out his powers of perception:

> I decided today to go for a run on a route that I normally do, but I decided to do it in reverse just to see what it was like. I didn't really expect anything different, but in the spirit of trying to make a conscious effort to see so to speak I thought maybe this could be an interesting exercise. (S7, D17)

This was a conscious decision, as was his decision to really look at the world around him while running, at nature's sheer beauty, and also to take in the damage that was being done through the thoughtlessness of human beings. A fellow student undertook a similar exercise in trying to live in—and be fully aware of—the here and now. Looking at and really *seeing* what he was looking at helped him in his spiritual project of mindfulness and living in the present (S10, D6). This encouraged changes not only in his belief and convictions, but also in his attitudes and perceptions.

At the same time, the experiment was about querying existing habits. One student focused on food waste and in doing so suddenly found herself wondering about the edge of the pizza "left over": "I just gave my crust to a friend.... However, it made me think of all the crust that I waste when I order a pizza for myself" (S12, D8). The student who had decided to live without using plastic tried to change some of the world around her: "Carrying a metal fork in your back pocket (to avoid using plastic silverware) ranges from slightly strange to very uncomfortable depending on the orientation of the fork" (S1, D2). This is a matter of breaking habits—and working on habits can take two forms, if one looks at it in a very fundamental way. Either one abandons a habit ("breaking a habit") or acquires a habit ("cultivating a habit"). It is reasonable for these two intentions to go hand in hand, because a habit is best disposed of by adopting an alternative habit. When someone gives up a habit, they most likely adopt another habit in place of the discarded behavior pattern; the new habit should respond to the same trigger. Of course, the most secure way to break a habit is to make its practice impossible, or at least complicated—hence, a way to overcome habits is to avoid situations that trigger them. Furthermore, a habit can change if one dislikes the immediate experience related to it. Also, rather than weakening the negative habit, one can try to reinforce the positive habit; for example, if one desires to eat less meat, focus on providing tasty, varied, and satisfying meatless dining experiences. And finally, be clear and consistent. The Spanish Jesuit Jerome Nadal, in his reflections on internal growth, suggested being careful about minor failures and having clear agreements with oneself; he also advised careful examination of why a resolution was broken.[104]

Consciously setting up certain ways of doing things means that it is easier to reach the goal one has set for oneself:

> Some practices make it easier to avoid using plastic that is thrown away after one use. For example, I don't wash my hair with anything except water (it's not as strange or as gross as it sounds, I promise) because doing anything more is unnecessary (shampoo creates build-up on your head that requires more shampoo to wash out) and harmful to the environment. By not needing plastic bottles for shampoo or conditioner, using bar soap instead of the bottled kind, using apple cider vinegar and coconut oil (both of which come in glass jars) as face wash and lotion, respectively, the need for plastic packaging diminishes. (S1, D3)

Sometimes other habits slow you down or stand in the way of your getting where you want to be, even if the habit in itself may seem morally acceptable and desirable: "Some sustainability practices, such as following a vegan diet, make it more difficult to avoid plastic because a lot of specifically vegan food is specialty food and is therefore individually packaged" (S1, D4). This points to the challenge of competing goods: the reality of lifestyle choices is not a scenario of choices between "good" and "bad," but rather between two forms of evil or two values. Even more so, different lifestyle options may be open to the same person at the same time; since people move between different contexts, a person may experience "competitive moral pluralism" as he or she struggles to achieve incompatible moral goods through mutually exclusive means. A well-known example of this challenge is the question: should we buy locally (but not organically) grown food, or should we buy organically grown food that has been trucked in from a long distance?

The issue of competing goods can also be found in the environmental burdens created by scientific research:

---

[104] J. Nadal, *Der geistliche Weg. Hg. J. Stierli* (Freiburg/Br: Knecht, 1991), 62 and 68.

I do research with proteins and DNA in a lab on campus twice a week and the amount of waste, especially plastic, that is produced there is enormous. Many of the containers and all of the pipette tips are plastic, and are thrown away after one use. They need to be, for sake of sterilization and avoiding cross-contamination, but the quantity is impressive. (S1, D7)

Here we have a moral question about the sense and purpose of research—and how it is carried out. The burden-of-proof question comes into play, as well as the question of levels of justification—or even the more fundamental question of what counts as justification.

An interesting aspect of habits in our society is the normative framework, that is, the laws in place, which may lead to damaging behavior. One student describes how she worked at a hotdog stand during a huge on-campus sports event in order to raise money for a good cause—three dozen bread rolls were left over and had to be discarded for legal reasons. "36 buns!!! Perfectly edible! Just tossed into the trash" (S12, D19). The same student experienced something similar while working for the university's catering service, which stipulated that after an event, all food, including "full trays of food, even if they were untouched" (S12, D19), had to be disposed of, a food hygiene measure, she thought, that had less to do with public health than with making sure there were no grounds for litigation. In order to give no one a legal reason to complain about the quality of the food, food had to be discarded. Legal changes (as with many other changes) might very likely have unintended or undesired consequences and implications. Legal provisions also structure the space of judging actions as "risky" or "prohibited" or "non-advisable," creating processes of reasoning that may not necessarily be adverse to a throwaway culture. This conundrum illustrates the interconnectedness between different spheres of life, such as the legal, social, and ecological realms.

One student managed to work out another type of interconnectedness, in recognizing the domino effect of habits: if you change one thing in your daily life it will inevitably impact another area of your life that you may not even have considered. Habits are interconnected, but not all of them in a clear way: "It's interesting to see the ways that different sustainability habits affect each other and make it easier or more difficult to add additional practices. Some, of course have basically no influence. Turning off any lights that are left on before leaving a room does not make it any easier or more difficult to abstain from using plastic" (S1, D3). A domino effect arises as a result of the fact that different areas of life depend on a specific constellation of activities in order to remain in the known form; when an element in that configuration changes, one thing leads to the other. This also means that fundamental changes in lifestyle can begin with a concrete and minor change in habits, a change that is part of a fabric of practices affected by an initial change on the local level.

Social Aspects

There is a social context for lifestyle experiments. Some students found social support to be a huge help; friends can and do provide a network of moral support, strengthening you in your resolve to overcome the little (and big) temptations life throws at you (S2, D4). Keeping to a vegetarian or vegan diet is easier if you have a mentor (S5, D3). Carrying this notion one step further, it should thus be advantageous to celebrate a vegan Thanksgiving dinner with vegans, because the people present share preferences and reconfirm the common values (S5, D24). One interesting aspect in the realm of food is gender stereotyping, which presents its own ethical questions: "It became very apparent when my friends who are girls were more accepting of me talking about veganism than my friends who are guys. And I would be lying if I said that one of the reasons I wouldn't want to become a vegan was because some would consider it 'unmanly' even though it is a silly reason" (S5, D30). This in turn leads us to wonder at the social significance of food, which plays a large role in a very personal and sensitive part of our lives, both at the ethical and social level: "I thought it was interesting that the speed at which people eat changes when they are by themselves and when they are with others. . . . I personally eat much faster when I'm by myself" (S12, D18).

Additional social factors are to be considered. One is that changing a habit depends on a supportive, "enabling" environment in which small, appropriate, concrete steps can take place. The design of the environment is therefore crucial. Writer Thomas Mann, for example, arranged such an environment: after breakfast he retired to his study at 9 a.m. to work there for three hours behind a locked door; his family had to tiptoe and be quiet as mice during this time.[105] Only at noon would he sound the all clear. The environment followed the habit, forming the framework for the cultivation of the writing habit. Ludwig Wittgenstein spoke of the "environment" of a linguistic statement.[106] A statement is understandable only in the context of the proper environment; a dog, for example, cannot "dissemble," because for this behavior the right environment—in this case, the presence of certain behavioral capabilities—is lacking. A

---

[105] Currey, *Daily Rituals*, 34–35.
[106] L. Wittgenstein, *Philosophical Investigations* (Oxford: Blackwell, 1967), 250 and 584, respectively.

change in habit also depends on an appropriate environment, physically and socially. Appropriate infrastructure, a supportive social environment, and the design of an everyday structure all contribute to making it easier to cultivate a habit. That is why communities and institutional arrangements such as monasteries were meant to support the cultivation and preservation of spiritually important habits.

Social issues are about not only support but also tensions and challenges. The students participating in this project were faced with delicate challenges: for instance, should they tell the others in their dorm that they are wasting resources, that they have bad habits (S6, D12)? Vegan or vegetarian diets can give rise to social tensions and even conflict, particularly in the context of someone inviting or being invited for a meal. Highly charged moments of turning down food that has been prepared can end nastily for all parties concerned: one student had a similar experience to that of Eve Schaub, although in this case it is waste and not sugar that caused the issue:

> When I began this experiment, I did not realize how much waste I created every time that I went to [this coffeeshop].... The next time I went back, I brought a plastic Tupperware container and asked if they could not give me a drink and put my food in the Tupperware instead. After a look of confusion, the woman agreed and gave my container to the cook. The cook also looked confused and the woman and the cook talked for a few minutes. In the end, they gave me my veggie burger in the Tupperware—I didn't create a single piece of waste! (S4, D4)

Again, the health code or other legal provisions may restrict the options in such settings.

In any case, alternative behaviors challenge cultural codes and boundaries, the distinction between being "in place" and "out of place." Finding one's own style is difficult enough; challenging the style of others even more so. It is a difficult process when (taken-for-granted) cultural worlds collide with new ones. Sometimes, ethical insights turn upside down our cozy picture of the world: "Why are we so addicted to convenience? Why I am putting convenience and not wanting to have another awkward conversation with my friends, over my morals, ethics, and the well-being of others? It's quite sad, pathetic, and selfish. This experiment is really opening my eyes to all of these things" (S4, D2).

A harmless situation can underline deep social grammar:

> My group of friends and I decided to have a movie night and watch the first *Lord of the Rings* (warning: it's incredibly and unnecessar-

ily long but it's an okay movie). One of my friends offered to bring snacks and asked if I'd want chips and salsa. Knowing that the chips would have been wrapped in plastic I said no, and he asked why not, wondering if this was part of the training plan I'm doing for a half marathon. And I didn't know how to answer him. I knew that if I tried to explain avoiding disposable plastic it wouldn't have made sense (after all, I can't avoid it completely and almost everything you do involves plastic and it doesn't make a difference to the temperature of the planet and all of the reasons that I know but that I find varying degrees of unimportant when compared to the idea that everyone should be as good as they can and act how they would want everyone else to act), so I didn't really say anything. (S1, D12)

The same student went on to write in another entry how important it is to talk about these things and give friends reasons for changes in habits. This process of transforming habits is also a matter of finding the appropriate language and questioning thoughtlessness through the art of substantial conversations. One socially and ethically relevant factor is the danger of spoiling the fun for others. One student was working hard on reducing the amount of water she used and had become highly sensitized to the subject:

My friend posted a throwback video of her and her dog playing with a hose in a summer time. It was a cute memory, but for half of the video, the dog was just running crazy from being excited by the water while the hose was uselessly pouring out water, flooding the grass it was laying in. Realized that I have probably done this a ridiculous amount of times with my own dog. (S6, D29)

This kind of summer fun no longer made her laugh. Can such cross-cultural experiments assume too serious a character and become socially unacceptable?

Another student focused on the quality of his personal relationships and suddenly realized the true meaning and value of "deep sharing," those one-to-one confidential conversations on delicate matters that, in order to occur, require the right place at the right time (S8, D26). A seemingly simple question such as "How are you?" takes on a new dimension because we know that it is not a question at all, and that any honest answer would probably startle us: this reveals a great deal about our cultural communication habits. One student went one step further: as she tried to pursue a life guided by the Holy Spirit, she asked herself, "Am I surrounding myself with the right people?" (S9, D11). The question may seem harsh, but it points to the reality that supportive social environments and relationships can support a sometimes painful change of habits.

Ethical Insights

Living ethically increases cognitive processing demands. The price of overcoming thoughtlessness is engaging in more and deeper reflective efforts. Fewer things can be taken for granted, and you need more time to arrange and plan. There are more decisions to be made—what to eat, what to avoid, where to shop. "I'm having to be much more intentional," one student noted (S2, D2). "Each day I must make a conscious decision," a fellow student writes (S5, D4). The student who had decided to slow down by taking part in a daily Ignatian exercise also opted to increase her expectations of herself with regard to self-scrutiny:

> I really had to remember why I wanted to do this experiment in the first place. I wanted to participate in a daily task that would increase my intentionality, especially considering this year being my last year at Notre Dame and the semester having gone so fast already to this point. I resolved at the beginning of the year to remember the big picture and not get caught up in the nitty gritty of the day to day so much so that I did not enjoy the year as a whole, missing the important moments, or dismissing them to move onto the next item on the to-do list. I didn't make any concrete plans to try to sustain this frame of mind, though. I see this daily Examen as an opportunity to come back to this plan, to really appreciate this month and slow down life for long enough to enjoy it, and to build this skill so that I can have it in the future months and even years. (S9, D1)

Questions about the pace, content, and meaning of life and its concomitant relationships inspired a number of students, including the one just mentioned, to choose to consciously live their lives in the here and now, in this moment in time (S10, D5). While there is an increase in the number of decisions to be made and the effort to realize them mindfully, the range of available options to choose from becomes narrower since the moral space has been restructured—that is, it has become the less-dense space of morally acceptable actions.

One challenge is to renegotiate not only "rules," but also "exceptions to the rules." Normally, celebrations and feast days are seen as exceptions, and celebrations come with intentional wastefulness and abundance. One student, however, found himself wondering about "enough" and "plenty" and realized that both had been drastically accommodated for:

"For Thanksgiving I went over to my friend's house. Their spread was rather ... excessive, I would say. There were 10 pies and 27 pounds of turkey for 10 people!!! Not to mention all the other side dishes!" (S12, D24). The underlying category here may be the category "*lagom*," a Swedish word that means "exactly the right amount." Some diary entries talk about the ecological burdens and the unwritten laws of hospitality the students suddenly become aware of—and the cultural expectation to move beyond the *lagom*.

Students continually found themselves in ethical dilemmas, such as how to avoid throwing away perfectly good food (S12, D11). Or, more difficult, if you are trying to cut down on plastic or waste but know a friend is having a really tough time, do you get him a little something, nicely packed and wrapped, to cheer him up (S3, D16)? And what would you do in the following situation?

> I've mentioned before the interesting dilemma that presents itself when I am faced with wasting food or doing something else I am trying not to do. For example, if I accidentally take too much food in the dining hall, should I overstuff myself or just throw out the extra food? Today, I was working a late shift in the law school café and knowing that they were closing early for Thanksgiving, they had extra ham sandwiches that were not going to be eaten. Any I did not take home would be thrown away. Even though I haven't been eating meat, I decided to take one of the sandwiches. My reasoning: I am eating a vegetarian diet because I want to reduce waste and protect the environment. By taking the sandwich and saving it for later, I am not only reducing waste by saving the sandwich, but also by reducing my need to buy food on the go. Instead of eating a protein bar or buying a pre-packaged sandwich or salad for lunch later this week, I will instead be able to eat the sandwich. Even if this logic is flawed, at least I am being intentional about my food decisions. (S2, D21)

In a similar experience, another student wanted to spend a month making conscious decisions and choices regarding her eating and "trash" habits; she decided she would go vegetarian for that month but soon found herself faced with one dilemma after the other.

> I made a Belgian waffle, and I found it very difficult to finish the whole thing. Very full and with just a few bites remaining, I wondered to myself what was worse, wasting a few bites of food or eating the rest

of the food to the point that I felt uncomfortable and overstuffed. I ended up eating the rest because I really dislike throwing away food, but was it still wasted if I didn't need it? (S2, D5)

The effort of honoring a commitment can create moral costs of a second order, that is, painful compromises of moral standards. Here again is the question of acceptable moral compromises and less acceptable compromises—"rotten compromises," as Avishai Margalit put it: compromises that betray ideals and standards of integrity.[107] Where is the line between the nonnegotiable and the negotiable, between the prophetic and the provocative, given social and cultural expectations? The prophet may not be beloved in her hometown because she might challenge standards of normalcy and convenience. These are questions about ethical decisions and moral calls.

The question of what we do with our time when we have a choice is also ethically relevant, particularly when it has to do with those "special times" in our lives; the challenge of big occasions like weddings and birthdays was a key issue in Eve Schaub's experiment. One student noted,

> Today, I didn't do very well with keeping my sustainability practice. It was my best friend's birthday, and I wanted to bake her a cake. ... I debated just making a cake from scratch because my roommate and I have the ingredients in our room. In the end, I found myself with a box of pre-made cake mix, a tube of frosting, and an extra tube of icing for letters. I realized I just didn't have time to make a cake from scratch, and doing it this way was much more convenient and I wish I had made the cake from scratch. (S3, D18)

Thanksgiving is perhaps the most important annual family gathering in the United States, and without exception each student noted the pressure it put on their good intentions and the challenge it posed to their consumption targets. Over the holiday, for example, one student was faced twice with moral decisions: one was about whether he should eat the leftovers of a spaghetti meal rather than throw it away,[108] and the other

---

[107] A. Margalit, *On Compromise and Rotten Compromises* (Princeton, NJ: Princeton University Press, 2010).

[108] Note the fine line of reasoning in this argumentation: "I arrived home today not having eaten any dinner. It was really late, so I looked in the refrigerator to see what there was to eat. There was some pasta with meat sauce sitting in the fridge, and my mom requested that I eat it, since we were going to have leftovers from Thanksgiving dinner soon and the pasta would not get eaten. I decided that it was okay for me to eat the meat in this

was about not being able to say no to a steak his father lovingly prepared just for him (S2, D27).

We are confronted here with the moral cost of the pain caused by the lifestyle habits we choose: as one student asked, "Can anyone truly live a cruelty-free diet in this country?" (S5, D7). Then there is the "painful" awareness that a vegan lifestyle is costly both in terms of money and time (S5, D18), which in turn may create the impression that moral choices are only for the rich and privileged. One student asked herself "why I was doing this in the first place. It's not about my moral edification and keeping up a standard. It's about God's beautiful world which He crafted in such love, and which calls for us to care for it as well" (S3, D17). Another reflected that it is worth remembering "why I became a vegan in the first place and the call for me as a Christian to Care for God's Creation" (S5, D20).

Such spiritually motivated reasoning goes deeper than any moral, psychological, or philosophical considerations, which underlines the deep significance of the *Magis* (more) of Catholic Social Teaching. The student who undertook the Ignatian *Examen* found that this one exercise, this new habit, strengthened her relationship with God:

> Something that I have noticed as I progress through my month of using the daily Examen is that I am starting to notice God's active presence in my life. I see Him more than just in the times that I seek him out through prayer or through the kind words of others. I feel more of his grace and supportive powers that foster these general feelings of happiness. He lightens my disposition. He enables these meaningful interactions with others. He may not be interceding for me in flashy, conspicuous, or grandiose ways, but I feel like I am more consistently recognizing Him willing me forward and towards happiness; towards Him. (S9, D10)

This example also hints that the *Magis* of social teaching is not just about nature but also about creation, not only about happiness but also about grace, and not only about success but also about service.

---

situation. Eating it would not increase the demand for meat or cause anyone to purchase more meat. The dish had already been created, and the meat had already been used; it was either going to be eaten or be wasted. As I have reflected before, I think that it is better to consume already produced less-than-ethical food than to let it go to waste. Although, that being said, I think I have to be careful, even about eating something that would otherwise be wasted, if it means that I might be causing more demand for that food" (S2, D23).

Experiments and Growth

Gandhi's experiments with truth were a tangible expression of his spiritual search. He characterized his experiments with truth in the spiritual field with these words: "If the experiments are really spiritual, there can be no room for self-praise."[109] There is also an exhortative element in Gandhi's account: "The experiments narrated should be regarded as illustrations, in the light of which everyone may carry on his own experiments according to his own inclination and capacity."[110]

Experiments with habits are experiments with the good life. Experiments are purposeful changes that trigger a dynamic where one step leads to the next. Life is like a book; it forms a text, a fabric (*textum*) in which the individual parts are connected. For example, Leo Hickman, an English journalist who lived in London with his family at the time of his experiment, wanted to change his middle-class life.[111] He had the vague feeling of needing to live differently. He suffered from the "sugar pea moment," the guilt that tells you that you are doing something bad when you buy a small package of sugar snap peas that have been imported long-distance from another country. Hickman wanted to change his lifestyle, but he did not know where to start, so he invited three experts in ethical consumption and environmental issues to his home. They ransacked his refrigerator, his trash can, and his bathroom cabinet, questioned him about his lifestyle habits, and finally gave him a clear suggestion for how to begin changing his life: he should start with trash, food, chemicals, and transportation. His trash can, refrigerator, and cleaning products, along with the issue of transportation, become the keys to a lifestyle change. The first step soon led to a second and a third. Changed travel habits led to changes in work habits (incorporating remote work from home), changed vacation habits (such as traveling by train from England to Italy), and also to changed relationship structures (Hickman's wife was so unnerved on their arrival in Italy after the tiring train journey that she ordered an air-conditioned rental car for herself and the baby, while blaming her husband for the ordeal). By changing his habits, Hickman became more attentive, which caused him to question other habits, such as temperature-control levels in his residence. As a result, he just turned the heat down in the winter, saying to himself, "'After all, I could just put on a sweater,' as my grandmother used to say."

---

[109] Gandhi, *Autobiography*, x.
[110] Ibid., xii.
[111] L. Hickman, *A Life Stripped Bare: My Year Trying to Live Ethically* (London: Transworld, 2005).

Life forms a tapestry, and when you pull on one of its threads, it affects the whole tapestry. The first step, the phase in which you begin to pull on that thread, is decisive. Hickman experienced the first step of his experiment as an "interrogation" and "inventory": the three experts invaded his family's privacy to get an accurate picture of his life. A few years after his experiment, Hickman described the beginning of his habit change dramatically:

> We opened the door for them, invited them to sit down, served lunch, led them through our house, and then they spent three hours snooping around all over the house. They went into our bathroom, opened all the cabinets and boxes, looked at all the medications and their packages, at our shampoo, at everything. Then they marched into the kitchen, opened the refrigerator, looked in, then took out all the food, checked all the labels and the packages, everything. Then they sat down with us in the living room and asked about our last vacation, about our means of transportation, about where we buy our clothes, about everything. They really tested us. At the end, my wife and I almost wanted to hit them in the face and throw them out of the house.[112]

Here again we are reminded of the fine line between the prophetic and the provocative.

Hickman came to understand a key idea of this chapter: the longer a habit change lasts, the deeper the practice has to become. At the beginning of a habit experiment, there may be a certain euphoria stemming from the freshness of the decision, the allure of the new, the colorful vision of a different life, the sense of achievement—if a day went well. But over time, the distance from the original decision increases, the charm of the new fades, the vision is corrected by reality, and the experiences of success lose intensity pursuant to the law of the hedonistic treadmill: you need more and more of a good to achieve the same happiness effect. A decision is made faster than a habit is changed; being in charge of a decision is easier than being in charge of a new habit. After deciding, hard work is necessary, stamina is needed. In Latin, "*perseverantia*" is the ability to remain continuously engaged in a well-founded project; likewise, "*persistere*" needs to be used here with its meaning of "standing still" or "remaining." People with perseverance are people who can remain focused on the same thing for a long time. Stamina and patience—but also resistance and the ability

---

[112]L. Hickman, "Living the Sustainability/CSR Agenda to the MAX," in Clemens Sedmak et al., eds., *Marktwirtschaft für die Zukunft* (Vienna: LIT, 2013), 195–204, at 196–97.

to endure pain—are necessary. Stamina demands endurance and a clear view of the target at the end of the path; patience is a form of moderation, of being content with small steps and small successes and not demanding too much too fast. Resistance is the readiness to stand up to an obstacle to defend the recognized good, never taking the path of least resistance. Perseverance is a special virtue, which addresses a moral-psychological paradox: I need the virtue (habitual attitude) of perseverance in order to acquire other virtues. In other words, I need to already have good habits in order to acquire good habits—or to hold onto a habit even if there is the temptation to make an exception, which could weaken the habit. The virtue of perseverance makes a person "persist firmly in good, against the difficulty that arises from the very continuance of the act." It also takes "constancy" that helps a person "persist firmly in good against difficulties arising from any other external hindrance."[113]

One particular challenge to moral and spiritual change is weakness of the will, *akrasia*. A weak-willed person knows what is good and knows that he should aspire and want the good, but he cannot bring himself to do the good. According to Aristotle, the weak-willed ("akratic") man is not a bad person, but he acts like one.[114] Harry Frankfurt assigned central importance to the concept of "wholeheartedness."[115] Whoever does something "with all her heart" is mustering the required effort, overcoming weakness of will, and persevering since there is firmness of commitment.

Laudato Si' calls for a revision of habits, admonishing "the unjust habits of a part of humanity."[116] The encyclical also calls for an education that does not fail "to instill good habits."[117] It encourages the overcoming of old habits, like "the habit of wasting and discarding"[118] or the "harmful habits of consumption."[119] It is clear about the need for conversion and for the development of new habits, noting that an awareness of the gravity of today's cultural and ecological crisis must be translated into new habits.[120] Such change, however, is not simply a matter of individual willpower; it is also a matter of the appropriate environment.

> In those countries which should be making the greatest changes in consumer habits, young people have a new ecological sensitivity and

---

[113] Aquinas, *Summa Theologiae* II-II, q.137, a.3, resp.
[114] Aristotle, *Nicomachean Ethics* 1151a10–11.
[115] H. Frankfurt, "Identification and Wholeheartedness," in H. Frankfurt, *The Importance of What We Care About* (Cambridge: Cambridge University Press, 2007), 159–76.
[116] *LS* 93.
[117] *LS* 211.
[118] *LS* 27.
[119] *LS* 55.
[120] *LS* 209.

a generous spirit, and some of them are making admirable efforts to protect the environment. At the same time, they have grown up in a milieu of extreme consumerism and affluence which makes it difficult to develop other habits. We are faced with an educational challenge.[121]

Experiments are a particular way of learning: acquiring "knowledge by acquaintance." At the same time, experiments with truth are experiments with one's vocation, with one's calling; the person needs to inhabit the space of truth in a personal way. And understanding the truth of the need for an "ecological conversion" is not enough; it has to be enacted:

> The ecological crisis is also a summons to profound interior conversion. It must be said that some committed and prayerful Christians, with the excuse of realism and pragmatism, tend to ridicule expressions of concern for the environment. Others are passive; they choose not to change their habits and thus become inconsistent. So what they all need is an "ecological conversion," whereby the effects of their encounter with Jesus Christ become evident in their relationship with the world around them.[122]

An ecological conversion is an invitation to fresh thinking and new habits; living the social dimension of the faith is a commitment to accepting the permanent need for a conversion; and enacting human dignity (i.e., respecting the dignity of others and respecting one's own dignity through a "decent and dignified" life) means enacting a mystery that can never be exhausted. Here again we reach the idea of an Advent spirituality that was mentioned in the introduction. Enacting Catholic Social Tradition is expressed in the readiness to see with fresh eyes like the man born blind in the Gospel of John who was told, "You have seen the Son of God" (Jn 9:37).

---

[121] *LS* 209.
[122] *LS* 217.

5

Catholic Social Teaching as *Regula* and Therapy

Catholic Social Teaching as an expression of the social dimension of the Christian faith is also an articulation of the order and rules of our coexistence. Obviously, a society is not a monastery. But we can entertain the thought that the Catholic social imagination, with its emphasis on the common good (and its ultimate goal, the highest good) and on personal growth within a well-ordered community, has adopted some key aspects of a monastic rule for the macro level of politics. Catholic Social Teaching expresses rules for a form of life, that is, rules for "good living," and can in this sense be likened to the idea of a *regula*.

Catholic Social Teaching, as I have tried to argue, is definitely not first and foremost a catalogue of clauses and subclauses; rather, it is a users' guide to a way of life. Perhaps *regula* could be perceived more as a "specifications statement," less an index of rules and regulations to be learned by heart and obeyed and more a manual, a guide of best-practice recommendations that any monk or nun can live by. Giorgio Agamben describes the connection between rules *and* life, and rules *for* life, in his work on monastic life.[1] The basic tenets of monastic life and its traditions can be seen as an interweaving of rules and life in such a way as to see the pattern of life woven into the words of the rules, and the words of the rules giving tangible expression to the way of life they describe. Both result in a rich tapestry—in which thread and color cannot be separately discerned. In sharing their lives together, monks create a unique way of "communal living." For monks, this living together is not about wearing the same clothes and living in the same place, it is about *habitus*: appropriating a way of life so that it becomes second nature, a habit. In other words, a monk is a human being living life consciously. This conscious

---

[1] G. Agamben, *The Highest Poverty: Monastic Rules and Form-of-Life*, trans. A. Kotsko (Stanford, CA: Stanford University Press, 2013).

living embraces time and space, chores and concerns. The *regula*, this guidebook or manual, becomes a way of life, an everyday routine—a life tapestry so intricately woven that the threads and seams are no longer visible to the naked eye. It is the shape and form that counts.

This idea of *regula* can also serve as a mirror for moral reflection. Moral theories are not just about developing across-the-board theories or passing concrete proposals; they are also about life rules, to be employed and applied as one would the rules in a manual, even though there is no automatism at work; "rules" are located between "general principles" and "particular judgments."

The general principle to respect the dignity of the human person can be translated into the rule to be particularly attentive to basic bodily functions (like the digestive process and human waste management). And this rule will lead to judgments about particular situations—like the sometimes unnecessary use of diapers in nursing homes, done for the staff's convenience. A deep practice of human dignity will not be committed to convenience or efficiency as the highest moral standards in social situations. The rules that translate general principles can guide practices that can become established and habitual and can even shape the way social realities are being perceived. The Golden Rule is not an abstract principle but a guidepost to human behavior, and it shapes the way we see actions and interactions. It can moderate the space between an abstract principle like "respect" and a concrete action like organizing a meal train for a family in need.

In making Catholic Social Teaching one's own and thus relevant for one's personal life, it can help if one views the normative guidelines expressed in the Catholic Social Tradition as *regulae*, or invitations into a form of life. It is not enough to be able to quote Catholic Social Teaching documents. If a bishop merely recites the text before him in his role as teacher exercising the ordinary magisterium, he is not practicing what could be called a "deep communication" of the matter. Deep communication of Catholic Social Teaching requires a personal appropriation. Pope Francis repeatedly draws our attention to the fact that it does not do to simply repeat what has been said elsewhere, even if these texts carry a great deal of authority. In *Evangelii Gaudium*, he warns, "A missionary style is not obsessed with the disjointed transmission of a multitude of doctrines to be insistently imposed. . . . The message has to concentrate on the essentials, on what is most beautiful, most grand, . . . while losing none of its depth and truth, and thus becomes all the more forceful and convincing."[2] This clearly refers to a process beyond

---

[2] Francis, *Evangelii Gaudium*, "The Joy of the Gospel" (2013), no. 35, hereinafter *EG*.

rote learning, a much deeper practice of integrating and internalizing. There are even particular theological dangers in repeating the Word without personal appropriation. As Francis notes, "The message is one which we often take for granted, and can repeat almost mechanically, without necessarily ensuring that it has a real effect on our lives and in our communities."[3] We must be aware "how dangerous and harmful this is, for it makes us lose our amazement, our excitement and our zeal for living the Gospel of fraternity and justice!"[4] If our acceptance of the message gets stuck at this entry level of rote repetition, we will never experience the light the teaching proffers in its deepest sense, a light that awakens personal inner transformation and makes us stand in "compassionate" awe.

Archbishop Óscar Romero

One particularly striking example of the interiorization of Catholic Social Teaching in the sense of its being applied as *regula*, as a way of life, is that of Óscar Romero, archbishop of San Salvador, who was assassinated while celebrating Mass on Monday, March 24, 1980. He was well known for the way he prepared his homilies, juxtaposing the contemporary political agenda with scripture and in doing so praying for divine guidance. Romero's assimilation of Catholic Social Teaching was so deep that it pervaded his entire perception of the social world. What we see happening here is less a process of application than one of interiorizing, of embracing with body and soul. It is a deep conversion in its true sense: a movement from knowledge by description to knowledge by acquaintance, which enables a person to cross that threshold from reflection to judgment, from passive thinking to actual action. The categories of human dignity, common good, and option for the poor shaped Romero's judgments and actions. These categories were like rules he lived by, making them his own in a similar way to how a monk would live the *regula* (rather than merely following the *regula*). Romero lived the social teachings of the church. Looking at his example can provide a thick description of embodied Catholic Social Teaching.[5]

We know from a diary entry Romero made on January 7, 1980, that his analytical understanding of social and political issues was driven en-

---

[3] *EG* 179.
[4] *EG* 179.
[5] See R. Bergman, *Catholic Social Learning* (New York: Fordham University Press, 2011), 92–117.

tirely by the Holy Spirit, a ubiquitous presence in the life and narrative of Romero, himself a singular person in the political history of his country.[6] Romero's key concern was about being free to judge actions in the light of the Gospels.[7] His own assimilation of Catholic Social Teaching was well known, with government bodies consulting him on various matters; just weeks before his death, the under secretary of agriculture sent him a draft proposal for agricultural reform for him to critique in the light of Christian Social Teaching.[8] Social teaching was Romero's normative source for assessing matters of fairness and justice.

Romero's testimony bears substantial weight because he had realized the significance of the social teachings of the Church before 1977, but had not applied them then in the way he did after what many call his "conversion."[9] He was, of course, well acquainted with the 1968 social encyclicals and the texts of the Medellín Conference in Colombia, but, as one scholar writes, "Romero's acceptance of these teachings had been abstract and theoretical."[10] Romero was therefore still appropriating Catholic Social Teaching at a level that was neither creative not concrete, not yet viably incorporated—and integrated—into everyday life. He was familiar with the principles but lacked the theological and spiritual strength to make concrete decisions that would lead to concrete change. This would change during his years as archbishop of San Salvador.

Romero was appointed archbishop at a time of great political and economic hardship. "Faced with this situation, he believed that the chief task required of him by his episcopal vocation was to shed the light of Christ on 'even the most hideous caverns of the human person: torture, jail, plunder, want, chronic illness.'"[11] His key calling was to make Christ visible in and to the world. In his homily of January 20, 1980, Romero called on Christian communities to be role models for civil society in general. This appeal can best be illustrated if we look at Romero's final Sunday homily of March 23, 1980,[12] which draws attention to the Church's offer of refuge to those who were being persecuted, regardless of their political leanings; the offer was all about providing a safe haven for human beings

---

[6] O. A. Romero, *Su diario: Desde 31 de Marzo 1978 hasta Jueves 20 de Marzo 1980* (San Salvador: Librería Mons. Luis Chávez y González, 2000), 350.

[7] "De libertad para juzgar las actuaciones de todos desde la luz del Evangelio" (ibid., 355).

[8] Ibid., 392.

[9] S. Wright, *Oscar Romero and the Communion of Saints* (Maryknoll, NY: Orbis Books, 2009), 53.

[10] M. Ashley, "Oscar Romero, Religion and Spirituality," *The Way* 44, no. 2 (2005): 113–33, at 115.

[11] Ibid., 113.

[12] March 23, 1980, was Romero's last *Sunday* homily, while the following day, March 24, 1980 was the date of his last homily.

in dire straits—nothing more, nothing less. In this next section, I would like to reconstruct key aspects of Romero's personal interiorization of Catholic Social Teaching and the way he went on to put it into practice, very much based on his own experiences.[13]

Romero's thought and judgment processes are permeated by this social teaching; he weaves core points of Catholic Social Teaching into the text of his homilies with absolute ease. This style of preaching was shared by Father Rutilio Grande, whose assassination shook Romero to his very core. In his homily of August 6, 1970, on the feast of the Transfiguration of Our Lord, Grande cites *Gaudium et Spes* 1 in elaborating on his call for solidarity as part of a wider process of the deep transformation of humanity.[14] In his last homily (February 13, 1977), as Romero would do in a similar manner several years later, Grande explicitly used the words of Pope Paul VI during the latter's visit to Jerusalem in January 1964.[15] Both Grande and Romero work with the Gospels and Church documents. Romero's homilies particularly are steeped in direct allusions to social teaching—he bridges the gaps between social teaching and the Gospels, and with this bridge strengthens the status of the social message he wishes to convey, as when he cites Pope Paul VI's words to the newly appointed Salvadoran ambassador to the Vatican with the angels' message to the shepherds in Bethlehem.[16]

Romero voices a deep trust in the guiding power of social teaching—how enlightened the world would be, he says, if we were to all allow social teaching to guide us in our social existence, our social conduct, and our political and economic obligations.[17] He puts forward social teaching as a third source of inspiration, alongside faith and love;[18] social issues and dilemmas must be viewed and tackled in the light of social teaching, particularly in the manner and method of linking human obligations and

---

[13] I refer to the following sources: ORD: O. A. Romero, *A Shepherd's Diary*, trans. I. B. Hodgson (London: Catholic Fund for Overseas Development [CAFOD], 1993); H I: O. A. Romero, *A Prophetic Archbishop Speaks to His People: The Complete Homilies of Archbishop Oscar Arnulfo Romero* (Miami, FL: Convivium, 2015); H II: O. A. Romero, *A Prophetic Archbishop Speaks to His People: The Complete Homilies of Archbishop Oscar Arnulfo Romero II* (Miami, FL: Convivium, 2015); and VV: O. A. Romero, *Voice of the Voiceless: The Four Pastoral Letters and Other Statements* (Maryknoll, NY: Orbis Books, 1985). Homilies are also quoted from the list of Spanish and English homilies to be found at www.romerotrust.org.uk.

[14] R. Grande, *Homilies and Writings*, ed., trans., and annotated by Thomas Kelly (Collegeville, MN: Liturgical Press, 2015), 22.

[15] Ibid., 113.

[16] H II, 179.

[17] H I, 61.

[18] H I, 406.

human rights.[19] Romero considers specific issues through the lens of such texts, for example, in a January 1978 homily, focusing on the education of children based on the core ideas expressed in Medellín.[20] Moreover, he highlights the "magisterium" of social teaching and how it expresses the authority of the Church as such; there cannot be "two" churches since, as Romero sees it, a dedicated church is one founded on Vatican II and the texts of Medellín.[21] Romero lived out of an attitude of being faithful to the teachings of the Church and of obeying his conscience.[22] For him, it was clear that social teaching is not an optional rider, not some sort of appendix, but an integral part of any understanding of the Gospel of the Lord. Loyalty to these teachings is a sign of loyalty to the Church and to the unity of the Church's hierarchy.[23] Again and again Romero repeats his deep sense of loyalty to and solidarity and with the pontiff.[24] During Holy Communion to celebrate the eightieth birthday of Pope Paul VI, Romero gives a special prayer not only to commemorate the birthday but to emphasize his own sense of union with the pope.[25]

Catholic Social Teaching is authentic *magisterium*, which questions the existing powers and social conditions that prevail but is never subversive.[26] Romero regards the mission of teaching as a prophetic one, and as such, it must inevitably agitate and stir up murky waters, such as when it defends Divine Right and human dignity. Just as inevitably, it will be persecuted for doing so.[27] On August 14, 1977, Romero cited Jeremiah 20:9 in his Sunday homily in order to bring home the message that prophetic speaking is not what we—or indeed the prophet—might want it to be.[28] A prophetic lifestyle requires a shift away from one's comfort zone into an uncomfortable space of inconvenience, both for those on the receiving end and for the one uttering the prophetic words. There always seems to be a temptation to read the gospel as a kind of housekeeping manual with all the uncomfortable bits left out, but this must be decidedly fought against;[29] at the same time, it seems that the social teaching of the Church also has the power to generate spiritual, moral, and epistemic unease and discomfort. This "uneasiness with culture" takes on a prophetic dimension.

---

[19] Ibid.
[20] H II, 207.
[21] H I, 344.
[22] D. Marcouiller, "Archbishop with an Attitude: Óscar Romero's Sentir con la Iglesia," *Studies in the Spirituality of Jesuits* 35, no. 3 (2003): 1–52.
[23] See H I, 248; H II, 129.
[24] H I, 104; H II, 358.
[25] H I, 321.
[26] H I, 82–83.
[27] H I, 135.
[28] H I, 253.
[29] H I, 163.

The Church must resist the temptation to get involved in power-grabbing games; as is clearly stated in Medellín, she must forgo all economic and political power, and in line with Matthew 16:18 stand indomitably, strong as a rock.[30] In an important homily on January 6, 1978, Romero quoted Pope Paul, who

> pleads for a constructive dialogue whose objective should not be to obtain some advantage or privilege.... The Church must renounce all of these things when her witness in this relationship might be tarnished.... The Church promotes and encourages these aspirations, within the sphere of her specific competence.... She always wishes to respect the competences of the temporal power in its sphere and to accept a constructive dialogue with the civil authorities.... Therefore, there should be no conflict between these two authorities who ought to promote the common good and provide for the happiness of people on earth.[31]

Indeed, religious and civil authorities should be united and inseparable in their commitment to the mission of standing up for the downtrodden and despised.

Again and again Romero makes a bridge to the "Church of the Poor," which was upheld and defended by Pope Francis, thirty years after Romero's death. One particular homily, on April 16, 1978, reiterates that a Church of the Poor is not one made up of thieves and organized gangs intent on making a living illegally, at others' cost: a Church of the Poor is one that can be identified by the modest houses the people live in, by those same people feeling no different from others living around them and not excluded in any way because all have been created in God's image.[32] In his homily of February 10, 1980, Romero emphatically underlined the implications for a church of the poor: we must be prepared to take the same risks and to suffer the same fate as the poor, the despised, and the persecuted.

For Romero, the message of the Church is a spiritual one, bringing forth peace from within. Those who are happy to criticize Church writings and texts (such as those of the Second Vatican Council and Medellín) should be advised to study the documents in question with the intention to reveal their spiritual wealth and the message of peace contained within.[33]

I see Romero as someone who perceived social teaching as an expression

---

[30] H I, 169.
[31] H II, 182–84.
[32] H II, 380.
[33] H I, 107.

of faith, articulating an ecclesiology, a sense of the vocation and mission of the Church in the world. In his third pastoral letter and especially in the section "The Duty and Danger of Speaking Out," Romero clarifies "yet again the attitude of the Church to human situations that, by their very nature, involve economic, social, and political problems," but not from the perspective of a scientist or an expert in the field.[34] The Church has a duty to express the results of consultations in the same way that the Apostolic Council of Jerusalem did, as outlined in Acts 15.[35]

The Church cannot remain silent in the face of injustices.[36] The Church "has the duty to proclaim the liberation of millions of human beings, many of whom are her own children—the duty of assisting the birth of this liberation, of giving witness to it, of ensuring that it is complete. This is not foreign to evangelization."[37] In considering the very point and purpose of the Church's social teaching, it must first and foremost be seen as incommensurate with callous indifference. As the Medellín document confirms, the Church can never be indifferent to the screams of millions.[38] Romero harks back to this quote in his first pastoral letter when he writes that the world can be transformed by following the Easter Message. In the same letter he refers to *Evangelii Nuntiandi* 31: "Between evangelization and human advancement—development and liberation—there are in fact profound links."[39]

On August 6, 1977, in his second pastoral letter, he describes the relationship between the Church and the world as being strikingly reciprocal and interdependent: the Church constantly sees the world with new eyes and reveals sinfulness for what it is in the true light of day, and yet does not stand in the way of the world questioning its actions and querying its understanding of sinfulness—a surprising admission of reciprocity.[40] In its encounters with the world, the Church learns about, and in fact it is in encounter that the Church gains a deeper understanding of sin, a deeper sense of incarnation, and a deeper understanding of faith, Romero points out in his Louvain address of February 1980.[41] The Church lives in the human world and is herself so human that it must make all the pain and suffering that exists around it its own, whether the tummy ache of a small child, the huge debt that cannot be paid off, or the burden of

---

[34] VV, 87. Cf. VV, 95.
[35] Cf. H I, 103.
[36] H I, 219.
[37] Paul VI, *Evangelii Nuntiandi*, "In Proclaiming the Gospel" (1975), no. 30, hereinafter *EN*.
[38] VV, 59.
[39] VV, 60.
[40] VV, 65.
[41] VV, 183–85.

unemployment.[42] The Church is not only "there," it is in close proximity. It shares in all that is human, and it identifies with all human beings who are busy building and designing new bridges for the world.[43] It therefore comes as no surprise that Romero sees no dichotomy between the history of Christian salvation and secular history.[44] The kingdom of God should be there to see on every page of every history book, in Romero's reading. Finally, the example of Romero also makes it clear that any tangible manifestation of social teaching will inevitably lead to conflict if social change, a process that always tips the balance of power, is seriously set in motion. The prize of moral clarity then is twofold: conflict and sacrifice.

Seven Criteria and Two Perspectives

Looking at Romero's writings and preaching we can identify some key criteria that he used to apply Catholic Social Teaching to the context of social and political analysis. These criteria, even though fundamental principles, serve as rules that shape the perception and the judgment of situations.

First, as in his homily of January 6, 1980, Romero strives to identify the value of *equality* by citing the Letter to the Galatians: "There is no longer Jew or Greek, there is no longer slave or free, there is no longer male and female; for all of you are one in Christ Jesus" (3:28). He emphasizes that this is the great equality that Christianity preaches and that is so needed amid all of the problems in El Salvador—the equality of the children of God. Second, in his commentaries, analyses, and assessments of the political reality around him, Romero harkens back repeatedly to the principle of participation as a key criterion in his assessment of development. He interprets this "sense of Participation" as a "sign of our Time," in which human beings have the right to participate in building up and working toward a common goal of the common good.[45] In his Sunday homily of March 5, 1978, Romero elaborates upon the message of *Octogesima Adveniens* and *Rerum Novarum* and their understanding of political participation.[46]

Second, along with the aspiration for equality is the commitment to this *participation* in creating a common good. Christians have a duty to

---

[42] H I, 212.
[43] H I, 230.
[44] H I, 239.
[45] H I, 186.
[46] H II, 279.

become politically involved,[47] since it is this participation that bears the fruit of pluralism. In his third pastoral letter, Romero vigorously defends the human right to "congregate" and join forces for a united front on particular issues, and backs up his arguments with references to the United Nations' Universal Declaration of Human Rights and *Pacem in Terris* 23.[48] Connected to participation is concern with dialogue. On January 2, 1980, he makes a plea for serious, open dialogue to seek the best possible and most peaceful solution to the conflict for the country as a whole. Here the Church acted as mediator between government and opposition, with Romero often finding himself directly involved. On January 27, 1980, Romero was still calling for a middle-of-the-road approach from both sides and the rejection of a polarized and blinkered mind-set; he was even discussing possible ways and means with the radical FPL (Fuerzas Populares de Liberación [Farabundo Martí]), which was "greatly feared" and responsible for a series of abductions. On February 21 he notes in his diary, "We have been able to enter into dialogue with them for the purpose of expressing the views and the thinking of the Church and to make them understand that the respect for these Christian sentiments of the majority of the people would be a necessary condition for them to have the popularity they lack now, when they are attacking these feelings."[49] A commitment to inclusive participation rings through Romero's approach to processes of political deliberation.

A third criterion for the archbishop was the *preferential option for the poor*. Romero frequently refers back to Medellín, as in his second pastoral letter regarding an option for the poor[50] or again in his third pastoral letter.[51] He focuses on Medellín whether he is addressing social issues or a "sinful situation."[52] He reminds his flock to keep an eye on the proper balance between rights and obligation—in other words, to also consider the obligations of the poor themselves.[53] A destructive sense of inertia (*acedia*) and futility only intensifies the existing injustices of the poor. Romero pinpointed this trap in his homily for the Feast of the Divine Saviour of the World on August 6, 1977.[54]

The preferential option for the poor is a theme that runs through all of Romero's thoughts and writings. It is expressed particularly strongly

---

[47] H II, 280.
[48] VV, 90.
[49] ORD, 498.
[50] VV, 66.
[51] VV, 93.
[52] H I, 217.
[53] VV, 98.
[54] See H I, 233.

in the closing lines of his address of acceptance for an honorary degree awarded by the University of Louvain in Belgium: "Early Christians used to say *Gloria Dei, vivens homo* ('the glory of God is the living person'). We could make this more concrete by saying *Gloria Dei, vivens Pauper* ('the glory of God is the living poor person')."[55] He mentioned the 1979 bishops' conference at Puebla, Mexico—first in February 1980 during a lecture in Louvain, in which he reiterated the importance of the option for the poor,[56] and again one week later in a letter to President Carter, in which he underlined his views with regard to US intervention and demanded of the president, "To forbid that military aid be given to the Salvadoran government; To guarantee that your government will not intervene directly or indirectly, with military, economic, diplomatic, or other pressures, in determining the destiny of the Salvadoran people." Romero continued, "It would be to violate a right that the Latin American bishops, meeting at Puebla, recognized publicly when we spoke of 'the legitimate self-determination of our peoples, which allows them to organize according to their own spirit and the course of their history and to cooperate in a new international order.'"[57] Such rights are rooted in the here and now, in this life in this world; Christianity calls upon all people to "collaborate" to work toward a humane life fit for all human beings, especially the poor and disadvantaged. Part of a preferential option for the poor is also a realism about human needs; the reality of material goods is something to be taken seriously. As human beings we cannot survive without these material goods, and such goods obviously need to supervised and distributed in some way,[58] particularly because human suffering is not God's will and happiness is not something to be obtained only in the afterlife. Romero quotes *Gaudium et Spes* 43: "The Christian who neglects his temporal duties, neglects his duties toward his neighbor and even God, and jeopardizes his eternal salvation."[59]

A fourth key criterion used by Archbishop Romero to read and judge the signs of the times was the *common good*, a major theme in his writing. The common good as the raison d'être of the government becomes the primary point of reference to judge political leadership decisions. On January 1, 1980, Romero noted in his diary that he needs to admonish government officials and civil servants to remember that they are serving the people and should think of the people for whom they are working.[60] A

---
[55] VV, 187.
[56] VV, 179.
[57] VV, 190.
[58] H I, 314.
[59] H I, 269.
[60] ORD, 430.

clear reference point is vital if any notion of social welfare is to be given any political credence. Making inroads into social welfare comes at a cost and personal sacrifice; this was the message Romero conveyed to Rubén Zamora, the Christian Democrat leader who came to visit Romero on January 11, 1980, "in a private capacity looking for a little strengthening, for comfort and guidance.... I tried to tell him how, as a man of faith and of hope, he has to serve the country generously and accept the difficulties and risks with the right intention."[61]

Perhaps the most outstanding and memorable example of how political reality should be perceived through a common-good lens is in the homily Romero gave on March 9, 1980, the third Sunday in Lent, voicing his own analysis of the government's reform proposals and the nationalization of the banks. He draws his listeners' attention to the agricultural land reform program:

> The appropriation of land has begun and land holdings greater than 500 hectares are being taken over.... This new law no longer allows a small minority to possess all the land and these individuals will receive payment for the land that is being taken from them and this is only just. This law is not drastic and demonstrates that this reform is being carried out according to a moderate capitalist plan.

So far, so good, in Romero's view. However, he does have his doubts about whether these reforms go far enough and will be successful in accomplishing their goals:

> If these reforms are unable to establish means that will stop the repression of the *campesinos* and if these same reforms are not supported by the people ... then these reforms will not resolve any problem and their failure will become another reality.... We hope that the good elements of this reform are preserved and that the doubtful and dangerous elements are eliminated.

Romero was addressing the overriding issue of procedural justice. A problem lies in the fact that the majority of the population hardest hit by these reforms had not been consulted in any way, shape, or form; in other words, they have had no say in the political process. Romero concluded, "There are some serious doubts about this process.... What is the meaning of these reforms in the general plan of the government?" Making this argument even more valid is the context: "One of the essential elements

---

[61]ORD, 442.

... appears to be bloody and deadly repression of those who propose a different national plan." He goes on to say that people who are opposed to the official plan should not automatically be treated as enemies, which long term would "lead to a systematic militarization of the Republic through a series of militarized estates. Thus we see the very real possibility of systematic control that would involve repression and spying, actions directed against the popular forces." Romero's analysis is based on the application of criteria for the common good, an option for the poor, and universal participation, so that a liveable reality for all can be achieved.

A fifth criterion Romero used was the *kingdom of God*: "Our duty as Church is to keep hope alive,"[62] to live in the here and now even though this sometimes demands us to be citizens of two worlds—being in the world but not of this world. In proclaiming the kingdom of God, the Church is taking a positive stance. In his work "Signs of the Times," Romero clearly defines what he means by a system of values such as those found in Catholic Social Teaching documents, and he makes a political analysis primarily focused on the kingdom of God. What stands out most in his analysis is the strong orientation toward the commonweal and an option for the poor. In addition, Romero sees private property as having a social function.[63]

Jon Sobrino lays out the four principles on which Romero builds his appraisal of the national reality:

> 1. The church is not the same thing as the Kingdom of God; it is the servant of the Kingdom.... 2. The poor are those for whom the Kingdom is primarily intended.... 3. As the servant of the Kingdom, the church ought also promote the values of the members of the Kingdom, both while the new society is being built up and when it is at length achieved.... 4. For the church in any way to impede or thwart either the Kingdom of God or the members of the Kingdom is sinful.[64]

The kingdom of God is a perspective that allows us to see social realities in a sacramental way, in a way that connects the visible with the invisible, the tangible with the intangible, the material with the spiritual.

A sixth criterion is probing for *truth*. The Church is intent on getting to the bottom of crimes and bringing facts (and fake facts) to light in

---

[62]ORD, 453; "nuestro deber como Iglesia es mantener esperanza" (Romero, *Su Diario*, 364).

[63]H I, 325; H II, 266–67.

[64]J. Sobrino, *Archbishop Romero: Memories and Reflections*, trans. R. R. Barr (Maryknoll, NY: Orbis Books, 1990), 84–85.

order to render well-informed judgments.[65] Meetings of the Priests' Senate must be held "more frequently in order to analyze the very difficult situation of the country and how to carry out the mission of the Church in the best way possible—a very frank analysis."[66] This analysis is pursued in the light of the kingdom of God and therefore is not affiliated to any particular political side. Analyzing the politics of the situation requires evidence provided by the social sciences. In view of the escalating political situation, Romero called a meeting on February 22, 1980: "A pre-revolutionary situation exists in El Salvador, but it is progressing rapidly toward a revolutionary phase."[67] The voice and presence of truth are imperative. The situation is delicate and dangerous, like an incendiary device. The Church asks that "the saner part of the government" help to create the credibility so desperately needed for progress of any kind to be made. The Church wants "nothing more than to cooperate with transformations that will benefit the poor," but "cannot cooperate with a project in which there is, at the same time, the reality of repression."[68] The commitment to reality and truth is a motif that Ignacio Ellacuría—rector of the University of Central America (UCA), with whom Archbishop Romero worked closely—also forcefully proposed. Both Ellacuría and Romero were committed to understanding history in theological terms and theology in historical terms. In an influential contribution from 1975, two years before Romero became archbishop of San Salvador, Ellacuría described three ways to engage reality: being present within and thus aware of reality, comprehending reality ethically, and acting accordingly.[69] This is close to the "see-judge-act" scheme. The second step is clearly the stage for engaging Catholic Social Teaching explicitly—for the sake of action and social transformation. Ellacuría deeply respected Archbishop Romero, as his essay "Monseñor Romero" shows, where he again discusses salvation as a historical process.[70] Truth, then, becomes both "incarnational" (Christ) and historical (reality).

A seventh and final criterion is *peacefulness*—that is, "a solution that is not based on blood, hate or violence," Romero wrote on January 26, 1980;[71] any solution arrived at via gunfire and bloodshed is untenable.

---

[65] On January 22, 1980, Romero noted the perplexing state of affairs: "The truth is very confused. As for the Church, we have calmly begun an investigation in order to make an informed judgment" (ORD, 455).
[66] ORD, 459.
[67] ORD, 499.
[68] Ibid.
[69] I. Ellacuría, "Laying the Philosophical Foundations of Latin American Theological Method," in *I. Ellacuría: Essays on History, Liberation, and Salvation*, ed. Michael E. Lee (Maryknoll, NY: Orbis Books, 2013), 63–91.
[70] I. Ellacuría, "Monseñor Romero: One Sent by God to Save His People," in ibid., 285–92.
[71] ORD, 461.

Again and again, Romero spoke out against violence, his views firmly rooted in the tradition of Catholic Social Teaching.[72] His strong stance against violence creates yet another source of moral clarity for Romero, who does arrive, even though the issues are complicated and the deliberations multilateral, at clear positions. Indeed, his clear position against violence probably signed his death sentence, when he exhorted soldiers to turn to their consciences and disobey immoral orders to kill in his last Sunday homily on March 23, 1980.

Romero offered his "examinations of the collective conscience" in conversation with the reference points of equality, participation, the option for the poor, the common good, the kingdom of God, truth, and peacefulness. These criteria underlying Romero's analyses become ever more pronounced, especially in the last months of his life. In the three months preceding that tragic event, he voiced a tangible intensity in his life through his personal diary and in his last homilies; both bear witness to the way he himself experienced the political situation in El Salvador, and at the same time tried to assess and explain it along the lines of Catholic Social Teaching. James Brockman characterized those final weeks as follows:

> Romero's last Sunday homilies are among his most memorable. The country's growing violence, the disappearance of alternatives to violence, his anguished, driven response, and his growing realization that the violence would almost surely touch his own person, as it had struck so many friends, so many of his priests and co-workers—all this gave his words an eloquence that drew frequent applause from his hearers.[73]

Romero is an exceptional and exemplary model of the interiorization of social teaching, because in consciously setting out to pursue a particular path, he appropriates Catholic Social Teaching in his own individual way, as only he could approach and adopt it. To my mind, two elements define his style: hermeneutic coincidence and transfigurative political analysis.

Hermeneutic coincidence is the conviction that an exegesis of biblical texts will yield fruit if the conditions described clearly correlate with the situation in the here and now; semantic coincidental circumstances can be perceived as if the text were speaking directly to us here in the present. Applying biblical texts to the here and now is that fine thread weaving its way through all of Romero's writings—right up to his homily of February 24, 1980 ("Lent: God's Saving Plan in History"), in which he

---

[72]E.g., Paul VI, *Populorum Progressio*, "On the Development of Peoples" (1967), nos. 30–31, hereinafter *PP*.

[73]J. R. Brockman, *Romero: A Life* (Maryknoll, NY: Orbis Books, 1990), 229.

elaborated on his reading of Deuteronomy 26:4–10, which underlines the significance and power of Israel's creed: "Israel's faith was the faith of its political life. Faith and political life were turned into a single act of love for the Lord. Their political life breathed God's graces and promises." He went on to say that the people of El Salvador have the same duty to God, a duty that brings them closer to God and illuminates their political path. Here, Romero is clearly shedding light on the delicate relationship between faith and politics.

On March 9 of the same year, for Lent, Romero continued his key message: that the history of El Salvador is a vehicle for God's plan. Thus we see a hermeneutic coincidence in the situation of Israel compared with the situation of El Salvador—they are not so very different and are united in God's plan for salvation. "What would Jesus do if he were living in 1977, in El Salvador today?" is the question from which Romero built his homilies for 1977.[74] He placed great emphasis on the Gospels not being read as bedtime stories of a distant land in a long-ago time, but as events happening now, in the present, in El Salvador; in other words, they need to be transferred and transformed,[75] and in doing so they become sources of our own epiphany and hope. When Romero employs Galatians 6:14, he is doing so on behalf of all those faithful to the Church in El Salvador;[76] when he quotes Luke 9:18, he is transforming its message to take it directly to the people: "Who do Salvadorians say that I am?"[77] The prophetic mission of the Church in El Salvador is directly juxtaposed to the words and deeds of Jeremiah,[78] and, too, those of Habakkuk[79] and Amos in their contemporary relevance: "Sisters and brothers, do you not believe that this reality is here, among us now in 1977, even if the text is referring to a situation which happened centuries ago?"[80] Romero conveyed the love of land expressed in the Bible and transformed it into a prophetic message for and in the present,[81] describing Jesus of Nazareth as an "authentic patriot."[82] Such expressive statements ratify the union of love of land and love of the Word. The Beatitudes become a model of understanding and, indeed, a roadmap for farmers working toward a better world.[83]

---

[74] H I, 248.
[75] H II, 153.
[76] H I, 177.
[77] H I, 231.
[78] H I, 254.
[79] H I, 347.
[80] H I, 325.
[81] H II, 172.
[82] H II, 314.
[83] H II, 229.

Romero aptly applied the message and meaning of "Blessed are the peacemakers" (Mt 5:9) to the "peacelessness" holding sway in El Salvador.[84] Similarly, he united Moses's song of praise and thanks to God—for having led his people out of Egypt and saving them from the pursuing Egyptian army—with a long-term perspective.[85] Romero returned to this theme of exodus on February 2, 1980, in his last great address, given at Louvain University on his being awarded an honorary doctorate. He quoted Exodus 3:9, calling it the starting point of a new way of looking at the world.[86] Biblical texts not only provide a means and source of prophetic criticism, as we can see here in the Exodus example, but also a source of mystic hope and life-shaping exhortations, as in the direct application of 2 Timothy 1:7–8 to the circumstances of the people in El Salvador.[87] These dynamics of applying biblical texts to contemporary circumstances can be found in many of Romero's constructions, for example, when he employed the parable of the Good Samaritan to illustrate his deeper perspective of the country.[88] Hence we see a fertile dialogue between biblical sources and political analysis, which makes the Bible politically relevant and the political analysis sacramental. This is also true for Romero's reading of the transfiguration.

The second aspect of Romero's personal style that I would like to point out is the *transfigurative political analysis* he offers. His analysis of the immediate social and political situation is one of transfiguration; it is not descriptive ("things are") and it is not normative ("things should be"), but dependent on Divine Grace rather than human intervention to transform reality. Such an approach allows for the completely unexpected if and when it should arise ("things could be"), and expresses a willingness to become involved in the transformation process no matter what the cost.[89] This is an analysis firmly rooted in faith—in the gospel and in the word of the gospel that allows the political reality to become flesh. In a July 2, 1978, homily, Romero reminded listeners that actions speak louder than words, and he underscored the enormity of "transforming" words into acts, which sounds much, much easier than it is in reality: "To follow faithfully the Pope's magisterium in theory is very easy. But when you try to live those saving teachings, try to incarnate them, try to make

---

[84] H I, 178.
[85] Ex 15:1–18; H I, 246.
[86] VV, 179.
[87] H I, 352.
[88] H II, 342–43.
[89] This corresponds to Romero's theology of transfiguration, which also embraces our understanding of the Passion of Christ. See M. Pfeil, "Oscar Romero's Theology of Transfiguration," *Theological Studies* 72 (2011): 87–115.

them reality in the history of a suffering people like ours—that is when conflicts arise. Not that I have been unfaithful . . . Never!"[90]

Romero's reading of a situation or set of circumstances is not a political one; rather, it is based on a firsthand pastoral understanding of the context. The nation should be like the antechamber to the kingdom of God, he stated in his homily of February 24, 1980. In other words, the kingdom of God stretches straight into the political here and now. The narrative of a country is indivisible from the narrative of salvation, and this narrative and indeed the history of salvation are inseparable from the historical events taking place in El Salvador. "Conversion" becomes a political category when, in the same homily, Romero talks about the need for fighting forces on both sides of the war to "turn around" and repent; he repeated this same message just two weeks later.

In his homily of January 13, 1980, Romero reminded his congregation that Christians are citizens of two worlds: "Baptism makes citizens of a nation on earth citizens of the kingdom of God." This is a clear statement based on a theological cornerstone that enables a sacramental perspective of reality. As Christians and citizens of nations on earth we are duty-bound to embrace and avail ourselves of every aspect of reality this world can provide in our work toward the common good. At the same time, of course, our view of the reality of this world is guided by an overriding sense of sanctity and the knowledge that our priority is to work toward the kingdom of God. The criteria laid down in the Gospels should likewise guide political thinking and judgment, which of course also means that the common good is the focus of all decision-making, not swayed by the interests of one particular group or section of the population. Analysis of the spirit of the gospel message should not be one of emotional reaction or indeed of fear; it should be a concerted effort to see and understand objectively. The human person in his and her completeness and development must be at the heart of such analysis, as Romero declared in his homily of January 20, 1980. This analysis is also the main message of his homily ("God Invites Us to Build Our History with Him") a few weeks later, on February 10, emphasizing that the gospel message is not something we can twist and bend until it fits our needs; it is a shield, certainly not to hide behind but to assist us in our battle to overcome our own indifference toward others.

Bearing the criterion of participation in mind, Romero adopted similar

---

[90] "Es fácil predicar teóricamente sus enseñanzas, seguir fielmente el magisterio del Papa en teoría. ¡Es muy fácil! Pero cuando se trata de vivir, cuando se trata de encarnar, cuando se trata de hacer realidad en la historia de un pueblo sufrido como el nuestro esas enseñanzas salvadores, es cuando surgen los conflictos."

measures in his assessment of the nationalization of the country's banks. This reform would hit the oligarchs hard, and the draft reform bill brought with it two possible problems: "First, it is part of a more general plan which is supported by the United States and includes repression," which is unacceptable if people remember the Catholic Social Teaching principles of subsidiarity, participation, and human dignity. "Second, it runs the risk of being carried out in such a way that the majority of people receive no benefit from this reform," which would be a breach of the common-good criterion. Romero remained understandably cautious; he allowed that while both measures might be productive, reform would only come about if repressive measures are abandoned and replaced by dialogue. One week later, Romero continued with his transfigurative analysis of the planned land reform by highlighting the theological significance of "land," for example, by referring to the promised land (Jos 5:9a, 10–11).[91] He went on to emphasize the necessity of land reform, since it is not theologically tenable that the land of an entire nation be held in the hands of a small minority. As land is God-given and therefore holy, it should be used in such a way as to bring human beings closer to God. Romero's analyses ultimately come down to the human relationship with God, and in his fifth and final Lenten homily on March 23 of the same year, he pointed out that structural or social sin cannot be divorced from—or discussed as though it had nothing to do with—personal sin. They go hand in hand.

In his Sunday homilies, Romero put forward his analysis of the political situation of his home country by reading reality with a sacramental perspective, or in other words, unifying the tangible with the intangible. This perspective allows circumstances and contexts to be seen in a new light, to be to a certain extent "transfigured," since at the end of the day, it is not about *having* more of something but *being* more of something.[92] Earthly reality is viewed through the lens of faith and with the perspective of Christ (resurrected, ascended, and seated at the right hand of God, the Father).[93]

Looking ahead to the final judgment is a perspective that only faith can offer; Romero was convinced that in God's final judgment of humanity, not only would individual deeds and conduct be held to account, but social and structural trespasses would be as well.[94] The injustices in El Salvador, the torture and the suppression, and the betrayal of the common good

---

[91] Romero approached the issues of land reform as witness and reminder of the sacramental view—see M. P. Whelan, *Blood in the Fields: Óscar Romero, Catholic Social Teaching, and Land Reform* (Washington, DC: Catholic University of America Press, 2020), part 3.
[92] VV, 133.
[93] H I, 117.
[94] H I, 245.

are the expression and manifestation of sin and sinfulness,[95] and a secular analysis of such conduct does not have such categories at its disposal. It must be admitted that theological analysis does depend on social expertise; Romero mentioned *Populorum Progressio* 30, which bears witness to the sufferings of the country and puts the responsibility fairly and squarely at the door of terrorism, bloodshed, and social injustice.[96]

A transfigurative political analysis generates a deeper understanding of core concepts of ethical and political thinking, concepts such as "development," "peace," "poverty," and "liberation." In line with *Populorum Progressio* 19, development has important moral and ethical aspects that cannot be overlooked; in the Christian understanding of the word, development is a gift from God, to be transformed into hope of a transcendental God.[97] Toxic *avaritia* (greed) stands in the way of development, as outlined in *Populorum Progressio* 18,[98] and the development of humanity depends on the development of individual human understanding.[99] Authentic development, according to *Populorum Progressio* 14, is the development of the individual in her entirety.[100] This is the lens through which Romero reads the written word of God.[101] The Church has to take a global perspective on human development, according to Romero; a national view does not suffice.[102] Mainly focused on being in harmony with God's Divine Plan,[103] "peace" is the fruit of justice.[104] "Poverty" is an aspirational, ideal condition as seen through the lens of Christianity, rather than the poverty commonly witnessed on the streets that is the result of injustice.[105]

A transfigurative political analysis looks at political realities with a sacramental view of life in mind—what is happening "on the outside" and "in this life" is inextricably linked to what is "happening in people's interior lives" and "in the life yet to come."

Particularly in the last months of his life, Romero emphasized the meaning of hope and employed his homilies as the medium to put forward this message. It is an expression of a sacramental view of things, to be

---

[95] H I, 171.
[96] H II, 234.
[97] H I, 221.
[98] H II, 224.
[99] H II, 201.
[100] H I, 359.
[101] As on October 9, 1977, when he addressed 2 Cor 5:14–17; 2 Tim 2:8–13; and Lk 17:11–19.
[102] H II, 181.
[103] H I, 251.
[104] H I, 178.
[105] H I, 301.

able to see and find hope in situations that according to purely human categories are absolutely irresolvable. The blood shed by the people—the message of his homily on the second Sunday in 1980—is united with the blood of Christ, and thus paves the way to resurrection. Lent is the time of transfiguration, and Jesus ascending Mount Tabor is a powerful sign of liberation—which is basically what transfiguration is all about. Hope is at the heart of his very last homily on March 24, 1980. In this Mass on the first anniversary of the death of a friend's mother, he reflected upon the necessity for death in making life possible: "The harvest comes about only because it dies, allowing itself to be sacrificed in the earth and destroyed. Only by undoing itself does it produce the harvest." In words that perhaps more than any others are his legacy, he quoted a passage in *Gaudium et Spes* focusing on the creation, and the kingdom of God in this life and the next,[106] and then added: "This is the hope that inspires us as Christians. We know in our hearts that all human effort to make the world a better place, to change a world in which injustice and sin are so deeply ingrained, is both desired and blessed by God."[107] This hope gave Romero life and empowered him in his mission.

***

As I have tried to show, Archbishop Romero developed his own style with regard to the application of social teaching. He spoke the language of social teaching fluently—and perhaps here we are reminded of Iris Murdoch's observations about language learning, which she concedes is an exercise in humility; in order to learn any language, one needs to know the rules and the grammar if one wishes to speak it fluently. Romero was a strong believer in loyalty and commitment to the Church. On January 28, 1980, he described his last visit to Rome as a returning to the cradle, as coming home, as going back to the source—the source, heart, and mind of the Church.[108] He worked for balance in all things, especially balance between striving for social justice and commitment to the mission of the Church, and he outlined this balance in his last meeting with Pope John Paul II on

---

[106] John XXIII, *Gaudium et Spes*, "Pastoral Constitution on the Church in the Modern World" (1965), no. 39, hereinafter GS.

[107] "Esta es la esperanza que nos alienta a los cristianos. Sabemos que todo esfuerzo por mejorar una sociedad, sobre todo cuando está tan metida en la injusticia y en el pecado, es un esfuerzo que Dios bendice, que Dios quiere y que Dios nos exige."

[108] "Rome for me means a return to the cradle, going home, returning to the source, to the heart, the brain of our Church. I have asked the Lord to preserve my faith and my loyalty to Rome, which Christ chose to be the seat of the universal pastor, the pope" (ORD, 464) ["Roma significa para mí volver a la cuna, al hogar, a la fuente, al corazón, al cerebro de nuestra Iglesia] (Romero, *Su Diario*, 374).

January 30, 1980. Romero saw social teaching as a tangible expression of this balance between social justice and commitment to the Church, between serving this world and the kingdom of God. He made use of the Gospels and other biblical sources to identify certain political realities as social and spiritual pathologies, and he used Catholic Social Teaching to address them. Catholic Social Teaching became his rule of life that inspired his engagement with biblical texts and shaped his political judgments.

Romero lived each day as archbishop of San Salvador in light of Catholic Social Teaching, appropriating it as his *"regula vitae."* He also made use of this *regula* to address problems or pathologies, offering a therapeutic reading of Catholic Social Teaching. This is the second aspect of social teaching that I would like to highlight in this chapter: Catholic Social Teaching as diagnosis of and therapy for social pathologies.

Catholic Social Teaching as "Therapy"

One important task of any social analysis is a diagnosis of social pathologies. Archbishop Romero identified a number of social pathologies during his three years as archbishop of San Salvador. He found a language to name them and analytical tools to interpret them. Social philosophy has paid considerable attention to such pathologies as well. The Frankfurt School of philosophy, to give a prominent example, has analyzed and reconstructed social pathologies through Theodor Adorno's analysis of the "administered world" and bureaucracy, Herbert Marcuse's concept of the one-dimensional man, and Jürgen Habermas's reconstruction of the colonization of life-worlds. Axel Honneth, the most prominent voice in the discourse on social pathologies, uses the Marxist category of "alienation" (from oneself, from the product of one's labor, from fellow humans) as an analytical tool to pinpoint social pathologies and, following a reading of Rousseau, whom he credits with founding social philosophy, the erosion of self-presentation and the virtue of compassion.[109] Honneth's reading of social pathologies refers to pathological deformations of life-worlds that undermine the possibility of self-realization and flourishing, that is, contaminated sources of recognition. By using a medical metaphor,[110] Honneth is compelled to introduce a concept of "normal" ("healthy") versus "abnormal" ("pathological") development. Social pathologies are

---

[109]A. Honneth, *Disrespect: The Normative Foundations of Critical Theory* (Cambridge: Polity, 2007), 10 and 14.

[110]See A. Honneth, *The Struggle for Recognition: The Moral Grammar of Social Conflicts*, trans. J. Anderson (Cambridge: Polity, 1995), 135.

forms of social suffering and destructive forms of social development that inhibit human flourishing.

According to Christoph Zurn's reconstruction of Honneth's approach, such pathologies operate "by means of second-order disorders, that is, by means of constitutive disconnects between first-order contents and second-order reflexive comprehension of those contents, where those disconnects are pervasive and socially caused."[111] Here again, we are made aware of the incongruity between levels of experience and levels of reflexivity. This analysis views a social pathology in terms of "ideology," that is, as false beliefs on a first-order level connected with the social inability to identify (let alone satisfy) the need for reflexivity on a second-order level. A social pathology prevents a person from understanding the mechanisms that caused it; the person experiences something and is unable to categorize it because of conditions that shape both experience and reflection. When we understand human dignity as a form of life and as a way of "seeing" the world, we can understand the extent and gravity of the challenge we face: social pathologies deprive the persons living under those conditions of the possibility of seeing their toxic living conditions as toxic. People get used to degradation, humiliation, and dehumanization.

The diagnosis and analysis of social pathologies can be seen as the proper place for social philosophy insofar as "Social philosophy is primarily concerned with determining and discussing processes of social development that can be viewed as misdevelopments (*Fehlentwicklungen*), disorders or 'social pathologies.'"[112] Prominent misdevelopments can be traced in phenomena such as loss of community, denigration of cultural practices, cultural impoverishment, and denial of equal rights. Social lifeworlds become desolate and devoid of meaning; erosions of *Self*, perversions of the *Social*, and distortions of *Reason* emerge as three prominent forms of social pathologies in the philosophy of the Frankfurt School.

These considerations are clearly relevant for theology; there may even be a specific place for social theology and Catholic Social Tradition in the realm of social analysis. Social philosophy primarily deals with social pathologies in a diagnostic manner. Social theology, with its basis in communities and practices, may be in a different position to offer a contribution.

---

[111] C. F. Zurn, "Social Pathologies as Second-Order Disorders," in D. Petherbridge, ed., *Axel Honneth: Critical Essays* (Leiden: Brill, 2011), 345–70, at 345–46. In Honneth's rejoinder in the same volume (417f), he accepts this analysis as exceptionally fruitful. A more basic reconstruction of Honneth's concept of social pathologies is provided by Jean-Philippe Deranty, *Beyond Communication: A Critical Study of Axel Honneth's Social Philosophy* (Leiden: Brill, 2009), 319–24.

[112] Honneth, *Disrespect*, 4. Social pathologies are developments that prevent members of society from having a "good life" (ibid.). Social philosophy emerged as a representative of an ethical perspective in the territory of society (ibid., 33).

With this foundation, social theology and Catholic Social Teaching can move in the direction of therapy. I suggest that social theology in general and Catholic Social Teaching in particular offer therapeutic responses to social pathologies by stretching and deepening the social and political imagination—through a moral imagination shaped by a commitment to a deep practice of human dignity.

A Therapeutic Reading of Catholic Social Teaching Documents

Catholic Social Tradition has responded to "the wounds of the time" over the centuries; the first official social encyclical. *Rerum Novarum* (1891), reacted to the plight of workers and their miserable working conditions.[113] Catholic Social Teaching differs from a social-philosophical construction of social pathologies by

- Being an instrument of evangelization, with a clear commitment to transformation and pastoral concerns.[114]
- Basing its claims on theological and not merely philosophical grounds[115] by acknowledging biblical revelation and the tradition of the Church as normative sources.[116]
- Referring to a form of life and particular social practices grounded in the Church.

Catholic Social Tradition transcends the boundaries of analysis, and although social analysis may be part of Catholic Social Teaching documents, it is not an exercise in descriptive or reconstructive social hermeneutics. Catholic Social Teaching is theological reflection and instruction as much as it is part of the mission of the Church.[117] As an element of the Catholic magisterium, Catholic Social Teaching documents share its therapeutic

---

[113] Leo XIII, *Rerum Novarum*, "Rights and Duties of Capital and Labor" (1891), hereinafter *RN*.

[114] See Cardinal Angelo Sodano's letter to Cardinal Renato Martino of June 29, 2004 (N. 559.332) on the status of Catholic Social Teaching; Pontifical Council for Justice and Peace, *Compendium of the Social Doctrine of the Church* (2004), 10, and chap. 2, hereinafter *CSDC*.

[115] *CSDC* 72; John Paul II, *Sollicitudo Rei Socialis*, "On Social Concerns" (1987), no. 41, hereinafter *SRS*.

[116] *CSDC* 74.

[117] In order to understand the nature of Catholic Social Teaching documents one, needs to offer a (missiological) ecclesiology. See S. Bevans and R. Schroeder, *Constants in Context: A Theology of Mission for Today* (Maryknoll, NY: Orbis Books, 2004), 10–31 (describing the idea that the Church is missionary by its very nature).

dimension, in which the magisterium is seen in the light of a soteriological and sacramental understanding of the Church.[118] The magisterium is a "remedium" to help a person see the truth; doctrinal clarifications have an existential, life-guiding, pastoral dimension.[119] Seen thus, Catholic Social Teaching documents have a curative aspiration.

I suggest exploring a therapeutic reading of Catholic Social Teaching documents based on three assumptions:

- Catholic Social Teaching documents can be framed as "exhortative language games," that is, as language games whose rules demand that the boundaries of speech be transcended in order to enter the realm of human action.
- Catholic Social Teaching propositions can be interpreted as *"wichtige Sätze"* (existential propositions) in Bernard Bolzano's sense, that is, as propositions that exercise a systematic influence on personal virtue-building and the good life.[120]
- On the basis of the first two assumptions, Catholic Social Teaching documents can be seen as a means of fighting social pathologies.

These three assumptions help us to identify the specific contribution of Catholic Social Teaching documents to the healing of social pathologies. What can Catholic Social Teaching contribute to the prevention, al-

---

[118]See, for example, Paul VI, *Lumen Gentium*, "The Dogmatic Constitution on the Church" (1964), no. 1, hereinafter *LG*; Paul VI, *Dei Verbum*, "The Dogmatic Constitution on Divine Revelation" (1965), no. 10, hereinafter *DV*.

[119]Elmar Klinger puts forward a pastoral reading of doctrinal texts in the light of the Second Vatican Council and pleads for a connection between dogma and ministry; see E. Klinger, "Der Glaube des Konzils," in E. Klinger and K. Wittstadt, eds., *Glaube im Prozeß: Christsein nach dem II. Vatikanum* (Freiburg: Herder, 1984), 615–26, at 615. A similar connection is suggested by Gerhard Stanke, *Freiheit und religiöser Gehorsam des Willens und des Verstandes: Zum Verhältnis von Gewissen und kirchlichem Lehramt* (Frankfurt/Main: Josef Knecht, 1993), 22–23. The International Theological Commission suggested in its 1989 document "The Interpretation of Dogma" (with reference to *LG* 25) that the Second Vatican Council provides a "valorization of the pastoral character of the Magisterium" by calling the bishops "to be primarily the heralds of the Gospel," thus subordinating their role of teachers to that as evangelists (II.2). Number II.4 of the same document states, "The Magisterium in practice should tend towards realizing her own pastoral character. Her task of witnessing authentically to the truth of Jesus Christ is at the heart of the larger mission of the care of souls. With this pastoral character in mind, the Magisterium will meet with prudence and judgment new social, political and ecclesial problems."

[120]Bolzano sees *wichtige Sätze* as having a general and systematic influence on virtue and eternal happiness (Bolzano, *Lehrbuch der Religionswissenschaft. Teil I.* [Stuttgart: Frommann Holzboog, 1994], 49–50; see also E. Morscher, "Bolzanos Logik der Religion," in W. Löffler, ed., *Bernard Bolzanos Religionsphilosophie und Theologie* (St. Augustin: Academia, 2002), 35–90, at 50–51. With Catholic Social Teaching propositions in mind, it makes sense to transcend Bolzano's individualized account and introduce a social dimension.

leviation, or eradication of social pathologies? As occasion-based texts, Catholic Social Teaching documents confront "illnesses of a time" and provide a particular reading of challenging signs of the times; they set out to change the way issues are looked at, such as an invitation to rethink narrow concepts of "development"[121] or to reframe the relationship between minor and major structures.[122] The perspective of the authority behind Catholic Social Teaching documents is not the perspective of a neutral observer, but the perspective of an agent speaking in a mode of self-involvement. Catholic Social Teaching texts are "anchored" in the social practices of the Church, which themselves are meant to bring the "good news."

An important aspect of the good news is a deepening of the imagination. With such creative thinking, Catholic Social Teaching documents can be seen in the tradition of "therapeutic arguments,"[123] which offer a different way of framing experiences and events. It is consoling, for instance, to understand the connection between the ultimate horizon of a new heaven and a new earth and our engagement in this world now.[124] In some instances, the therapeutic analysis consists of showing a deeper sense of the tragedy of social pathologies by making use of concepts such as sin or human brokenness. One could even be tempted to say that Catholic Social Teaching provides a "wound of knowledge" that deepens the sense of social pathologies during therapy. A deep imagination of the social tragedies that we face may be necessary to create momentum for social change. "Imagination" is the capability to conceive of alternatives to the status quo or of possible or impossible states and circumstances; this capability involves a sense of the real (as a reference point for the construction of alternative worlds) and a sense of the possible. Immanuel Kant conceived of "imagination" as the faculty bridging understanding and sense, the faculty that can represent an object without sensing its presence intuitively.[125] The senses lack intellectual content, understanding lacks sensual content, and imagination connects the two. The "Catholic Social

---

[121] *PP* 14–15.

[122] Pius XI, *Quadregesimo Anno*, "On Reconstruction of the Social Order" (1931), no. 79, hereinafter *QA*.

[123] Martha Nussbaum developed an understanding of therapeutic arguments in conversation with Stoic philosophers using a medical analogy; just as medicine stands for the body, philosophy stands for the soul (Nussbaum, "Therapeutic Arguments," in Nussbaum, *The Therapy of Desire: Theory and Practice in Hellenistic Ethics* [Princeton, NJ: Princeton University Press, 1994], 13–47). Therapeutic arguments express an attempt to change the outlook of a person, in that they provide a different way of framing experiences. They are instruments for a new way of looking at seemingly tragic or even hopeless experiences.

[124] See *GS* 39.

[125] Immanuel Kant, *Critique of Pure Reason*, B 151.

Imagination" connects a close reading of the signs of the times ("senses") with conceptions of alternatives to the status quo ("understanding"). *Laudato Si'* is an excellent example of a document that reads the present situation[126] and offers bold alternatives.[127]

The imagination is a powerful tool to rethink but also to re-form one's way of life. John Paul Lederach has characterized the moral imagination as a powerful way to transcend violence and to overcome destructive practices. Specifically, he sees the moral imagination as a way of weaving together different capacities:

> Stated simply, the moral imagination requires the capacity to imagine ourselves in a web of relationships that includes our enemies; the ability to sustain a paradoxical curiosity that embraces complexity without reliance on dualistic polarity; the fundamental belief in and pursuit of the creative act; and the acceptance of the inherent risk of stepping into the mystery of the unknown that lies beyond the far too familiar landscape of violence.[128]

The moral imagination, then, is a way to embrace complexity, paradox, creativity, and risk; it is a way to think beyond the established patterns of thought and to transcend established practices. The status quo is not left to have the final word. The moral imagination can be used to "imagine oneself into a new reality," in the way that a deep understanding of dignity and a commitment to a deep practice of human dignity can lead to moral and social transformations. The moral imagination, however, is not disconnected from realities and commitments; it is shaped by particular traditions and a particular way of life with its experiences and access to a particular range of examples. Looking at the Catholic Social Tradition we can say that the imagination is anchored in principles and faith commitments. The understanding of human dignity is based on ordering principles that "bind" imagination in a particular way, and create what could be called "bounded imagination," an imagination based on explicit commitments. A new kind of imagination, a refined "sense of possibilities"—especially possibilities with a normative force, insofar as they are acknowledged as points of orientation and direction—opens up a new way of "being in the world."[129]

---

[126] Francis, *Laudato Si'*, "On Care for Our Common Home" (2015), chapter 1, hereinafter *LS*.
[127] *LS* chapter 6.
[128] J. P. Lederach, *The Moral Imagination: The Art and Soul of Building Peace* (Oxford: Oxford University Press, 2005), 5.
[129] A moving example of these dynamics is the story of Shin Dong-hyuk, who was born

Catholic Social Teaching has shaped the Catholic imagination. In his apostolic exhortation *Evangelii Gaudium,* Pope Francis lays out a vision of ecclesial *metanoia.* The document has been read as a papal Magna Carta for Church reform. Whether this is the case or not, the document clearly develops a vision of what the Church should be and should do regarding the signs of the times. It cannot be denied that the tradition of Catholic Social Teaching has contributed to Pope Francis's ecclesiological imagination as manifested in the document.

Evangelii Gaudium explicitly recommends that the *Compendium of the Social Doctrine of the Church* be studied in depth.[130] One could entertain the assumption that key elements of Pope Francis's document on how to read the signs of the times could not have been expressed without the wealth of resources provided by Catholic Social Teaching. In particular, we can see the following ideas that were conceived within the Catholic Social Teaching tradition:

- The social dimension of redemption.[131]
- A concept of true development[132] and a broader and deeper vision of the good life beyond "dignified sustenance."[133]
- The need to draw practical conclusions[134] and a commitment to social change.[135]
- A connection between peace and the rights of peoples, and a social reading of human rights.[136]
- A sound definition of peace based on justice.[137]
- An understanding of the need to grow in solidarity.;[138]
- The concept of alienation leading to erosion of self and of solidarity.[139]

---

inside Camp 14, a huge political prison north of Pyongyang, the son of two prisoners. He was raised in the camp but was never given a sense of "context" or "alternatives"; only with the arrival of another inmate, who told him about the outside world and the possibility of escape, was his imagination ("sense of possibilities") triggered for the first time, with a whole new way of being in the world opening up before him (B. Harden, *Escape from Camp 14* [London: Pan Books, 2013].)

[130] *EG* 184.
[131] *EG* 178, referring to *CSDC* 52.
[132] *EG* 181, referring to *PP* 14.
[133] *EG* 192, referring to *Mater et Magistra* 3 (John XXIII, "On Christianity and Social Progress," 1961).
[134] *EG* 182, referring to *CSDC* 9.
[135] *EG* 183, referring to *CSDC* 12.
[136] *EG* 190, referring to *CSDC* 157.
[137] *EG* 219, referring to *PP* 76.
[138] *EG* 190, referring to *PP* 65.
[139] *EG* 196, referring to *Centesimus Annus* 41 (John Paul II, "On the Hundredth Anniversary [of Rerum Novarum]," 1991).

- The option for the poor as a theological category.[140]
- Charity as a principle for both micro and macro relationships.[141]
- An understanding of the state and its responsibility to promote the common good.[142]
- A vision of four central principles derived "from the pillars of the Church's social doctrine, which serve as 'primary and fundamental parameters of reference for interpreting and evaluating social phenomena' ";[143] these four principles are unpacked in the exhortation: time is greater than space, unity prevails over conflict, realities are more important than ideas, and the whole is greater than the parts.

So, clearly, Pope Francis's vision of the Church has been shaped by key ideas from the tradition of Catholic Social Teaching, ideas that form and widen the ecclesiological imagination. This imagination connects different languages, different sources, and different normative inputs. The "therapeutic imagination" offered by the Catholic Social Tradition to respond to social and political pathologies is nurtured by three main sources: (1) the experience of social realities such as social inequality, labor conditions, corruption, war, and poverty; (2) the doctrinal (theological and philosophical) approach making use of terms such as "subsidiarity," "common good," and "overdevelopment"; and (3) the biblical sources that have inspired and accompanied the Christian Social Tradition, which offers a specifically therapeutic response to social pathologies because of its foundation in the good news.

The Catholic Social Tradition has biblical roots that make it very clear that it is not a philosophy or a political program. The preferential option for the poor is not an abstract "difference principle," but a commitment to discipleship based on the fundamental praxis of Jesus, a praxis that is the foundation of forms of life that would not be possible without Jesus, the Christ. As teacher and healer, Jesus does not only show or model a way of life, he also enables a new way of life, that of discipleship. And this new way—based on the fundamental praxis of Jesus—was mentioned in the book of Acts in several places.[144]

The good news is not only the basis of Catholic Social Tradition; its teachings should also express and be good news in themselves. For instance, *Sollicitudo Rei Socialis* uses the pericope of poor Lazarus and the rich man from Luke 16 as the basis of a special attention to the weakest

---
[140]*EG* 198, referring to *SRS* 42.
[141]*EG* 205, referring to *Caritas in Veritate* 2 (Benedict XVI, "Charity in Truth," 2009).
[142]*EG* 240, referring to *CSDC* 168.
[143]*EG* 221, quoting *CSDC* 161.
[144]Acts 9:2; 22:4; 24:14.

members of the community.¹⁴⁵ This special attention to the poor is also based explicitly on the example of Jesus and "the program announced by Jesus himself in the synagogue at Nazareth, to 'preach good news to the poor . . . to proclaim release to the captives and recovery of sight to the blind, to set at liberty those who are oppressed, to proclaim the acceptable year of the Lord' (Luke 4:18–19)."¹⁴⁶ This is not just a quotation, but indeed an expression of Catholic Social Teaching.

Catholic Social Tradition is a therapeutic response to woundedness and vulnerability. We are wounded by life, as we should be. Paul Auster writes in *In the Country of Last Things*, mentioned in chapter 2 of this volume, about the vulnerability of encounter:

> What happens when you find yourself looking at a dead child, at a little girl lying in the street without any clothes on, her head crushed and covered with blood? What do you say to yourself then? It is not a simple matter, you see, to state flatly and without equivocation: "I am looking at a dead child." Your mind seems to balk at forming the words, you somehow cannot bring yourself to do it. For the thing before your eyes is not something you can very easily separate from yourself. That is what I mean by being wounded: you cannot merely see, for each thing somehow belongs to you, is part of the story unfolding inside you.¹⁴⁷

For good reasons Pope Francis has chosen to use for the Church the metaphor of a "field hospital." This image is a powerful one for the project of enacting Catholic Social Tradition.

The Church as Field Hospital

Pope Francis compares the Church to an army field hospital, one "that welcomes all those wounded by life." In reaffirming the mission of the Church in his Morning Meditation of February 5, 2015, he recalled, "A few times I have spoken of the Church as a field hospital: it's true! How many wounded there are, how many wounded! How many people who need their wounds to be healed!" There is a sense that the image of the field hospital emphasizes "compassion" and "accompaniment."¹⁴⁸ The field

---

¹⁴⁵ *SRS* 42.
¹⁴⁶ *SRS* 47.
¹⁴⁷ P. Auster, *In the Country of Last Things* (New York: Penguin, 1987), 19.
¹⁴⁸ See Francis, "Address to the Members of the Pontifical Commission for the Protection of Minors," September 21, 2017: "The Church is called to be a place of piety and compassion, especially for those who have suffered. For all of us, the Catholic Church continues

hospital metaphor is also linked to the ideas and values of reconciliation and forgiveness, as Pope Francis underlined in his homily in the Tokyo Dome on November 25, 2019, during his apostolic journey to Thailand and Japan: "The proclamation of the Gospel of Life urgently requires that we as a community become a field hospital, ready to heal wounds and to offer always a path of reconciliation and forgiveness. For the Christian, the only possible measure by which we can judge each person and situation is that of the Father's compassion for all his children." It is very clear that the theological foundation for this metaphor is divine love and the Church's mandate to live out (of) this love.[149]

A very tangible aspect of this metaphor is connected to actual medical services, which are one expression and an essential aspect of Catholic Social Tradition. In his message for the Twenty-Sixth World Day of the Sick 2018, Pope Francis illuminates this connection:

> In countries where health care systems are inadequate or non-existent, the Church seeks to do what she can to improve health, eliminate infant mortality and combat widespread disease. Everywhere she tries to provide care, even when she is not in a position to offer a cure. The image of the Church as a "field hospital" that welcomes all those wounded by life is a very concrete reality, for in some parts of the world, missionary and diocesan hospitals are the only institutions providing necessary care to the population.

The first time Pope Francis reflected upon this image was in an extraordinary interview with Antonio Spadaro, SJ, in August 2013. On announcing his resignation, Pope Benedict XVI had said, "The contemporary world is subject to rapid change and is grappling with issues of great importance for the life of faith." In turn, Pope Francis commented,

> The thing the Church needs most today is the ability to heal wounds and to warm the hearts of the faithful; it needs nearness, proximity. I see the Church as a field hospital after battle. It is useless to ask a seriously injured person if he has high cholesterol and about the level of his blood sugars! You have to heal his wounds.... And you have to start from the ground up.[150]

---

to be a field hospital that accompanies us on our spiritual journey. It is the place where we can sit with others, listen to them, and share with them our struggles and our faith in the Good News of Jesus Christ."

[149]See W. Cavanaugh, *Field Hospital: The Church's Engagement with a Wounded World* (Grand Rapids: Eerdmans, 2016).

[150]Antonio Spadaro, SJ, "A Big Heart Open to God: An Interview with Francis," conducted in several meetings in August 2013 and published in several Jesuit journals around

In his address to the parish priests of Rome on March 6, 2014, Pope Francis underscores the fine line between the medical treatment administered in a field hospital and that researched in a laboratory: "The priest is called to learn this, to have a heart that is moved. Priests who are—allow me to say the word—'aseptic,' those 'from the laboratory,' all clean and tidy, do not help the Church. Today we can think of the Church as a 'field hospital. . . . There are so many people . . . wounded by the world's illusions."

On September 19, 2014, in his address to the participants in a meeting sponsored by the Pontifical Council for Promoting New Evangelization, Pope Francis compared the on-the-ground work of a field hospital with that of the up-close-and-personal work of the Church in providing "closeness and warmth." He noted, "I have also said several times that the Church seems to me to be a field hospital: so many wounded people who ask us for closeness, who ask us for what they asked of Jesus: closeness, warmth. And with this attitude of the scribes, of the doctors of the law and of the Pharisees, we will never give a witness of closeness."

In his address to participants in the General Assembly of the Focolare Movement on September 26, 2014, Pope Francis drew draws his listeners' attention to two main obstacles to healing the wounded in a field hospital: quibbling over theological details and nitpicking. These are two "tempting" obstacles that stand in the way of our "going out" to do what needs to be done. While "we cannot be content with half measures, we cannot hesitate but . . . broaden our gaze." This condition of not being able to do justice to the mission at hand, of not being able to cope with the tasks the field hospital requires, comes up again in his homily during morning meditations in the Chapel of the Domus Sanctae Marthae on April 1, 2014. Pope Francis pinpointed the malaise of "spiritual *acedia*," which "cripples apostolic zeal" and "causes Christians to come to a standstill," and that of people following a culture of "formalism," that is, those people whose main concern and notion of "the Christian life" is reduced to "a matter of having all one's documents in order!"—so much so that "they close to [sic] the door to the grace of God."

In a keen message made in the run-up to World Health Day one week later, he went on to underline the dangers of blinkered vision, of a familiarity breeding contempt, which stalls the "apostolic zeal" that enables us to "draw near to so many wounded people in this field hospital, to those who often have been wounded by men and women in the Church." From Pope Francis's observations and exclamations it becomes clear that we are living in an age in which many people have been wounded in their daily

---

the world, including *La Civiltà Cattolica* and *America*.

lives. These people need assistance; the mission of the Church is to reach out and find these people, to treat them and help them get better. This can only be done on the spot; long-distance assistance does not work when a life is at stake. Such work requires a merciful mind-set, a compassionate eye for what is required in the here and now.

As the pope says, working in "physical proximity" means being physically present in the vicinity of the person needing help. This is not a stationary state, and it does not suggest immobility; in fact, it is quite the opposite. It is being mobile, on the move, going out, getting around, and making connections. Physical proximity means being there, in the midst, in the fray, which can only be done if the helper is on the spot; it can and must never be a long-distance diagnosis. Proximity work is in the here and now, and it is accepting and giving at the same time: the acceptance of what is, now, and giving of ourselves by being here, now. The capacity to see the fundamentals is honed by a compassionate eye. In his aforementioned September 19, 2014, address, Pope Francis emphasized that it is not about simply doing more, but about the quality of what one does:

> At times it seems that we are more concerned with redoubling activities than with being attentive to the people and their encounter with God. Pastoral care which does not pay attention to this becomes, little by little, sterile.

In *Evangelii Gaudium*, Pope Francis harkens back to a Doctor of the Church, Thomas Aquinas, quoting his assertion, "'In itself mercy is the greatest of the virtues, since all the others revolve around it and, more than this, it makes up for their deficiencies. This is particular to the superior virtue, and as such it is proper to God to have mercy, through which his omnipotence is manifested to the greatest degree.'"[151] There is no room here for distortion or reduction, or being "obsessed with the disjointed transmission of a multitude of doctrines to be insistently imposed."[152] We are invited to "see God in others and to go forth from ourselves to seek the good of others." Moreover, he continues, "If this invitation does not radiate forcefully and attractively, the edifice of the Church's moral teaching risks becoming a house of cards, and this is our greatest risk. It would mean that it is not the Gospel which is being preached, but certain doctrinal or moral points based on specific ideological options."[153]

---

[151] Thomas Aquinas, *Summa Theologiae* II-II, q. 30, a. 4 (quoted by Francis in *EG* 37).
[152] *EG* 36.
[153] *EG* 39.

"*Misericordia*" means having a heart for the poor and at the same time having a poor heart—the heart of a poor person. It all comes down to that core message, sharing with "the poor in spirit."

True mercy and compassion are "knowingly seeing"; they tug at the cords of cozy and convenient blindness born of a lackadaisical, lukewarm mind-set; an ingrained mentality of disinterest; and a refusal to get up and get involved. Compassion is none of these; compassion is the "fragrance" found in love and respect, the deep desire to see and know and the effort this requires. Compassion drives us to divine the essential and discard the inessential, to no longer differentiate between doer and deed. The compassionate gaze is neither blurred nor bleary-eyed; it is a clearly focused take on what is spiritually and morally at stake. Compassion is judgmental.

In his remarkable essay in the Festschrift on the occasion of Karl Rahner's sixtieth birthday in 1964, Vladimir Richter reminds us that we are required to know a lot about things before we can acknowledge that most things are in fact a mystery or an enigma.[154] The word "mystery" is not an expression of intellectual capitulation but the acknowledgment that our capacity to understand is just beginning; it is an admission of our lack of understanding. Compassion makes a similar acknowledgment; it is not the organic result of "not-being-botheredness." Quite the reverse, compassion challenges us to be very bothered about things and requires us to make judgments, and the answers we come up with are the tangible expression of that "being-botheredness." As Luke 6:36 tells us, "Be merciful just as your Father is merciful." Mercy is never blind but requires seeing, human care and knowing attention, and a clear head to take stock of the life context of the person in need of compassion. Beginning with a quote from Saint Augustine, Francis wrote,

> If we were in peril from fire, we would certainly run to water in order to extinguish the fire. . . . In the same way, if a spark of sin flares up from our straw, and we are troubled on that account, whenever we have an opportunity to perform a work of mercy, we should rejoice, as if a fountain opened before so that the fire might be extinguished. This message is so clear and direct, so simple and eloquent. . . . Why complicate something so simple? . . . Conceptual tools exist to heighten contact with the realities they seek to explain, not to distance us from them. We should not be concerned simply

---

[154]V. Richter, "Logik und Geheimnis," in J. B. Metz, W. Kern, A. Darlapp, and H. Vorgrimler, eds., *Gott in Welt. Festgabe für Karl Rahner. Bd. I: Philosophische Grundfragen. Theologische Grundfragen. Biblische Themen* (Freiburg/Breisgau: Herder, 1964), 188–206.

about falling into doctrinal error, but about remaining faithful to this light-filled path of life and wisdom. For "defenders of orthodoxy are sometimes accused of passivity, indulgence, or culpable complicity regarding the intolerable situations of injustice and the political regimes which prolong them."[155]

In a nutshell, mercy is proximity; it is knowingly seeing with compassion what counts. It is feet on the ground; it is a field hospital in action. The metaphor of the field hospital is directed against indifference; it involves a sense of urgency; it calls for attention to wounds, woundedness, and vulnerability; and it is concerned with accompaniment. The field hospital metaphor can also point to the need to fight for each life and to uphold a respect for human dignity, even under adverse circumstances.

We should also mention important limits to the metaphor. It does not reflect the underlying structural causes, it does not suggest sustainability, it uses us-versus-them language, it presents patients as passive victims, it leaves out the question of perpetrators, and it raises the political issue of neutrality. These are important aspects to keep in mind when we take a closer look at the image of the field hospital in a constant state of emergency.

The Reality of a Field Hospital

Unfortunately, we do not need to look far to find a twenty-first-century field hospital: they can be found in Syria, Congo, and Eritrea, and in Haiti after the earthquake of 2010. The COVID-19 pandemic has added field hospitals in many parts of the world.

Pope Francis's field hospital is not comfortable, fireside evening viewing; his field hospital is a 24/7 mobile army surgical hospital, a "self-contained, self-sufficient health care facility capable of rapid deployment and expansion or contraction to meet immediate emergency requirements."[156] It needs to be there, on the ground, ready to face what comes and to do what needs to be done.

We can list five key characteristics for a field hospital or a mobile care facility:

---

[155] *EG* 193–94. The last passage in quotations is from the Congregation for the Doctrine of the Faith, Instruction *Libertatis Nuntius* (August 6, 1984), XI.18.

[156] World Health Organization, "Guidelines for the Use of Foreign Field Hospitals in the Aftermath of Sudden-Impact Disaster" (Washington, DC, 2003), 20.

- A sense of urgency and emergency and meeting proximity needs.
- Adapting to one-off local conditions.
- Minimalism of norms and structures.
- Inner strength and robust concern.
- Tiny gestures of tenderness.

A field hospital is called for in unexpected circumstances, during states of emergency or in periods of conflict and adversity caused by a war, needing on-the-spot, on-the-ground action. There is a sense of urgency, a sense of exceptional circumstances. A field hospital is the tangible expression of the reaction to those needs. It is a reaction to human affliction that can no longer be transported to a safe place for treatment; since neither time nor circumstances allow such transport, care must be given ad hoc. Consequently, medical treatment has to be mobile and has to adapt to the proximity of the case and context, and not vice versa. Then the questions become: Where is there dire need? Where is there need of a mobile facility, where the hospital must go to the patient because the patient cannot be brought to the traditional hospital for traditional forms of treatment? Where must field hospitals go?

If a mobile medical facility needs to be adapted to actual local conditions, then logistics will play a lead role; a field hospital only works if it can withstand the conditions in situ. Is there a water supply? What energy sources are available? Communication is paramount; how can this be achieved with what is at hand? If there has been an earthquake or a tidal wave, the unit has to provide and incorporate certain features not usually found in hospitals. In other words, local conditions are crucial reference points for decision-making. A field hospital is always a one-off, unique to its situation. At the same time, medical care demands that certain standards be met even in a field hospital. In this regard and in the same way as logistics and resources need to be considered and adapted, the work force or medical team available also needs to adapt to be able to work together, usually under the auspices of one organization but at times together with other teams.[157] All forces on the ground—local and foreign—need to be united, since the endeavor can only work if it is a joint effort on all sides. There is no time for petty arguments. There has to be a sense of the essential, the most important. There is also no space for competition. Irfan Noor, a doctor in a field hospital in Pakistan, noted in his diary how vital it is that agencies do not "duplicate efforts."[158] Field

---

[157] Red Cross Canada, ed., "Inter-Agency-Collaboration: The Future of Field Hospitals in Disaster Response," discussion paper (Sidney, BC, 2014), 7.

[158] Irfan Noor, "Doctor's Diary: Healthcare without Hospitals," BBC News, October 24, 2005.

hospitals require high degrees of cooperation; teams must work together to meet "the health needs of a population without hospitals."

A field hospital has to work with minimal equipment and resources at every level. In other words it has to cope well with minimal norms, with thin legal frameworks and not an extensive list of guidelines. Quick, almost instant decision-making is required, often only in mere minutes or seconds, as there is not time for sophisticated bureaucracy and complex regulations. It requires raw thinking. The skill of improvisation becomes a key competence. Creativity, especially in teamwork, becomes imperative. The protocols have to be clear and concise.[159] The fewer the norms, the clearer and more pronounced those remaining have to be. Clarity is essential, so basic rules need to be kept to a minimum.

A field hospital needs personal stability, a strength of will, inner robustness. It needs patience, peace, and boldness, and—as far as humanly possible—it should be a fear-free zone. Patients and staff are under enough strain and stress without unnecessary fuss about nonessential matters. Irfan Noor writes about doctors reduced to tears. It takes inner strength to endure. Inner strength is born of conviction that one knows one is doing the right thing. Dang Thuy Tram, a twenty-seven-year-old doctor in a field hospital in Vietnam during the war, did her utmost to protect and support her patients; she was killed during an air attack on the hospital. On August 5, 1969, she had written in her diary, "Perhaps I will meet the enemy, and perhaps I will fall, but I hold my medical bag firmly regardless."[160] She held fast to what she believed in, to what she was fighting for, to her vocation. Such a stance requires boldness and deep inner strength. Hamza Khatib, a doctor in a field hospital in Aleppo, writes that although he could probably find a safe and secure job somewhere else, he knows he has a responsibility to work in the field: "It would be shameful to leave, thinking of a better life."[161] Robust concern (one definition of love) is the reason for this strength to keep going. Robust concern is an expression of the commitment to the deep practice of human dignity that this book has discussed. Such concern is fortified by mindful prayer, meditative moments, and a mobile store of inner wealth.

In a field hospital, it is also the little things that count, especially in the face of medical hopelessness; a field hospital thrives on *tiny ges-*

---

[159]M. C. Bricknell, "Command in a Field Hospital," *Journal of the Royal Army Medical Corps* 149, no. 11 (2003): 33–37.

[160]D. Thuy Tram, *Last Night I Dreamed of Peace: The Diary of Dang Thuy Tram*, trans. A. X. Pham (New York: Harmony Books, 2007), 146.

[161]Lena Masri, "Diary of an Aleppo Doctor: 'The Child in Front of Me Could Be My Daughter,'" ABCNews, October 11, 2016.

tures of human kindness and warmth, and gentleness works wonders in a cold, hostile environment. All too often, the medical care required comes too late, and no more can be done to repair the wounds. But it is in such circumstances when nothing can be done—medically or surgically—that human need is at its greatest, that there is an acute awareness that people are people, giving and receiving. The commitment to a deep practice of human dignity can be expressed in big decisions like legislation in favor of a culture of life, but also in small details. A smile or a hand on a cheek can be powerful confirmations of a person's dignity. This aspect of proximity work, a micro world of tiny gestures, is what Pope Francis is talking about when he describes the Church as field hospital. In her final diary entry, just a few days before her death, Dang Thuy Tram wrote,

> I am no longer a child. I have grown up. I have passed trials of peril, but somehow, at this moment, I yearn deeply for Mom's caring hand. Even the hand of a dear one or that of an acquaintance would be enough. Come to me, squeeze my hand, know my loneliness, and give me the love, the strength to prevail on the perilous road before me.[162]

A tiny gesture can make a world of difference.

Enacting the Catholic Social Tradition means understanding the needs of wounded persons and moving toward appropriate responses. Processes like raw thinking and experiments with truth and life can be expressions of this wrestling with the challenge of finding appropriate diagnostic and therapeutic responses to social pathologies and the wounds of the time. We need (to interiorize) the *regula* of Catholic Social Teaching to make proper judgments, as we have seen in the example of Óscar Romero as he attended to the wounds of his time and place. Enacting Catholic Social Teaching can be understood as akin to working in a field hospital. Fighting for a culture that respects the dignity of a person, holding onto the core value of dignity, and seeing the connection between "the cry of the poor" and "the cry of the earth"[163] is field-hospital work in a nutshell. To use a different metaphor, this is the life of a Christian as a pilgrim.

During World War I, Edith Stein worked in an Austrian field hospital, and in 1915 she wrote in her diary, "I no longer have a life of my own."[164]

---

[162]Tram, *Last Night I Dreamed of Peace*, 225.

[163]See, for example, Leonardo Boff, *Cry of the Earth, Cry of the Poor*, English trans. (Maryknoll, NY: Orbis Books, 1997); and Pope Francis, *Laudato Si'*.

[164]See more on Edith Stein at www.vatican.va.

She is, of course, right, in that our lives do not belong to us alone; each life is a gift from God, and so, as God-given, it is God's life. And it also belongs to the community, which is a key point of Catholic Social Tradition. Our lives are indeed not our own.

Index

Abbas Makarius of Egypt, 71
acedia (moral exhaustion), 26, 168, 190
Adam (biblical figure), 51
Adams, Rachel, 30
Adorno, Theodor, 180
Advent spirituality, xv, xxxvii, 158
Affordable Care Act, xxxi
After Virtue (MacIntyre), xxxiv
Agamben, Giorgio, 159
agency, 3, 13, 23
  basic human capabilities, discourse on, 14
  Gaudium et spes, agency of children in, 82–83
  The Jungle, analysis of stakeholders' agency in, 60
  scrupulosity, danger of agency loss with, 26
  solidarity in acknowledgment of, 49, 57
  tax system, trust in the agency of, 96
aggiornamento, theological process of, 80
akrasia (weakness of the will), 157
Alcides Carrión, Daniel, 127
Amoris Laetitia (Joy of Love), 86
Aphothegmata Patrum (Makarius), 71
Apostolic Council of Jerusalem, 166
Aquinas, Thomas, 66, 88, 91, 92, 191
Arendt, Hannah, 80
Arinze, Francis, 85
Aristotle, 124, 157
Assman, Aleida, xxiii
Assumption of the Blessed Virgin Mary, 85–86
Attard, "Mary and Jodie" (twins), 74–77
Aubenas, Florence, 4
Augustine of Hippo, 88, 92, 143, 192
Auster, Paul, 60, 188

Bacon, Roger, 126, 127
Badard, Ana T., 63
Bartholomew I, Patriarch, 88
Barton, Sheila, 25–26
Basil of Caesarea, xviii
Beck, Martha, 30
Benedict XVI, Pope, 88, 189
Berenstain, Nora, 78
Berger, Theresa, 83–84
Betancourt, Ingrid, xxi–xxiii
Bieri, Peter, xxiv
Blood, Benjamin Paul, 127
Bolzano, Bernard, 183
Bonanomi, Andrea, 62
Bonhoeffer, Dietrich, 56
bounded imagination, 185
Bouyid, Said, 16–17
The Boy in the Moon (Brown), xxxv
Boyle, Gregory (Fr. Greg), 51–53
Brandom, Robert, 88
Brockman, James, 173
Brown, Ian, 30
Brown, Peter, xviii
Brownlee, Kimberley, 30

Cain and Abel, 49–50
Calvino, Italo, 29
Caritas in Veritate (Charity in Truth), 33, 95, 103
Carter, Jimmy, 169
Castañeda-Liles, Maria Del Socorro, 116
Castiglione, Cinzia, 62
Catechism of the Catholic Church (CCC), 84, 123–24, 125–26
Catholic social imagination, 159, 182, 184–85
Catholic Social Teaching, 33, 73, 177
  children, no major role in, 81–82
  common good and, 58–64, 68

199

context in applying, 15–21
diversity in Catholic social theology, 65–68
habitual practice of, 119–21, 124, 127
human dignity, honoring, 1, 7–15, 31, 126
just wages, standing up for, 97–113
Laudato Si' case study, 136–43
raw thinking as a process in, 77–84, 116
regula, applying as, 117, 159–61, 180
Rerum Novarum as introducing, 89
social and political analysis, key criteria for, 167–79
social pathologies, analysis of, 180–82
solidarity as a principle of, 47–58
taxation as a case example in, 90–97
as therapy, 180–82, 182–88
cemetery workers' strike, xxvi–xxix
Centesimus Annus (On the Hundredth Anniversary), 103
Cézanne, Paul, 37
Chevalkov, Mikhail, 122
"Christian Anthropology and the Theory of Gender" (Eijk), 73
Coady, Roxanne, xxxvi
Cocks, Frederick S., xxxiv
Coetzee, John M., 8
Colombian Peace Accords Matrix, 120
common good, 46, 110, 134
   Catholic social imagination, emphasis on, 159
   in Catholic Social Teaching, 34, 38, 187
   children as contributing to, 82
   civil authorities, working with to promote, 165
   common bad, comparing to, 68–72
   diversity and, 64, 67
   ecology of daily life, role in promoting, 136–37
   El Salvador, betrayal of the common good in, 177–78
   just wages in the framework of, 98–99, 104, 106
   Kingdom of God and, 176
   Mary's Meals program as committed to, 53
   measurements and indicators of, 62–64
   neighborliness, building up for, 120–21
   participation in creating, commitment to, 167–68
   portrait of the concept of, 58–62
   Romero focus on, 161, 170, 171, 173
   signs of the times, reading in light of, 169
   solidarity in, 93, 96
   in *Sollicitudo Rei Socialis,* 47
   taxes as contributing to, 91, 92, 94, 95, 97
Compendium of the Social Doctrine of the Church (CSDC), 7, 64, 84, 102, 103, 186
competitive moral pluralism, 146–47
Conferences (Cassian), 122–23
Congregation for the Doctrine of the Faith (CDF), 84, 120
COVID-19 pandemic, 8, 71, 193
Coyle, Dan, 23
Critique of Judgment (Kant), xxxi
Crowe, Martin, 95
The Curious Enlightenment of Professor Caritat (Lukes), 62
Curran, Charles, 95
Currey, Mason, 124

Day, Dorothy, xxvii–xxx
De Beer, Stephen, 139
De Civitate Dei (Augustine), 92
Deckmar, Maud and Fred, 23–27
deep sharing, concept of, 150
De Gaetano, Vincent, 18
Deiparae Virginis Mariae (Virgin Mother Mary), 85
Dei Verbum (Dogmatic Constitution on Divine Revelation), 81
De Kock, Eugene, xxiii
Delp, Alfred, xx, xxxvi
DeLugo, John, 92–93
Dershowitz, Alan, xxxv
Dewey, John, 123
DiAngelo, Robin, 142
Dicastery for Promoting Integral Human Development, 120
Dickinson, Anson, 37
dignity. *See* human dignity

Distributive Justice (Ryan), 101
diversity, 64, 65–68, 113

Ecclesia in Europa (The Church in Europe), xxx
ecological conversion, 88, 158
Economic Justice for All pastoral letter, 94–95
Eijk, Willem Jacobus, 73
Elias-Jones, Alun C., 74–75
Ellacuría, Ignacio, 172
ethical lifestyle insights, 151–54
Ethics (Spinoza), xxxi
"Ethics, Human Rights, and Globalization" (lecture), 1
European Court of Human Rights (ECHR), 16, 19
euthanasia, 11, 61
Evangelii Gaudium (Joy of the Gospel), 31, 186, 191
   complacency and self-indulgence, warning against, 86
   diversity and reconciliation in, 67
   missionary evangelization, offering corrections on, 160–61
   the poor, on the opportunities for, 42–43
   serving others, on the commitment to, xvii
   throwaway culture, chastisement of, 138
Evangelii Nuntiandi (In Proclaiming the Gospel), 166
Evangelium Vitae (Gospel of Life), 82, 121
Everett, Edward, 37

Farabundo Martí (FPL), 168
Farha, Leilani, 70
Faulkner, William, 125
Federal Republic of Germany Basic Law, 5
Fides et Ratio (Faith and Reason), 119
field hospital concept, 188
   Focolare Movement, in address to assembly of, 190
   gestures of human kindness in, 195–96
   key characteristics for a field hospital, 193–94
   reconciliation and forgiveness, as linked to, 189
Finnis, John, 92
Firth, Stubbins, 127
Floyd, George, 8
Food and Agriculture Organization (FAO), 47–48
Forte, Bruno, 115
Francis, Pope, 66, 144, 161
   Albanian students, addressing, 55–56
   change in lifestyle, calling for, 136
   Church of the Poor and, 165
   concrete situations, preferring to the abstract, 34
   convenience mindset, resisting, 141–42
   CST, vision of the Church shaped by, 186–87
   field hospital, comparing the Church to, 188–93
   globalization of indifference, lamenting, 51
   intentionality, promoting, 135
   on poor people as teachers, 38
   single human family, upholding vision of, 48–49
   throwaway culture, commenting on, 138
   World Food Day, commemorating, 47
   See also Evangelii Gaudium; Laudato Si'
Frankfurt, Harry, 157
Frankfurt School of philosophy, 180–81
Frankl, Viktor, 125
Fratelli Tutti (On Fraternity and Social Friendship), 48–49
Freud, Sigmund, 125
Fuerzas Armadas Revolucionarias de Colombia (FARC), xxi

Gallaher, Brandon, 35
Gandhi, Mohandas K., 118, 127, 155
Gaudium et Spes (Pastoral Constitution on the Church in the Modern World), 44, 94, 179
   children, on their role in family welfare, 82–83
   on duty towards your neighbor, 169
   just wages, addressing, 103–4
   solidarity, calling for, 163

Genova, Lisa, 22
Glass, Ruth, 68–69
globalization of indifference, 13, 48, 51
Gobodo-Madikizela, Pumla, xxii–xxiii
Goffman, Erving, 46
Goodridge, Sarah, 37
Grande, Rutilio, 163
Gregory, David, xxviii
A Grief Observed (Lewis), 114–15
Guardini, Romano, 89
Gump, Johannes, 37

Habermas, Jürgen, 180
habits, 2, 49, 91
  concept and dynamics of, 121–26
  CST, habitual living in, 116–17, 119, 135
  culturally established habits, 138, 141
  eating habits, 132–33, 140, 149, 152, 154
  experimenting with, 127–30, 130–32, 155–58
  Gandhi and the art of proper habits, 118
  habits and behaviors, 143–48, 150–51
  habitus of communal living, 159
  harmful habits of consumption, 136
  Laudato Si', evaluating habits in light of, 139
  personal growth and development of habits, 97
  in a portrait of principles, 46–47
  principles, translating into habits, 120
Hammer, Victor, 34–35
Hanvey, James, 50
Heads, Henry, 127
Heller, Agnes, 122
hermeneutics, 60, 89, 141, 173–74, 182
Hickman, Leo, 155–56
Himes, Kenneth, 101
Hoffman Davis, Jessica, 39–40
Hollenbach, David, 60, 68, 69
Holmes, Richard, 41
Honderich, Ted, xxxii
Honneth, Axel, 4, 180–81
human-beingness, Christian tradition of, 115

human dignity, 158, 161, 181
  in adverse conditions, 116
  baby Issa as an example of, 56
  bounded imagination as linked with, 185
  in *Caritas in Veritate*, 103
  Christian understanding of, 14
  in concept of mystery, 50
  in CST, 7–11, 15–21, 34, 105, 177
  deep practice of, 22–31, 44, 115, 160, 182, 195, 196
  dignity-conductive habits, 126
  enacting human dignity, 1–2
  facelessness as showing contempt for, 72
  false universalism as undermining, 65
  in field hospital metaphor, 193
  four central aspects of, 11–13
  humiliation, going through, 2–7
  just wages and, 98, 101
  prophetic defense of, 164
  research methods, respect for human dignity in, 78
  sanitation-related dignity issues, 45–46
  uniqueness, recognizing and honoring, 87
  violations of, assessing, 70, 74
Humboldt, Alexander von, 127
Husserl, Edmund, 122

Ignatian *Examen*, practice of, 143, 151, 154
Ignatieff, Michael, 6–7, 9
imago Dei concept, 7, 22, 23
Institutes (Cassian), 122–23
"Instruction on Certain Aspects of the 'Theology of Liberation'" (CDF), 84
In the Country of Last Things (Auster), 60, 188
Into the Wild (Krakauer), 131

Jesus Christ, 158, 177, 179
  authentic patriot, describing as, 174
  diversity of chosen disciples, 65
  in field hospital scenario, 190
  human dignity of Jesus, 24
  incarnational Christ as truth, 172
  Jesus Prayer, 117–18

as a laborer, 104
the poor, special attention on, 188
praxis of Jesus, 187
prayer in the spirit of Christ, 125
Romero, making Christ visible to the world, 162
Sacred Heart of Jesus, devotion to, 55
solidarity, pushing the envelope on, 58
trust in God and, 16
unity in Christ, 167
Job (biblical figure), 51, 114
John Paul II, Pope, 119, 121, 126
ecological conversion, calling for, 88
Extraordinary Synod of Bishops, convening, 85
Romero, meeting with, 179–80
superdevelopment, introducing term, 32–33, 110
John XXIII, Pope, xxx
Jones, David Albert, 73
judgment, necessity of, xxix–xxiii
The Jungle (Sinclair), 58–60
Justice in the World synod (1971), xvii

Kant, Immanuel, xxxi, 184
Kasser, Tim, 144
Katongole, Emmanuel, 40
Keegan, Marina, 50
Keehan, Carol, xxxi
Ketteler, Wilhelm Emmanuel, 110
Khatib, Hamza, 195
King, Martin Luther, Jr., 117
Kingdom of God, 167
in *Gaudium et Spes,* 179
politics not a part of, 172
Romero, understanding of, 173, 176, 180
social realities, viewing through, 171
kinship, concept of, 51–52
Kittay, Eva Feder, 14, 28
Koh, Germaine, 38
Korczak, Janusz, 27
Krakauer, Jon, 131
Kreisau Circle, xv
Kroc Institute of International Peace Studies, 119–20
Kuch, Hannes, 6
Kurdi, Aylan, 49
Kurihara, Albert, 28

Laborem Exercens (Through Work), 103
lagom (exact right amount), xiv, 152
Laing, Olivia, 51
Laudato Si' (On Care for Our Common Home)
change in lifestyle, making appeal for, 136–37
footnotes to text, revelations of, 87–89
globalization of indifference, condemning, 48
habits and behaviors, on revising, 143–48, 157
home building, offering reference points for, 81
intentional living, on transitioning to, 135
perception and categorization as themes in, 137–43
signs of the times, influence on reading of, 185
on superdevelopment as dehumanizing, 32
Law, Bernard Francis, 85
Lawrence-Lightfoot, Sara, 39–40
Lederach, John Paul, 185
Lemmens, Paul, 18
Lenten sacrifices, 128, 129
Leo XIII, Pope, xviii–xix, 89, 93–94
Levine, Judith, 129–30
Lévi-Strauss, Claude, 80, 87
Lewis, C. S., 114
"lived ethic of thinking," concept of, 76
A Living Wage (Ryan), 100
Logico-Philosophicus (Wittgenstein), xxxi
London: Aspects of Change (Glass), 68–69
The Lonely City (Laing), 51
Lozza, Edoardo, 62
Lucie (artwork), 35
Lukes, Steven, 62

MacFarlane-Barrow, Magnus, 53–54
MacIntyre, Alasdair, xxxiv
Magis (sense of more), 12, 22, 28, 154
magisterium, 88, 113, 160, 164, 175, 182–83
Mahoney, Paul, 18

Maine de Biran, Pierre, 123
"Male and Female He Created Them" (Congregation for Catholic Education), 74
Mann, Thomas, 148
Marcuse, Herbert, 180
Margalit, Avishai, 5, 153
Mater et Magistra (On Christianity and Social Progress), 82, 94
Maugham, Somerset, 125
McCandless, Chris, 131
Medellín Conference, 162, 164–66, 168
mercy, 48, 50, 58, 86–87, 117, 191–93
metanoia (conversion), 126, 186
Möllers, Christoph, 50
More, Thomas, 10
Moreau de Tours, Jacques-Joseph, 127
Moskowitz, Peter, 69
Munificentissimus Deus (Defining the Dogma of the Assumption), 85–86
Murdoch, Iris, 179
Murphy, Liam, 96

Nadal, Jerome, 146
Nagel, Thomas, 96
Nancy, Jean-Luc, 36
neighborliness, practice of, 120–21
Neuringer, Allen, 128
Nguyen, Martin Nam, 35
Nicodemus, conversion of, 130
Noor, Irfan, 194–95
Not Buying It (Levine), 129–30
Notes from the Warsaw Ghetto (Ringelblum), 2–3

Obama, Barack, xxxi
O'Brien, Issa Grace, 54–58
Octogesima Adveniens (Eightieth Anniversary), xxxii, 167
"The Opposite of Loneliness" (Keegan), 50–51
Opus Maius (Bacon), 126
Ordinatio Sacerdotalis (On Reserving Priestly Ordination to Men Alone), 88–89
Our Lady of Everyday Life (Castañeda-Liles), 116

Pacem in Terris (Peace on Earth), 42, 168

Painting of the Social Network (artwork), 35
parable of the Talents, xiii
Paris, John J., 74–75
Paul VI, Pope, 84, 88, 163, 165
perseverance, virtue of, 47, 156–57
pilgrims, thinking as, 113–15
Piombo, Sebastiano, 36
Pius XII, Pope, 85
Plath, Sylvia, 124
polyphony of life, concept of, 56
Populorum Progressio (On the Development of Peoples), xiii–xiv, 84, 94, 178
prayer, 48, 116, 195
  CCC on, 125–26
  habit of mealtime prayer, 122
  Jesus Prayer, 117–18
  in Job narrative, 114
  Romero, prayers of, 161, 164
preferential option for the poor, xix, 9, 187
  Church of the Poor, 165
  CST, as a principle of, 34, 98–99
  oeconomicae et pecuniariae quaestiones on, 120
  principle of common welfare and, 95
  Romero, orientation toward, 161, 168–69, 171, 173
  standpoint epistemology approach, 67
principles, 76, 84, 98
  ability-to-pay principle, 92, 93, 106
  "desert" principle in wage structure, 108
  fiction, using to think through, 60, 62
  habits, turning CST principles into, 119–21, 127
  of human dignity, 7, 10, 15, 19, 99
  mercy as a core principle, 86
  "painting principles," 41–47, 64
  personally inhabiting CST principles, 33, 34, 116
  principalism, portraits beyond, 34–41
  Romero and CST principles, 162, 167, 171–73
  of subsidiarity, 20, 24, 34, 66, 95, 177, 187
  testimonial elements, 54–58
  of the universal destination of goods, 100, 101

See also common good; solidarity
private property, 95
  living wage and private ownership, 100–101, 107
  in *Quadragesimo Anno*, 93–94
  in *Rerum Novarum*, 102
  social function of, 171
  in taxation framework, 91
  in *Utopia*, 61
The Problem of Pain (Lewis), 114
propria of the human person, 14
Proust, Marcel, 125
ptochotropheion (poorhouse/hospital), xviii

Quadragesimo Anno (On Reconstruction of the Social Order), 82, 93–94, 102, 109–10

racism, 8, 12, 69, 107
Rahner, Karl, 192
Ravaisson, Félix, 143
raw thinking, 93, 97, 196
  Catholic Social Tradition and, 77–84
  describing and defining, 73–77
  disciplined raw thinking, 84–90
  in field hospital-like situations, 195
  honest engagement via, xvii
  just wage scenarios, applying to, 98, 103, 111
  thinking as pilgrims and, 113–15
regula (rule of life), 117, 159–61, 180, 196
Rerum Novarum (Rights and Duties of Capital and Labor), 106, 167
  Catholic Social Tradition, introducing, 89
  on earnings and private property, 102
  Ketteler, influence on, 110
  laborers, reacting to the plight of, 182
  taxation, envisioning fair system of, 93
Richter, Vladimir, 79, 80, 192
Ringlebaum, Emmanuel, 2–3
Roberts, Seth, 128
Robinson, Mary, 1–2
Romero, Óscar, 164, 175, 180
  common-good lens, applying, 170–71
  CST, criteria and perspectives of, 161, 162–63, 167–79, 196
  on hermeneutic coincidence, 173–74
  hope, expanding the meaning of, 178–79
  Louvain address on pain in the world, 166–67
  participation, emphasis on, 176–77
  preferential option for the poor, 165, 168–69
  prophetic ministry of, xvii
Roth, Philip, 125
Rousseau, Jean-Jacques, 180
Rueckert, Gertrud, 22–23
Rule of Saint Benedict, 129
Ryan, John, 99–101

Sam, Anna, 4
Santori, Santorio, 127
Schaub, Eve, 130–35, 149
Schaub, Greta, 130–31, 132
Schenker, Heinrich, 34–35
Schmidt, Godfrey P., xxviii
Schütz, Alfred, 122
Scotus, John Duns, 79
Second Vatican Council, 81, 85, 103–4, 164, 165
security, 68, 107, 120
  of everyday life, 123, 125
  food security, UN efforts to provide, 48
  just wages helping to establish, 103, 106
  lack of, fiction as depicting, 60–61
  ontological insecurity, agency insecurity link to, 3
"see-judge-act" approach, xxxiii, 172
signs of the times, 15, 80, 169
  CST documents as providing a reading on, 184, 185, 186
  Extraordinary Synod of Bishops convened in light of, 85
  "Signs of the Times" sermon by Romero, 171
Sinclair, Upton, 58, 60
Skidelsky, Robert and Edward, 123
Sloterdijk, Peter, 90
Smith, Neil, 69
Sobrino, Jon, 171
social doctrine, four principles of, 187
social pathologies, 4, 180–84, 187, 196

Socrates, 80
Soldhju, Katrin, 127
solidarity, 12, 34, 38
  alienation leading to erosion of, 186
  in baby Issa case study, 54–58
  bridge concept as expressing, 50–53, 58
  for deep transformation of humanity, 163
  The Jungle, lack of solidarity in, 59
  portrait of solidarity, 47–50
  Romero, solidarity with Paul VI, 164
  tax compliance and, 90, 93, 95–96
  violation of the principles of solidarity, 70
Sollicitudo Rei Socialis (On Social Concerns), 47, 187–88
Spadaro, Antonio, 189
Spellman, Francis, xxvii–xxx
Stang, Dorothy Mae, 10
Stein, Edith, 196–97
Stein, Gertrude, 124
Steiner, George, 58, 79
Stier, Fridolin, 79
Still Alice (Genova), 22
Stoecker, Ralf, 21–22
Sultana, Farhan, xxiv
superdevelopment, concept of, 32–33

taxation, ethics of, 90–97
Temsch, Jochen, 21–23
Thoreau, Henry David, 131
Tolomei, Claudio, 36
Tractatus (Wittgenstein), 83
Tram, Dang Thuy, 195, 196
transgenderism, 73–74
"Truthfulness and Tragedy" (Yau), xxxiv
Uncle Dominique as a Lawyer (painting), 37

Uncle Tom's Cabin (Stowe), 39
UN Convention against Torture (1984), xxxiii

Universal Declaration of Human Rights, 5, 16, 81, 168
Utopia (More), 61

Van Gogh, Vincent, 37
Vanier, Georges, 117
Vanier, Jean, 117
Vatican II, 81, 85, 103–4, 164, 165
veganism/vegetarianism, 78, 146, 148, 149, 152, 154
Veritatis Spendor encyclical, 119
Villiger, Judge, 19–21
Vinter and Others v. The United Kingdom (2013), 17, 19–21
Virgen de Guadalupe, devotion to, 116

wages, 13
  criteria for establishing, 106–11
  ethics of a just wage, 91, 97–98
  in *Gaudium et Spes*, 103–6
  in *Quadragesimo Anno*, 102–3
  tradition, insight on wages from, 99–102
  trans-contextual justification for, 112–13
Waiting for the Barbarians (Coetzee), 8
Walden (Thoreau), 131
Waldron, Jeremy, xxxiii–xxxiv
Way of the Pilgrim (prayer manual), 117–18
Weimar Constitution, 5
Wetter, Friedrich, 85
White, Kimberly, 27–28
white fragility, concept of, 142–43
Whitmore, Todd, 78
wichtige sätze (existential propositions), 183
Wittgenstein, Ludwig, 15, 79, 83, 148

Yau, Darren, xxxiv

Zamagni, Stefano, 69
Zamora, Rubén, 170
Zurn, Christoph, 181